EFFECTIVE USE OF VISUALS IN TEACHING IN HIGHER EDUCATION

EDUCATION IN A COMPETITIVE AND GLOBALIZING WORLD

Additional books in this series can be found on Nova's website under the Series tab.

Additional e-books in this series can be found on Nova's website under the e-book tab.

EFFECTIVE USE OF VISUALS IN TEACHING IN HIGHER EDUCATION

ARIANNE JENNIFER ROURKE
AND
ZENA O'CONNOR

Nova Science Publishers, Inc.
New York

For permission to use material from this book please contact us:
Telephone 631-231-7269; Fax 631-231-8175
Web Site: http://www.novapublishers.com

NOTICE TO THE READER

The Publisher has taken reasonable care in the preparation of this book, but makes no expressed or implied warranty of any kind and assumes no responsibility for any errors or omissions. No liability is assumed for incidental or consequential damages in connection with or arising out of information contained in this book. The Publisher shall not be liable for any special, consequential, or exemplary damages resulting, in whole or in part, from the readers' use of, or reliance upon, this material. Any parts of this book based on government reports are so indicated and copyright is claimed for those parts to the extent applicable to compilations of such works.

Independent verification should be sought for any data, advice or recommendations contained in this book. In addition, no responsibility is assumed by the publisher for any injury and/or damage to persons or property arising from any methods, products, instructions, ideas or otherwise contained in this publication.

This publication is designed to provide accurate and authoritative information with regard to the subject matter covered herein. It is sold with the clear understanding that the Publisher is not engaged in rendering legal or any other professional services. If legal or any other expert assistance is required, the services of a competent person should be sought. FROM A DECLARATION OF PARTICIPANTS JOINTLY ADOPTED BY A COMMITTEE OF THE AMERICAN BAR ASSOCIATION AND A COMMITTEE OF PUBLISHERS.

Additional color graphics may be available in the e-book version of this book.

Library of Congress Cataloging-in-Publication Data

Effective use of visuals in teaching in higher education / editors, Arianne Jennifer Rourke, Zena O'Connor.
  p. cm.
 Includes index.
 ISBN 978-1-62081-442-0 (hardcover)
 1. Education, Higher--Audio-visual aids I. Rourke, Arianne. II. O'Connor, Zena.
 LB1043.E36 2012
 371.33'5--dc23
                          2012016601

Published by Nova Science Publishers, Inc. † New York

CONTENTS

LIST OF FIGURES

ACKNOWLEDGMENTS

Zena O'Connor would like to acknowledge the support kindly provided by Rory and Lou O'Connor. In addition, this book would not have been possible without the enthusiasm and dedication of my co-author Arianne Rourke.

Arianne Rourke would like to sincerely thank her family for all their support and patients during the process of writing this book. In particular she would like to acknowledge her father Emeritus Professor Ken Reinhard, for sharing his remarkable insights and knowledge of art and design education and Kathryn Coleman for her unwavering support and contribution to this book. This book also would not have eventuated without the hard work and wholehearted commitment of my co-author Zena O'Connor.

Chapter 1

INTRODUCTION

Research in recent years particularly in the realm of communication skills in computer technology has supported the argument that students should have multiple skills and forms of communication that encompass the capacity to comprehend and convey information in visual form (Salomon, 1997; Greeno and Hall, 1997). McLoughlin and Krakowski (2001) argued that: "Although visual images are part of human cognition, they tend to be marginalised and undervalued in education" (p.3). This book addresses this concern, by examining specifically how visuals can be utilised in higher education to promote meaningful enriched learning. It argues that educators should allocate more time and effort towards developing student's visual literacy skills, which will assist them with understanding visual material used in teaching, as well as help with deciphering the visual messages in the world around them. It acknowledges that all students are different and bring with them different perspectives and levels of previous knowledge and understanding to the learning process. Students also adopt different learning styles and learn at different paces, with some learning through experiential learning activities while others learn best through more teacher-directed instruction, which will be discussed in detail.

The important role that visual memory plays in learning is analyzed and it is argued that it is imperative that educators in higher education become knowledgeable about effective methods for utilising visuals to promote the retention of learning. Visuals can be used to stimulate understanding of a discipline, promote discussion and student input as well as encourage creative problem solving and collaborative learning. Decades earlier Seels (1994) suggested that one of the reasons why visual literacy had not at that time achieved a sound theoretical basis was that it was not a construct that had operational specificity or did it have a discipline or profession. It will be argued that art and design education in particular should adopt the theoretical basis of visual literacy within the discipline, as an essential skill for students to develop. It will also be premised that other disciplines that utilise visual material to teach disciplinary knowledge should also consider including training in visual literacy skills for both students and teachers. For as Seels (1994) concurs, visual literacy amalgamates personal experience and imagination with social experience, technology and aesthetics as such it is a worthwhile attribute to develop in students in higher education.

According to McLoughlin and Krakowski, (2001), "Today's graduates require both visual and verbal thinking skills and need explicit practice in representing, interpreting and manipulating the visual aspects of their knowledge in multiple forms" (p.5). This book provides discussion of many pertinent research studies (including the author's own) that give evidence to support the need for effectively utilizing visuals in higher education to promote learning. It also provides guidelines and numerous practical teaching and learning examples to assist educators to achieve this objective. There are exemplars to demonstrate how visuals can be used in teaching to promote higher order thinking skills, learner confidence and motivation as well as self-directed and collaborative learning. Rieber (1995) argued that instructional material should promote visually oriented problem solving approaches as well as generate multiple representations, instead of restrict the learner to abstract visual strategies.

This book discusses what changes educators can make to their visual instructional material to achieve the type of problem solving Rieber (1995) suggests. It also puts forward the premise that there needs to be a connection between the learner's cognitive style and the mode of presentation used in instruction. As McKay (1999) has argued, performance is likely to be reduced where this is not present. In order to comprehend how educators could work towards achieving this objective they first need to understand what it means to be an effective teaching in higher education as well as the role reflective practice can play towards this phenomenon.

There will be an exploration of these notions in Chapter 2, which analyses what the literature says about what it means to be an effective lecturer in higher education. This includes a discussion on what makes a lecturer an effective teacher and teaching as a reflective activity with specific reference to the role visuals can play in this premise. It is acknowledged that there is no simple answer to the question of what makes an effective teacher in higher education. Teacher effectiveness embraces multiple perspectives (Marsh and Dunkin, 1997) including student and teacher expectations, teacher knowledge and experience, assessment practices as well as methodological issues, to name but a few. Both concept cartoons and mind maps are discussed as examples of learning and teaching tools that can be utilised to promote effective student learning in higher education.

In Chapter 3 the notion of threshold concepts is discussed, this theory has become quite a 'buzz' word in educational circles since its introduction by Myers and Land in 2003. It discusses how demonstrating to the 21st century design student that the threshold concept of learning the necessary knowledge and skills to recognise a designer's work or a design style and understand colour theory is a challenge for design educators in higher education. This chapter argues that utilising prototypical design examples and semantic cues to assist students to move beyond the threshold required to recognize a designer's work or design style has many benefits for the learner. It discusses a variety of methods for teaching threshold concepts to design students in particular in the disciplinary focus of teaching design history and colour theory. By providing a practical application of the theory of threshold concepts to a particular disciplinary focus it is envisaged that other educators will take what they have learnt from this exempla and apply it to teaching in their discipline.

The focus in Chapter 4 is on learning style modalities and visual literacy. It is acknowledged that learning is a complex and highly individual process that differs for every learner irrespective of age, gender or culture. This chapter discusses how each individual has their own preferred way of gathering, organising and considering new concepts presented to them in a learning context. It argues that educators have a responsibility to ensure a close match between their teaching approach and support materials and the range of possible learning styles. DePorter (1992) suggested when discussing learning styles that one of the basic problems was that "many people don't even realise they are favoring one-way or the other, because nothing external tells them they're any different from anyone else" (p.114). Hence it is imperative it is argued, that not only are students aware of their preferred learning style but educators in higher education provide a variety of learning instruction and activities to cater for their learners needs. Educators need to recognise that levels of visual literacy vary and they can play a key role in assisting students to develop their visual literacy skills to meet the challenges and demands of the visually cluttered digital era. Rakes (1999) notes, in the e-learning world of the 21st century it is imperative that we are able to think critically, manipulate and effectively process visual information so that we can interpret and draw reliable meaning from such information.

Online learning and teaching in higher education is discussed in Chapter 5, which specifically focuses on how educators can develop new engaging spaces through digital scaffolding that can provide the needed bridge for supporting students in the online learning process (Rourke and Coleman, 2010a). It provides an analysis on how visual cues were utilised in an online Postgraduate course to scaffold student learning and to promote active learner engagement and collaboration. It argues that educators should employ in their online course design assessment that not only enhances the learning experiences of students but also that engages them in real-world authentic tasks. It showcases a fully online course that was developed with the goal of having clear alignment between the learning outcomes, the assessment as well as method and materials of instruction. The course was designed to develop a model for learning where students were explicitly scaffolded using colour coding, cues and concept maps to enable learning research and writing skills that would culminate in a research paper directed by individual student interests. This chapter provides an example of how to effectively use visual cues to promote learning that could be adopted by other disciplines in both the face-to-face classroom as well as in blended and fully online courses.

To further explore the effective use of visuals in higher education Chapter 6 elaborates on what is visual literacy and defines the skills students need to develop in order to learn from visual material presented in lectures and other course material. It argues that it is crucial that teachers in higher education provide learning activities to promote visual literacy skills to assist students towards fully comprehending the many visual images utilised as teaching and learning aids. Rakes (1999) mentioned earlier argued: "Many students have difficulty interpreting visuals, yet the development of visual literacy still receives limited attention" (p.17). It will be argued that in higher education in the 21st century more attention needs to be given to this issue. A series of studies by Rourke and O'Connor (2008; 2009a, 2009b; 2010a; 2010b; 2010c) investigating this paradigm will be discussed in detail in Chapter 4. Specifically this chapter provides discussion on how to promote visual literacy skills with art and design students based on the author's research. How we cognitively understand visual material will also be analysed in terms of how we use our visual memory to assist educators towards reasoning how best to utilise visuals in education to promote productive long-term learning. Many of the problems and solutions discussed in the example of teaching art and design have generic application across many disciplines taught in higher education particularly as it is premised that visual images assist towards enhancing the effectiveness of both teaching and student learning.

In Chapter 7 the imperative role that colour and contrast play in the processing of visual information is discussed with particular reference to the Gestalt theories of perception in relation to the design of visual communications and presentations. There is an analysis of how human visual perception is underpinned by a search for visual cues within the visual field; a search that the Gestalt psychologists believed followed common patterns or 'laws'. This chapter describes the Gestalt 'laws' of perception and critically analyses how colour and contrast have the capacity to enhance or mitigate these 'laws' of perception. Colour and contrast are often integral in applied design in general, and visual communications in particular; therefore, knowledge about their role in respect to Gestalt 'laws' of perception may influence the effectiveness of the interface between visual communications design and human receptivity and response it is argued.

Visual perception and the role of colour and contrasts will also be discussed in detail in Chapter 8. It is argued that human visual perception and the ways in which humans process visual stimuli are integral to effectiveness of visual communications design. This chapter elaborates on the mechanics of human visual perception as well as cognitive processing of visual information. It analyses the Gestalt theories of perception in relation to how humans perceive, organize and cognitively process visual stimuli. In addition, colour and contrast are examined in some depth as these play key roles in visual perception and hence the design of effective visual communication materials. Colour models as well as common colour-related constructs are discussed along with perceptual effects as these have relevance to visual communications design. Information is also provided about current colour theories as well as common colour combination techniques as these provide insight and guidance for creating effective visual instruction. Finally, digital technology and issues relating to digital reproduction are discussed with particular reference to visual communications design.

Design factors and how these impact on visual communication materials are dealt with in Chapter 9 in some detail. Aside from the cognitive processing of information and the mechanics of human perception, there are a number of design factors that influence the effectiveness of visual communications. These include audience identification and analysis plus the clear definition of communication objectives. These serve to inform communication strategies and provide insight for the design and structure of visual communications. More specifically, design layout and various issues regarding typeface design and size also influence the efficacy of visual communications. Furthermore, the principles and elements of design and the way these are applied to visual communications can impact positively or negatively on the effectiveness of such communications. This chapter provides information to assist educators towards further understanding how design elements and principles impact on visual communication. With this knowledge educators are better equipped to design effective visual teaching material for facilitating learning.

Research has suggested that enhanced learning and retention is promoted when visual materials are used in teaching (Dwyer and Baker, 2001; Carney and Levin; 2002). Hence it is imperative that educators are aware of the most effective way of utilising visual material in teaching and learning activities to promote sustainable worthwhile learning outcomes in their discipline. It has been suggested, "that a use of a variety of teaching and learning approaches has the potential to enhance the learning and performance for a wider range of adult students" (Hawk and Shah, 2007, p.2). This book provides some useful teaching and learning methodologies to promote meaningful long-term learning. It argues that educators should be selective in their choice of which style and type of visuals to employ, providing suggestions as to how to create the most effective visuals for learning. Consequently using "a few well chosen and well executed illustrations can economically and powerfully convey a wealth of meaning" (p.150), according to Knupfer (1993).

Many students in higher education have difficulty distinguishing the meaningful visual messages imbedded in an image as well as recognising predominate visual factors that aid understanding. Stokes (2002) has suggested that if "visual literacy is regarded as a language, then there is a need to know how to communicate using this language, which includes being alert to messages and critically reading or viewing images as the language of the message" (p.12). According to Rourke and O'Connor (2009): "As educators we should promote in students an understanding of the connection between the disciplinary language that needs to be learnt, and the factors about the visual image that need to be remembered while linking this new information to the learners past acquired knowledge" (p.34). As educators we need to continue to reflect on how we could improve our teaching practice to promote learning while encouraging our students to have a 'love of learning' in our disciplines. As experienced design educators the authors feel they have a wealth of knowledge to contribute towards the 'effective use of visuals in higher education' to promote learning that they envisage will have relevance and application for other educators in higher education. They believe that visuals in education still have a vital role to play towards facilitating critical thinking skills and promoting understandings that are transferable to other learning situations. This book endeavors to further enlighten and encourage the 21st century educator in higher education towards advancing this goal.

REFERENCES

Carney, R.N. and Levin, J.R. (2002). Pictorial illustrations still improve student's learning from text. *Educational Psychology Review*, *14*(1), March, 5-26.

DePorter, B. (1992). *Quantum learning: Unleashing the genius in you*, New York: Dell Publishing.

Dwyer, F. and Baker, R. (2001). A systematic meta-analytic assessment of the instructional effects of varied visuals on different types of educational objectives. In Griffen, R.E., Williams, V.S. and Lees, J. (Eds.) *Exploring the visual future: art, design, science and technology*, (pp.129-134). Blacksburg, VA: The International Visual Literacy Association.

Greeno, J. P. and Hall, R. P. (1997). Practicing representation: Learning with and aboutpresentation forms, *Phi Delta Kappan*,*78*(5) 361–367.

Hawk, T.F. and Shah, A.J. (2007). Using learning style instruments to enhance student learning, *Decision Sciences Journal of Innovative Education*, *5*(1), 1-18.

Knupfer, P. (1993). From text to television: Hermeneutic textualisation and the challenges of visual technology in the teaching of history, *Verbo-Visual literacy: Understanding and Applying New Educational Communication Media Technologies*. Selected readings from the Symposium of the International Visual Literacy Association (Delphi, Greece, June 25-29, 1993).

Marsh, H.W. and Dunkin, M.J. (1997). Students' evaluation of University teaching effectiveness, *Journal of Higher Education*, 64, 1-18.

McKay, E. (1999,Sept.). An investigation of text-based instructional materials enhanced with graphics, *Educational Psychology*, *19*(3). 323-335.

McLoughlin, C. and Krakowski, K. (2001, Sept.). Technical tools for visual thinking: what does the research tell? Paper presented at the: *Apple University Consortium Academic and Development Conference*, James Cook University, Townsville, 23-26.

Meyer, J. and Land, R. (2003). *Threshold concepts and Troublesome knowledge,(1): linkage to ways of thinking and practicing within the disciplines, Improving student learning – Ten years on.* Oxford: OCSLD.

Rakes, G. C. (1999, Sept.). Teaching visual literacy in a multimedia age, *TechTrends*, *43*(4), 14-18.

Rieber, L. P. (1995). *A historical review of visualisation in human cognition Educational Technology, Research and Development*, *43*(1), 1042–1629.

Rourke, A. J. and O'Connor, Z. (2010b). The expectations-reality interface: Visual literacy levels, predominant learning modalities and preferences among first year design students, *Aspiration, Access, Achievement, 13th Pacific Rim First Year in Higher Education*, QUT publications, Adelaide, 27th-30th June, 2010, 1-5.

Rourke, A. J. and O'Connor, Z. (2010c). Visual Literacy Levels and Predominant Learning Modalities among First year Design Students: The influence of teacher intervention, *Design Principles and Practices: An International Journal, 4*(1), 347-360.

Rourke, A. J. and O'Connor. Z. (2009a). Look before you leap: testing assumptions on visual literacy and predominate learning style modalities of undergraduate design students in Australia and New Zealand, *The International Journal of Learning, 16*(8), 33-46.

Rourke, A. J. and Coleman, K. (2010). A learner support system: Scaffolding to enhance digital learning, *The International Journal of Technology, Knowledge and Society, 6*(1), 55-70.

Rourke, A. J. and O'Connor, Z. (2008). I can see it but I don't understand it!: Investigating visual literacy skills and learning styles in Higher Education design history students. *International Journal of the Humanities*, 6, 1-10.

Rourke, A. J., and O'Connor, Z. (2010a). Examining ways to improve visual teaching materials: The role of visual literacy and predominant learning modality. In M. L. Albertson (Ed.), *Developments in higher education* (pp. 1-37). New York: Nova Science.

Rourke, A.J. and O'Connor, Z. (2009b). Investigating Visual Literacy Levels and Predominant Learning Modality Among Undergraduate Design Students in Australia: Preliminary findings. *Design Principles and Practices: An International Journal, 3*(2), 17-28.

SalomonG. (1997). Of mind and media: How culture's symbolic forms affect learning and thinking, *Phi Delta Kappan*, 375–380.

Seels. B. (1994). Visual literacy: the definition problem. In D. M. Moore and F. M. Dwyer (Eds.) *Visual literacy: A spectrum of visual learning,* (pp.97–112), Englewood Cliffs, NJ: Educational Technology Publications.

Stokes, S. (2002). Visual literacy in teaching and learning: A literature perspective, *Electronic Journal for the Integration of Technology in Education, 1*(1), 10-19.

Chapter 2

Effective and Reflective Teaching: The Role of Visuals, Concept Cartoons and Mind Maps

Abstract

This chapter will explore what the literature says about what it means to be an effective lecturer in higher education. This will include a discussion on what makes a lecturer an effective teacher and teaching as a reflective activity with specific reference to the role visuals can play in this premise. It is acknowledged that there is no simple answer to the question of what makes an effective teacher in higher education. Teacher effectiveness embraces multiple perspective (Marsh and Duncan, 1997) including student and teacher expectations, teacher knowledge and experience, assessment practices as well as methodological issues, to name but a few. Both concept cartoons and mind maps will be discussed as an example of visual learning and teaching tools that could be utilised to promote student learning in higher education.

The Promoting Effective Teaching and Learning

Studies have been conducted on how teacher effectiveness might be defined in higher education (Braskamp and Ory, 1994; Young and Shaw, 1999; Theall and Franklin, 2001, Delaney, Johnson, Johnson and Treslan, 2010) through examining how students rate a competent teacher. The validity of using student ratings to evaluate lecturer effectiveness has been supported by the literature (Feldman, 1988, Marsh 1987, Entwistle, 1989, Marshal and Bailey, 1993, Greenwood and Gillmore, 1997). According to Theall and Franklin (2001) there is ample research to support the notion students are the most qualified sources to provide feedback on whether their learning experience was productive, informative, satisfying, or worthwhile. They stress however that student's views on these factors are not a direct indicator of instructor or course effectiveness but of student satisfaction. According to Ramsden (1992) students can "easily differentiate the empty performer from the good teacher" (p.91).

Student rating of teaching has also been found to correspond to lecturer personality traits. Students rated charismatic and expressive lecturers as highly effective while disregarding the substantive content of a lecture (Renaud and Murray, 1996). There is however, enormous ambiguity between studies on effective teaching, for in the study conducted by Renaud and Murray, (1996) where students as mentioned rated highly the 'charismatic and expressive lecturer', is this the same personality trait students commented on in Schwartz (1980) study, where the lecturer displays 'enthusiasm for their work'?

A strong relationship has been found however between student's ratings of lecturer effectiveness and their course grades. In a study by Greenwood and Gillmore (1997) it was found that the lecturers who were more lenient in their assessment received more positive student evaluations. However, a lenient assessor may not be an effective teacher. Although, "the most significant single influence on student's learning is their perception of assessment" (Ramsden, 1988, p.24) and an effective teacher is aware of this, for they construct assessment procedures to the objectives of the course including the skills, knowledge and understanding that they wish students to obtain. Adding to this, Booth (1993) discovered through questionnaires with seventy university students studying history that 60% felt that students should have a say in the type of assessment that they were required to undertake in their course. Based on this research, effective teachers are 'fair' in their grading (even lenient if you want to win in the popularity stakes!) of student's work, and they link the assessment to the course overall aim and objectives. The effective teacher also allows for flexibility so that assessment can be tailored to student interests by allowing them to have a voice in the type and methods of assessment used.

Young and Shaw (1999) discovered through qualitative research that examined student's ratings of University lecturer effectiveness that, "effective communication, comfortable learning atmosphere, concern for student learning, student motivation and course organisation" (p.682) were found to be highly related characteristics of effective teaching. In particular this study found that the value or worth of a course to the student (as well as lecturers) emerged as an important aspect of lecturer effectiveness. The notion of the 'value' of a course was tied into the importance of relevancy of the content of the course to the student and their studies as a whole and they rated a lecturer as effective if they were successful in teaching students to value their course. "Regardless of how difficult or mundane the course content is, the truly effective teacher of that course is assuming some responsibility for making it a valuable course for the students" (Young and Shaw, 1999, p.684). It also appeared in this study that effective lecturers could compensate for deficiencies in one or two areas by demonstrating exceptional skill in other areas.

An online survey conducted by Delaney, Johnson, Johnson and Treslan (2010), with over 17,000 graduate and undergraduate students at Memorial University of Newfoundland discovered that students identified nine behaviors that are characteristics of effective teaching. These included that effective teachers are: respectful of students, knowledgeable, approachable, engaging, communicative, organized, responsive, professional and humorous. This survey took into account the opinions of students on campus as well as online distant learners. Interestingly this study discovered that: "the characteristics of effective teaching transcend the mode of delivery" (p.66), however the only difference they identified between face-to-face teaching and online was that the distance learners had more concerns over the instructors quality of communication. Delaney *et al.* (2010) study also found that students valued more lecturers who were "respectful of them as people" (p.67) and as such appreciated them as individuals.

For Braskamp and Ory (1994), effective teaching was the "creation of situations in which appropriate learning occurs; shaping those situations is what successful teachers have learned to do effectively" (p. 40). In many ways the concept of the educator as facilitator rather than instructor captures this notion of guiding, supporting, directing and encouraging students in the learning process to be active collaborative learners. However with many courses now using online learning management systems (LMS) the notion of the educator as 'instructor' has come back into vogue, particularly as many of these courses provide all the course content and assessment online. Students in many online courses are expected to self-direct their learning while educators play the role as investigators checking progress and directing students to other online resources.

The emphasis on what makes an effective teacher changes when examining this phenomenon from the teachers rather than the students point-of-view. Lecturers above all are concerned about having 'mastery' of the course material. The goals for 'mastery' vary between lecturers, however 'the ability to communicate effectively' has appeared as an important characteristic of the effective lecturer regardless of their subject area (Goldsmid, 1977; Schwartz, 1980; Ramsden, 1992, Young and Shaw, 1999). This aspect of teaching generally covers: "clarity of speech, organisation of material, style of presentation and stimulation of thinking" (Schwartz, 1980, p.120). Feldman (1988) warns however, that the teacher having content-knowledge maybe rated highly by students (and lecturers), but knowing one's subject does not necessarily discriminate between good and poor teaching.

Although Schwartz (1980) discovered through questioning her students about the characteristics of the ideal teacher, that "knowledge of one's subject" was not high on the priority list, however this is important to the lecturer who was concerned with students 'mastery of course material'. Teachers in higher education are expected to have not only a solid grasp of the knowledge of their discipline but also be experts in their field, as such they need to keep up to date with current research in their area of speciality. Added to this, it will be argued that educators in higher education should also master the skills of teaching and understand the philosophies of learning, which will assist them to communicate their disciplinary knowledge and understanding to their students.

Schwartz (1980) also found that students rated evaluation of their work, including "fairness of tests, and promptness of grading and feedback" (p.121), as an important criterion of effective teaching after the lecturer's communication ability. Booth (1993) previously mentioned, discovered (through questionnaires) that university students valued highly any feedback they received on their assessment and he established that many students were perplexed by the variations they found in their feedback and grades between tutors within the same subject.

Schwartz (1980) suggested that "rapport with students based on mutual respect, availability and approachability" (p.121) was also ranked high along with 'enthusiasm for their work'. Students even went so far as to say that the effective teacher "displays self-confidence without arrogance, and dresses appropriately for their role" (!), in addition, "personal generosity (that is) giving of self" (p.121) was seen an essential characteristics of the effective teacher. Booth (1993) in his study discovered that students felt that the effective teacher also showed "sensitivity to students hopes and expectations" (p.228). Studies such as Schwartz (1980); Booth (1993) and Delaney *et al.* (2010), demonstrated that on student priority list of the characteristics of an effective teacher having a personal relationship with students through taking a genuine interest in them as individuals was of major concern.

However, Booth (1993) emphasised, along with other researchers (Brown and Atkins 1991; Ramsden, 1992) that students believed overall that success or failure in their studies largely depended upon their own efforts and that an effective teacher should promote independence of learning as students wanted some control over their learning. Students in the Booth (1993) study also went as far as to say that, of the seventy questioned some 80% felt they should have a considerable say in what content they were to learn, not only in their subjects, but also in the content of their degree. One student went further on the issue of students involvement in the learning process to stress that: "teaching methods should be to suit students and not the easiest option for the staff" (p.234). However, Booth (1993) stressed that student comments revealed that they wanted a "stronger consultation role rather than a controlling influence" (p.234).

It is imperative that educators in higher education engage in open communication with students where questions on the course content and assessment expectations can be asked and answered. Teachers need to 'take on board' students comments in order to improve the courses they teach which means viewing the course and it's teaching from the student's viewpoint. This feedback can be particularly useful when reviewing course material and when considering the best teaching methods to employ to communicate to students the main points to be learnt and to assist them towards developing a understanding of the course material.

An educator could only be considered an effective teacher it is generally believed, if ultimately meaningful learning has taken place. According to Novak and Cañas (2008) meaningful learning requires:

1. "The material to be learned must be conceptually clear and presented with language and examples relatable to the learner's prior knowledge.
2. The learner must possess relevant prior knowledge. This condition can be met after age 3 for virtually any domain of subject matter, but it is necessary to be careful and explicit in building concept frameworks if one hopes to present detailed specific knowledge in any field in subsequent lessons. We see, therefore, that conditions (1) and (2), are interrelated and both are important.
3. The learner must choose to learn meaningfully. The one condition over which the teacher or mentor has only indirect control is the motivation of students to choose to learn by attempting to incorporate new meanings into their prior knowledge, rather than simply memorizing concept definitions or propositional statements or computational procedures. The indirect control over this choice is primarily in instructional strategies used and the evaluation strategies used. Instructional strategies that emphasize relating new knowledge to the learner's existing knowledge foster meaningful learning" (p.4).

In order for meaningful learning to take place educators need to be trained in what teaching and learning methods to adopt that best facilitate worthwhile effective learning. This is an ongoing process, educators should continually update their knowledge and understanding of teaching and learning and be motivated to practice, evaluate and adapt their methods so that purposeful valuable learning is achieved. Institutions should dedicate more funds and provide a reward system that encourages academics be more motivated to want to learn and practice proven effective methods for promoting meaningful learning. Effective educators should be encouraged by their institution to share their teaching and learning knowledge and skills with their colleagues in a supportive, friendly, non-threatening, collaborative environment. If this can take place then educators in higher education may become more driven to want to provide a more valuable learning experience for students.

Young and Shaw (1999) discovered from questioning university students that, "regardless of how difficult or mundane the course content is the truly effective teacher of that course is assuming some responsibility for making it a valuable course for the students" (p.684). An effective lecturer in higher education should include a variety of well-selected visuals and through a well-constructed visual 'reading' of these, provide exemplars for students to follow which would hopefully assist them towards an understanding of the subject. This in turn could improve student use of visuals in their assignments, which may add immensely towards them valuing both the course and it's content.

There is no agreement on 'what makes an effective teacher' even the terms used to describe such a phenomenon are ambiguous and open to subjective interpretation. However as has been discussed, many agree that effective teachers motivate students, are effective communicators, provide fair and flexible assessment, provide relevant, prompt feedback and they value students as individuals. Most of these factors of the effective teacher in higher education it must be acknowledged come from the student not the teacher's perspective. Studies such as Schwartz (1980) revealed that students are less concerned about teachers having a mastery of their discipline, this was however a factor that concerned teachers. A more recent study conducted by Delaney, Johnson, Johnson and Treslan (2010) however revealed that students do in fact appreciate teachers that had "knowledge of content and pedagogy" (p.60). This reinforces the argument that there is no set agreement in particular from the student's perspective, on what is an effective teacher. The second area to be addressed in this chapter, 'the theories on reflective practice', are as enigmatic as those presented to characterise the effective teacher. Both these theories will be linked together to provide a basis for analysing next the use of visual material in teaching in order to critique their effective use in higher education.

The Reflective Educator: Examining the Effective Use of Visual Material in Lectures

The two paradigms, that of what constitutes effective teaching in higher education and teaching as a reflective practice, will be amalgamated in order to move from two generalist theories to later explore the realities of teaching practice. Many of the characteristics so far mentioned on the effective teacher will be fundamentally combined and applied to a study of the effective use of visuals in a lecture situation in a university setting.

Rakes (1999) has provided a number of strategies for the use of visuals in the classroom including, "creation, sharing and discussion of visual images in class, perhaps through the use of small group projects or co-operative learning groups" (p.17). She also suggests educators create visual projects that have a variety of options so that even those less artistic are confident sharing their thoughts visually. "Internet resources along with paint/draw programs. HyperCard-type programs and presentation software used with clip art, photographs (which can be scanned into the computer) and video clips allows students to use visual ideas easily as a communication tool" (Rakes, 1999, p.17). Since these suggestions were put forward by Rakes (1999) there has been a large mass of software available to assist both students and teachers to create visual teaching and presentation material. There is an avalanche of visual material that can be easily downloaded from the internet to use in teaching and for student assignments and presentations. We have become a visual 'cut and paste' society. What needs to be stressed in education to both teachers and students is that visuals should first be thoroughly research before being used in teaching or student's assignments. Students need to be shown how best to utilise visuals in their presentations to more critically illustrate a point rather than as 'decoration' to distract their audience or to relay superficial information.

Many researchers have discovered (Kozma, Belle and Williams, 1978; Brown, 1978; Brown and Atkins, 1991; Ramsden, 1992) that effective use of audio-visual aids has improved student learning in higher education. Visuals play an important role in delivering lectures in many subject areas in higher education. The communication of many key concepts and content in many disciplines in higher education rely heavily on visual illustration. These are not always effectively utilised to promote active long-lasting learning that has relevance to other areas outside the classroom. Through understanding the relevant theories of effective teaching, educators have a basis for critiquing their own teaching practice in order to reflect on what areas could be improved to enhance student learning. More than a decade ago Biggs (1999) recommended that reflecting on teaching and becoming aware of what is 'wrong' and how it may be improved, requires having an explicit theory of teaching. This is anoften neglected area in higher education, there are still educators who do not believe that it is necessary to develop a philosophy and rationale for teaching and learning or if they have one how to effectively apply it.

Many research papers that have been written over the past twenty years or so focusing on effective teaching in undergraduate university courses have based their assumptions and recommendations on years of teaching experience as opposed to controlled experiments. As Biggs (1999) claimed many university teachers, "through research and scholarship, have developed a perspective on their field of expertise that is not to be found in textbooks" (p.99). Reflective practice can be formally directed as a form of 'action learning' (Elliott, 1991; Kember and Kelly, 1993).

Effective teaching practice is not a static enterprise, good teachers are always looking for ways of improving their teaching and hence student learning as well as learning about themselves as teachers. "Essentially, action learning is being systematic about changing your teaching, and making sure the changes are in the right direction, specifically that your students are now learning better than they use to" (Biggs, 1999, p.6). The process of reflecting on one's teaching involves placing current practice under the microscope, so to speak, to identify both good practice and areas that need "fine tuning."

Many studies agree that many educators need to 'fine tune' their communication skills as good communication was ranked as an important attribution of the effective teacher in higher education (Goldsmid, 1977; Schwartz, 1980; Ramsden, 1992, Young and Shaw, 1999; Delaney, Johnson, Johnson and Treslan, 2010).

This section of this chapter will mainly focus on two specific aspects of this, the 'why's' and 'how's' of utilising visuals in teaching to promote learning. Specifically arguing that visual material assists the lecturer towards explaining complex multi-faceted information, stressing important points, providing an illustration of a subject as well as illustrating concepts that are not easily verbalised which can aid towards understanding. The effective use of visual material can assist lecturers towards efficiently and coherently communicating the content of the course. For according to Brown and Atkins (1991), the "main use of audio–visual aids in lectures is to improve clarity in explaining" (p.25).

Especially when as Heuvelman (1996) suggests, "the subject-matter is rather concrete, visualization that matches a simultaneously spoken text will not be problematic" (p.88). However there is much material being discussed in lectures in higher education that is not so concrete and straight-forward for the student, hence educators need to be mindful how they utilise visual material to explain highly complex concepts. In this case one or two carefully chosen visual examples discussed in detail could prove a better method for explaining complex content if the illustration is diagrammatic with limited text. Added to this when "the meanings of picture and sound do not match" (p.87), Heuvelman (1996) advises when discussing the use of television in education, "the viewers will not be able to pick up the message" (p.87). This can also be applied to lectures if visuals are not used appropriately to complement and reinforce the spoken words. As it is suggested, "at most only some visual fragments will be remembered, whereas the 'real' message was contained in the audio text" (Heuvelman, 1996, p.87), in the case of lectures if something can be explained clearly in auditory form then visuals may become only a distraction. However visuals are paramount when the content of the discipline is encapsulated in visual form that can not be explained by verbal form alone such as teaching art or design.

The concept of 'effective communication' and 'visual literacy' discussed later, need to be combined in many subject areas such as for example, teaching the concept of Post-Modernism to art and design students. When showing examples of this phenomenon, one should endeavor to teach students that pictures and symbols can have several meanings, for "meaning has a plurality of identities" (Hirsch, 1984, p.90). As can be seen in the visual below (Refer to Figure 2.1) of a Charles Jenck's silver Piazza tea and coffee service (1983) manufacturer by Alessi.

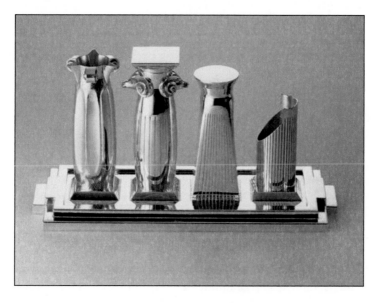

Figure 2.1. Charles Jencks Tea and coffee Piazza service, printed with permission from Di Palma Associati International Press Agency for Alessi, http://www.alessi.com/en/3/1415/silver-objects/tea-and-coffee-service.

Fluted columns represent classicism in architecture these have a function but have no function when used as a decorative element in a Post-modern tea and coffee service. To contextualize Post-Modern art or design it is useful to analyse a variety of examples and include definition and application of relevant vocabulary, for example terminology such as: pluralism, conceptualism, eclecticism and historicism would be applied. The teacher in this example could be an agent for transforming knowledge, by assisting students to interpret and to construct their own understanding (Biggs, 1999).

It is important however, as educators to remember that one cannot assume that their audience has seen what they see (Hall, 1975; Bligh, 2000). In order to avoid misinterpretation as well as misrepresentation, as previously mentioned, it is usually advisable in visually complex disciplines such as in art and design, to provide a variety of visual examples to explain a similar concept with the hope that at least one illustration will lead to an understanding of the concept.

A later chapter explores the notion of utilising a variety of visual prototypes to assist in teaching students to identify a specific art or design work. This approach could be adapted across other disciplines where a number of concepts could be embodied into a typical visual exemplar. Good teaching methodologies should have application in a variety of disciplinary contexts and the notion of the effective teacher should be seen as applicable regardless of the disciplinary focus. As these skills and understandings should be transferable to any teaching enterprise.

In the case of communicating knowledge regardless of the disciplinary focus, the effective teacher would use visual examples to illustrate terminology as well as an avenue for relating students existing knowledge and experiences to any new knowledge. For example, within a wider cultural context of the mass media, a pluralistic interpretation could be illustrated through reminding students of a scene in a popular film, television commercial or magazine advertisement. In the case of teaching art and design students this could then be drawn back to their art or design studio work and the role of the designer in mass media, implying a connection between the student's own interests, studio work (art or design processes) and the art or design profession. "It is not always appreciated that just as it is necessary to state a point in a number of ways, it is sometimes necessary to illustrate it in varying ways" (Bligh, 2000, p. 93).

This one example demonstrates how a teacher could facilitate a 'sharpening of perceptual skill' as well as developing student's fundamental visual and expressive vocabulary, through a more multi-faceted reading of a visual image by placing art or design language into a meaningful context. For "working with images…is a highly motivating way to lead students gently to engage with different theories and ideas" (Frederick, 2000, p.105).

Most of the literature suggests that students need to be motivated to learn and an effective teacher has methods, usually intuitive, for promoting enthusiasm for their subject (Reeve, 1996, Young and Shaw, 1999).

Showing visual examples provides a shift of the audience's attention from the physical presence of the lecturer, this in turn can assist towards providing a more comfortable atmosphere for the lecturer to 'relax in' and in turn 'promote enthusiasm' for their subject. One way of expressing enthusiasm and motivating students is through what Brown and Atkins (1991) terms 'transmission', where information is relayed through not only verbalisation but also through non-verbal cues (such as body language) and audio–visual aids which are utilised to convey both meaning and attitudes.

Figure 2.2. Cartoon of effective teacher by author's 10 year-old daughter.

There are also many external factors to consider that visual material can play a role in, for example for structuring of the course material. For effective teachers organise their lectures and courses to cover not only the required content but also to stimulate enthusiasm as well as to provide relevant links between the subject-matter, students interests and assessment. Visuals can play a vital role towards organising material into smaller digestible segments that can be linked to previous knowledge, as well as to new points (ideas, concepts), to create a pause (a moment for thought) or to provide a closure to a lecture. Brown and Atkins (1991) claimed that ideas linked through visual symbols were more likely to be retained in the long-term memory and since this should be a major aim for the effective teacher, time should be spent planning visual presentations so that key concepts, processes and relationships are clearly communicated.

According to Biggs (1999) by using visuals effectively in this way, cognitive growth can be encouraged through the restructuring that occurs when new knowledge becomes connected with previous knowledge. Teachers, Biggs (1999) claimed, should builds on the known, "for in deep learning, new learning connects with old, so teaching should exploit interconnectedness: make the connection explicit, choose familiar examples first, get students to build on their own experience, draw and explain parallels while teaching, use cross-references, design curricula that draws out cross connections" (pp.73-74). As shall be demonstrated later in this chapter, both concept cartoons and concept maps are effective visual learning and teaching tools to help achieve connectivity in the learning process.

Effective teachers, as previously mentioned, show 'mastery' (Schwartz, 1980) for their subject area through clarity, organization and style which visual material enhances. Stimulating thinking, was also an important aspect of effective teaching and visuals can be used persuasively to promote discussion, particularly in tutorials. According to Brown and Atkins (1991) "audio-visual aids may be used to confirm and reinforce the main points of a lecture, as a explanatory device in their own right, as an exemplar, or as a stimulus for thinking and discussion" (p.26).

The relevance of assessment to the students and the subject was a factor that the effective teacher considered according to before mentioned research. Within the humanities area especially in the arts, students use visuals (pictures, graphs, charts etc.) in their assignments to support their discussion and provide factual evidence, particularly in their essays and tutorial presentations. If lecturers effectively use visuals, students are provided with an exemplar that can assist in the appropriate use of visuals in their assignments. In order for students to grasp such an 'exemplar' of an effective use of visual material, it requires consistency and repetition on the lecturers part as 'perceptual sensitivity' can be improved upon through focused instruction, and according to Raney (1999) innate perceptual sensitivity can be sharpened by education or exposure.

One way of testing the effectiveness of the instruction would be to first examine student's use of visuals in their first written paper (that specifically asks for examples). The lectures following this could include emphasis (within the context of the lecture content), on effective ways of using visual example to support or provide evidence of a particular theory or theme. The student's next essay would then be examined to identify improvements in their use of visuals in this capacity. There is a usefulness to educators to discover if the effective use of visuals is a transferable skill that could be taught and in doing so, discover if students learn by viewing examples of good practice and then to examine if this has had any effect on improving student's visual literacy skills.

For visual aids to be effective, Brown and Atkins (1991) stated that: "illustrations, diagrams and summaries must be simple, brief and readable from the back of the class" (p.26). This statement appears to be 'common-sense', however it is often human nature to question this reasoning faculty. In teaching practice when explaining simple concepts, many educators often opt for verbal rather than visual elucidation. However, simply drawn black and white cartoons discussed later, can often capture student's attention more effectively than continuous monotonous discussion. "Ideally two or three simple illustrations are better than one that is complex" (Bligh, 2000, p. 93). As far as considering if visuals (pictures, diagrams, written lists etc.) can be 'readable from the back of the room', it is important that students are encouraged to fill the seats towards the front of the lecture theatre so they are more 'physically' engaged in the lecture. However as many lecturers have found, there are many 'back row dwellers' that refuse to move, who are willing to forgo their clear vision of the visual images. In this instance it would be useful to provide students with all the lecture visuals online so that they can be viewed on their own laptop computers during the lecture.

There are many useful ways of using visuals in teaching across the disciplines. Rakes (1999) suggests that in the social sciences a passage could be read from a book that contains numerical information, students could then be asked to create charts or graphs that visually represent that information. She also proposes that students could also take directions from text (such as steps for conducting a science experiment) and turn these directions into flow charts. Other suggestions by Rakes (1999) includes that the teacher locates: "several appropriate Internet sites. Ask students to describe the function of the graphics on that site. Describe the visual elements that require interaction with the user in order to explore the text" (p.17). To enhance student's visual literacy skills, educators need to provide activities such as those mentioned by Rakes (1999) that provide learning opportunities to develop their comprehension of the messages that visually convey as well as the semantic links between visuals and text. Rakes (1999) proclaimed that, "Teachers can create a positive atmosphere for using these strategies by providing enough class time to complete visuals and by including them in assignments and tests" (p.17). They could also provide examples of effective practice by showing students in class both good and poor examples of using visual material in assignments and presentations. As well the amount of time a lecturer spends on each visual example emphasises to the students their importance. Brown and Atkins (1991) also recommended, that if the illustrations are important for conveying knowledge and understanding of a subject then provide students with enough time to view them as well as if necessary to also copy them for later study.

There have been many studies conducted on the importance of note-taking in lectures (Hartley and Davies, 1978; Peper and Mayer, 1986; Kiewra. 1987; Isaacs, 1989 and 1994). It is generally agreed that note-taking of auditory as well as any visually presented material, could enhance student's short-term memory and in some cases recalling and connecting to previous lecture content in their long term memory. According to Kochkar (2000) taking notes in lectures can also provide students with training in listening as well as experience in taking down information quickly. Studies have found that copying down information both written and visual makes students more active participants. Issacs (1994) discovered that of the sixty-four lecturers that were questioned in his study, fifty-five wanted students to take notes in their lectures.

Lecturers agree, according to Issacs (1994), that note-taking serves to provide students with a basis for further study; helps students remember the lecture; provides a basis for revision of the subject and allows students to see the structure of the lecture. "Understanding is expected to occur later when the recipient has had time to analyse, synthesize and reflect upon the material which has been presented" (Woods, 1983). Often lecturers notice that the students towards the front of the lecture theatre, in the majority of cases, are not just writing down information but also copying visuals, particularly the graphs or diagrams shown. The 'back row dwellers' who have chosen a less than clear vision of the lecture seam less interested in recording the lecture through note-taking as a result they have forgone the aid of a 'memory jog' for later revision of the information presented in the lecture.

Recording visual examples in lecture situations is time-consuming for both the student and the lecturer. It requires the lecturer pausing in their dialogue so students can concentrate on accurately copying down the visual example. To avoid this disruption, Brown and Atkins (1991) suggested that if the illustrations are available in books, the lecturer should instead give a full reference, so that the student could photocopy them later. This is a useful method, as due to the time restraint of most lectures in higher education many lecturers do not provide 'silent time' for students to copy down visual examples, unless it is a simple diagram. As Brown and Atkins (1991) recommended, "the more that technologies allow lecturers to illustrate concepts, or large amounts of information in a way that students cannot record in their notes or immediately commit to long-term memory, the less efficient lecturing becomes" (p.26). Photocopied skeletal summary hand-outs, which require students to fill out only limited information during lectures could be an effective way of avoiding some of the above mentioned dilemmas (Brown and Tomlinson, 1980).

Honing visual literacy skills requires, as will be discussed in subsequent chapters, developing 'perceptual awareness', and exercises that require students to 'look intensely' could be used by the lecturer to draw attention to and promote such 'sensitivities'. Often this can simply be achieved by clearly indicating which feature to look for in a visual example.

Brown and Atkins (1991) also suggested that lecturers should "if possible, pose a question for the students to answer while they are watching, give them an opportunity for brief discussion afterwards, and then summarise the main points and link them to the relevant parts of the lecture" (p.27).This method could be applied to promote 'perceptual awareness' of the visual example, key questions could be asked to focus and draw students attention to the features they need to study that will aid in their understanding.

Brown and Atkins (1991) also recommended that an image should be held still for two or more seconds in order to avoid information overload. A longer time would be required however, if the illustration encapsulates vital or complex information that auditory alone could not clearly explain. It has also been argued that, using as few as ten slides or other still images in a one hour lecture to illustrate crucial steps, is more memorable and hence also more effective towards students later recalling information from their long-term memories (Brown and Atkins, 1991).

Visual overload for example in many arts disciplines is rarely a considered factor as the disciplinary knowledge is mostly encapsulated in the visual itself as a result a multitude of visuals are often utilised to explain the content. For within many visual art disciplines, ten visual examples to illustrate the variety, similarities and contrasts between art or designs or to illustrate, for example a stylistic change, would be an inadequate number, unless they were used to illustrate only one artist or designer's work. One visual type that can be utilised in teaching to assist towards cutting back on the amount of visuals needed to explain a complex concept is the use of 'concept cartoon' in instruction, which the next section of this chapter will elaborate on.

EXAMPLES OF EFFECTIVE VISUAL TEACHING AND LEARNING TOOLS

Using Concept Cartoons to Promote Student Learning

Cartoons can be utilised in education to assist in explaining many complex phenonemen or simply as a method for catching student's attention. They provide a method by which 'abstraction is used as a teacher', according to Arnheim (1974) who suggested that the least realistic images work well where only elements of interest are highlighted. Cartoons can be utilisd as educative tools to encourage the learner to link their previous knowledge to new knowledge, to visually simplify complex concepts, argue varied opinions, highlight sensitive issues, as well as to promote active student participation in the classroom.

Visuals such as cartoons have been effectively utilised in education for many years as one method for succinctly 'getting the point across' to the learner as well as to 'grab attention' while adding humour and entertainment value. See for example the cartoon below (Refer to Figure 2.3), which demonstrates how humour in cartoons can be used to promote a discussion on what we have gained and what we have lost in education with the introduction of the world-wide-web and computer technology. This topic can also be discussed in relation to computer sciences, psychology, history, education, or with design and art students as a discussion on the evolution of graphic design and copyright laws.

"I hope you've learned your lesson about cheating Billy. I guess you can go back to your computer now."

Figure 2.3. Cartoon computer and abacus by cartoonist Dan Rosandich (licensed to authors).

The image of the computer as a metaphor for 'making life easy' for the student and the abacus representing the laborious 'old ways' provides contrasts to promote discussion and debate in the classroom around these issues.

Rakes (1999) suggested that during a classroom discussion of a current issue or controversial topic the teacher could ask the students to create an editorial cartoon that describes their opinion of the issue. According to Rakes (1999), there are many useful editorial cartoons available online. It is always worthwhile for teachers to supply several examples of an assignment (both good and poor) or learning activities so that students do not misinterpret the required outcome. Examples are necessary when asking students to create cartoons for classroom discussions particularly as some learners are less accomplished or confident about communicating via visual representation.

As a learning tool, there has been much research on the use of concept cartoons as a useful strategy for promoting argument and debate in the classroom in science subjects (Feasey, 1998; Keogh and Naylor, 1999; Wellington and Osborne, 2001). The term 'concept' cartoons, was first used by Naylor and Keogh (1999) as a style of cartoon that could be used to assess what students already know about a specific concept. This particular type of cartoon usually illustrates competing views on a particular phenomenon. Concepts cartoons can be utilised according to Naylor, Keogh, de Boo and Feasey (2001), to support and justify arguments specifically through their use of characterisation, they assist the viewer to see alternative options as plausible while promoting the need for exploring supportive evidence. This approach takes on the Constructivist learning premise (Vygotsky, 1962)that advocates that students develop meaning of a subject based on their own existing knowledge and understanding. Concept cartoons are considered one way of promoting discussion especially when utilised to encourage students to engage in debates about their views, which can assist towards them developing further understanding of a subject (Refer to Figure 2.4).

Keogh, Naylor and Wilson (1998) suggest that in order for concept cartoons to be effective, they should have minimal text, be in dialogue form and apply ideas to everyday situations. They also need to provide alternative viewpoints that relate to student's understanding as well as to acceptable views if they are to be creditable. Alternative views, Keogh, Naylor and Wilson (1998) put forward, need to be given equal status in concept cartoons so that the learner is prompted to want to figure out which alternative is appropriate in the context represented. Research has also provided some evidence that using concept cartoons in teaching is an effective method for discovering student's misconceptions of the course material as Naylor, Keogh, de Boo and Feasey (2001) discovered. Another effective teaching method for identifying student's misconceptions of the material being taught is to utilise mind maps which provide a visual representations of the learner's thought processes, which the next section of this chapter will discuss.

Figure 2.4. Cartoon for teaching design history (created by author).

Utilising Mind and Concept as a Teaching and Learning Tool

Mind maps can be utilise in teaching to assist students to create a visual representation of their ideas and newly acquired knowledge and understanding of course material. Mind maps are "used for storing, processing, organizing and presenting information graphically"(Nada, Kholief, Tawfik, and Metwally, 2009, p.255).Arrows, linking words and squares or circles, colour coding and symbols can be used to make explicit the links and relationships between information. Usually mind maps start with a main or central idea, related subordinate ideas are then placed strategically around this starting point (Refer to Figure 2.5).Mind maps can start with a question being posed then the relevant literature is read and then a mind map is created to assist the student to plan as well as debate their answer. They usually have a hierarchical structure for the creator makes the decision when placing information on a mind map of its level of importance.

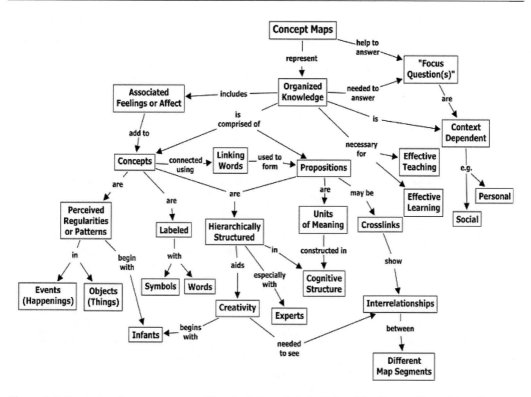

Figure 2.5. Example of a concept map, (Novak, J. D. and A. J. Cañas, The Theory Underlying Concept Maps and How to Construct and Use Them, Technical Report IHMC CmapTools 2006-01 Rev 01-2008, Florida Institute for Human and Machine Cognition. Available at: http://cmap.ihmc.us/Publications/ResearchPapers/TheoryUnderlyingConceptMaps.pdf.

Buzan (1991) suggests the following designing guidelines for structuring a Mind Map:

1. Start in the center with an image of the topic, using at least 3 colors.
2. Use images, symbols, codes, and dimensions throughout your Mind Map.
3. Select key words and print using upper or lower case letters.
4. Each word/image must be alone and sitting on its own line.
5. The lines must be connected, starting from the central image. The central lines are thicker, organic and flowing, becoming thinner as they radiate out from the centre.
6. Make the lines the same length as the word/image.
7. Use colors – your own code – throughout the Mind Map.
8. Develop your own personal style of Mind Mapping.
9. Use emphasis and show associations in your Mind Map.

Keep the Mind Map clear by using radial hierarchy, numerical order or outlines to embrace your branches.

Another feature of a mind or concept map that Novak and Cañas (2008) suggest is that they display cross-links that demonstrate where there are "relationships or links between concepts in different segments or domains" (p.20). Another important aspect of this feature of a mind map is that they "help us see how a concept in one domain of knowledge represented on the map is related to a concept in another domain shown on the map. In the creation of new knowledge, cross-links often represent creative leaps on the part of the knowledge producer" (p.20). These cross-links provide a method for succinctly and economically displaying thought processes.

According to Stevens (2009) recommendations, the first ideas need to be 'brain-stormed' on a piece of paper before any attempt is made to design a mind map. These thoughts are then used to create a skeletal form of a mind map then ideas are interlinked to the relevant category and certain elements are emphasised through various colours, fonts, underlining, bold or italics text. Steven (2009) suggests that a common problem is that people try to edit their ideas too soon before they have fully worked through the topic being mapped. He emphasises the importance of not making mind maps too cluttered with ideas as they may become incomprehensible to the creator and others trying to read them. Michalko (2006), concurred that mind maps should be studied over a prolonged period to allow for an insight to unfold into a complete idea. This method can assist the learner with recall of previous learnt information. Educators should encourage the learner to record previous learnt information on their mind maps and then connect this to any newly acquired knowledge. Then encourage students to use this new understanding on other learning activities to promote the use of transfer skills.

Mind maps can be a useful educational tool for providing a visual of students' thought processes as they display where an idea moves from the universal and abstract to the concrete and more explicit. According to Buzan (1991) mind maps are a type of cognitive map that has no formal restrictions on the types of links made between words. They also provide a structured format where ideas can not only be visually chartered but also deconstructed. Mind maps can free-up working memory, which allows for more short-term memory capacity for carrying out other learning tasks. By writing down thoughts and ideas in this way, it takes the stress off the learner to process new information within the limited capacity of their working memory. Mind maps can also be quickly reviewed, revised and added to as the learner rethinks their knowledge of a subject. This method allows for the student to become more self-directed and in doing so become more independent learners.

Mind maps also provide an easily accessible visualisation of a learner's thought process that teachers can use to identify any misunderstandings of a subject. They are an effective planning and organisational tool that students can use to map out their progressive thoughts about answering course assignments. This encourages the learner to view course assessment as an ongoing learning process that happens over time not as a 'rush job' completed the night before it is due. As well as a tool for encouraging students to make cross-disciplinary links while they problem-solve which can assist towards promoting the development of higher order and creative thinking skills.

Novak and Cañas (2008) suggested that, "there are two features of concept maps that are important in the facilitation of creative thinking: the hierarchical structure that is represented in a good map and the ability to search for and characterize new cross-links" (p.2). In order to achieve this, students need to be trained and shown how to create mind maps that are more than just recorders of knowledge. They need to be shown how to design mind maps that are innovative and creative so that they are used as a learning tool for problem solving as well as a means of enhancing understanding of a subject.

Mind maps can also be utilised to point out to the learner as Novak (1993) recommends that, "understanding is never complete. It is an iterative process where the learner moves gradually towards greater understanding" (p.53). Recording this process in a visual way provides at a glance this learning journey as it evolves over time. Mind maps can also be used to visually display where new knowledge has been understood, as well as being a versatile tool for linking what is known to newly acquired knowledge as previously explained, while also providing an avenue where independent thoughts can emerge.

As a teaching tool, mind maps provide a method for encouraging creative thinking when problem-solving. They are particularly effective for visual as well as kinesthetic learners who like to visualise and take a 'hands-on' active approach to learning. Mind maps can be utilised in the classroom to encourage learners to expand on and critically analyse what they have learnt and by doing this they develop higher order thinking skills as previously mentioned. For as Novak (1993) suggests, "educators need to empower learners by helping them organize and use carefully developed hierarchical knowledge structures" (p.53).

Mind maps if effectively utilised can provide a visualisation of the learning journey that students will travel through the course. They can also be utilised as a visual tool for charting out the relevance of the course content to the learner. The usefulness in education of utilising mind maps to promote learning has been appropriately summed-up by Nada, Kholief, Tawfik and Metwally (2009) who stated that:

> "With the fundamental goal of fostering learning they have been shown to be an effective tool for displaying students' prior knowledge, summarizing what has been learned, note taking, aiding study, planning, scaffolding for understanding, consolidating educational experiences, improving affective conditions for learning, teaching critical thinking, supporting cooperation and collaboration, and organizing unstructured knowledge content" (p.255).

As has been discussed, mind maps are a useful tool in education to encourage students to think more deeply about the material they are presented with and to provide a visual display of cognition and learning. Mind maps also provide a succinct way of linking ideas and emphasising key points. Mind maps as explained, can play a vital role towards improving students learning of disciplinary knowledge and as a visual display of group as well as individual student's understanding of the course material.

IMPLICATIONS FOR THE USE OF VISUAL MATERIALS FOR LEARNING

An important factor towards being an effective educator is to embrace multiple perspectives (Hirsch, 1984; Marsh and Dunkin, 1997). Well-selected visual examples can assist towards communicating this to students in a succinct manner without overloading them with irrelevant information. An important aspect of this, according to Brown and Atkins (1991) is that any illustrations, diagrams and summaries are simple, brief and readable even from the back of the classroom. Bligh (2000) recommends that: "Ideally two or three simple illustrations are better than one that is complex"(p. 93). When discussing visual examples educators should endeavor to be 'expressive' (Renaud and Murray, 1996) with how they utilise the tone of their voice. Taking an "actor on the stage" approach by also adding non-verbal cues (Brown and Atkins, 1991) can add 'charisma' to a lecture, a factor which, according to Renaud and Murray (1996) students appreciate.

Adding a 'story' behind the image can also assist the learner to become more actively engaged with the content material to be learnt. Stories are often remembered longer than factual information that has no link to student's previous knowledge. So where possible the educator should link to student's previous knowledge and experiences when giving 'learning' stories. Engels (2000) also suggested that, good stories, whether they are direct or indirect, could provide worthwhile insight into the 'sense-making' aspect of learning. The 'shared experience' aspect of stories told through visual imagery can assist educators towards creating a 'comfortable learning atmosphere', which according to Young and Shaw (1999) students appreciate.

Brown and Atkins, (1991) also proclaimed that, ideas linked through visual symbols are more likely to be retained in the long-term memory, so it becomes imperative therefore that if using metaphoric references to promote learning educators utilise obvious visual examples in instruction. According to Weick (1979) metaphors provide "language with flexibility, expressibility and a way to expand language" (p.47), which is a powerful way of reinforcing learning especially when linked to a memorable visual image. Chapter 6 will explore in more detail the notion of utilizing visual metaphors in instruction to promote long-term retention of learning.

As students value educators that are good communicators (Goldsmid, 1977; Schwartz, 1980; Ramsden, 1992, Young and Shaw, 1999, Delaney, Johnson, Johnson and Treslan, 2010) it is important that visual material is used to enhance discussion of a topic as well as to aid students towards comprehending the disciplinary content. An important factor of this is that as Hall (1975) and Bligh (2000) proposed, educators cannot assume that their audience has seen what they see, so being explicit is imperative. However as Bligh (2000) recommends, it is often necessary to state and illustrate a point in a number of ways. Visuals however should not distract from the main point being communicated or add complex knowledge beyond student's level of understanding; hence it is important that educators choose these wisely. As Brown and Atkins (1991) suggested, the main purpose of audio-visual aids in lectures is to improve clarity when explaining. Educators need to consider carefully if the visual material they utilise in lectures and classroom activities enhances understanding of the course content, if it does not then why use them in the first place?

However as has been argued visuals such as cartoons, mind maps and simple charts and graphs can be effective mechanisms for assisting students to remember the knowledge communicated in lectures. For as Heuvelman, (1996) discovered when testing effectiveness of recall of both realistic and schematic visuals that, "schematization of visuals illustrating abstract subject-matter would appear to be beneficial to viewers" (p.93) compared to realistic representations. In particular it was the 'concept related' graphics (Wileman, 1980) that showed the essence of the image as a stylized version of the real thing that proved the most effective communication tool.

The function visuals play as a teaching resource for facilitating student learning of a subject's content and for improving students overall visual literacy skills will be further explored in subsequent chapters. Research studies will later also be discussed that utilise both qualitative and quantitative data to provide evidence to suggest that, if visuals are effectively used in teaching, student's learning improves. The main objective for educators is to provide visual examples that encourage students to critically think about the course content and to develop further their skills for deciphering visual material in the world around them.

REFERENCES

Allen, D. (1994). Teaching Visual Literacy – Some Reflection on the Terms, *Journal of Art and Design Education*, *13*(2), 133-143.

Arnheim, R. (1974) Virtues and vices of the visual media, in: D.R. Olson, (Ed.) *Media and Symbols: The Forms of Expression, Communication, and Education.73rd Yearbook of the National Society for the Study of Education* Chicago: University of Chicago Press.

Biggs, J. (1999). *Teaching for Quality Learning at University*, Buckingham: SRHE and Open University Press.

Bligh, D.A. (2000). *What's the use of Lectures*, San Francisco: Jossey-Bass.

Booth, A. (1993). Learning History in University: student's views on teaching and assessment, *Studies in Higher Education*, *18*(2), 227-235.

Braskamp, L. A., and Ory, J. C. (1994). *Assessing Faculty work: Enhancing individual and instructional performance*. San Francisco, CA: Jossey-Bass.

Brown, G. and Atkins, M. (1991). *Effective Teaching in Higher Education*, London: Routledge.

Brown, G. (1978). *Lecturing and Explaining*, London and New York: Methuen.

Brown, G. A. and Tomlinson, D. (1980). How to improve handouts, *Medical Teacher*, *2*(5), 215-221.

Buzan, T. (1991). The mind map book. New York: Penguin.

Delaney, J. G., Johnson, A. N., Johnson, T. D., and Treslan, D. L. (2010). *Students' Perceptions of Effective Teaching in Higher Education*. St. John's, NL: Distance Education and Learning Technologies.

Elliot, J. (1991). *Action Research for Educational Change*, Milton Keynes: Open University Press.

Engels, S. (2000). The Stories children tell, making sense of the narratives of childhood. New York: WH Freeman and Company.

Entwistle, N.J. (1989). *Styles of Learning and Teaching*, London: Wiley.

Feasy, R. (1998). Effective questioning in science. In R.Sherrington (Ed.) *ASE guide to primary science education*, (pp.156-167). Hatfield: ASE/Stanley Thornes.

Feldman, K. A. (1988) 'Effective College Teaching from the student's and Faculty view: Matched or mismatched priorities'. *Research in Higher Education*. 28, 291-344.

Frederick P, J. (2000). Motivating students by active learning in the history classroom. Booth, A., and Hyland, P. (Ed.) *The Practice of University History Teaching*, (pp.102-112). Manchester: Manchester University Press.

Goldsmid, C. A., Gruber, J. E., and Wilson, E. K. (1977). Perceived Attributes of Superior Teachers (PAST): An inquiry into the giving of teacher awards. *American Educational Research Journal, 14*(4), 423-440.

Greenwood, A. G. and Gillmore, G. M. (1997). Grading leniency is a removable contaminant of student rating. *American Psychologist*, 52, 1209-1217.

Hall, W.C. (1975). *University Teaching*, Advisory Centre for University Education, Adelaide: University of Adelaide Press.

Hartley, J. and Davies, I.K. (1978). Note-taking: a critical review, *Programmed Learning and Educational Technology*, *15*(3), 207-224.

Heuvelman, A (1996). Realistic and Schematic Visuals, *Journal of Educational Media*, 22(2), 87-95.

http://cmap.ihmc.us/Publications/ResearchPapers/TheoryUnderlyingConceptMaps.pdf

Isaacs, G. (1989). Lecture note-taking, Learning and recall, *Medical Teacher*, 11 (3/4), 295-302.

Issacs, G. (1994). Lecturing Practice and Note-taking purpose, *Studies in Higher Education*, 19(2), 203-216.

Kember, D. and Kelly, M. (1993). *Improving Teaching through Action Research*, Green Guide No. 14, Camperdown, New South Wales: Higher Education Research and Development Society of Australasia.

Keogh, B. and Naylor, S. (1999). Concept cartoons, teaching and learning in science: an evaluation, *International Journal of Science Education,* 21(4), 431-446.

Keogh, B. Naylor, S. and Wilson, C. (1998). Concept cartoons: a new perspective on *Physics Education, 33*(4), 219-224.

Kiewa, K.A. (1987). Note-taking and review: the research and its implications, *Instructional Science*, 16(3), 233-249.

Kochkar, S.K. (2000). *Methods and Techniques Of Teaching.*New Delhi: Sterling.

Kozma, R.B., Belle, L.W., and Williams, G.W. (1978). *Instructional Techniques in Higher Education,* New Jersey: Englewood Cliffs Educational Technology.

Marsh, H.W, (1987). Students' evaluations of University teaching: Research findings, methodological issues, and directions for further research. *Journal of Educational Research*, 11, 253-388.

Marsh, H.W. and Baily, M. (1993). Multidimensional students' evaluations of teaching effectiveness. *Journal of Higher Education*, 64, 1-18.

Marsh, H. W., & Dunkin, M. J. (1997). Students' evaluations of university teaching: A multidimensional perspective. In R. P. Perry & J. C. Smart (Eds.), *Effective Teaching in Higher Education: Research and Practice*. New York: Agathon Press.

Michalko, M. (2006). Thinkertoys: A handbook of creative-thinking techniques, Toronto: Ten Speed Press.

Nada N, Kholief M, Tawfik S, and Metwally N. (2009). Mobile Knowledge Tool-kit to Create a Paradigm Shift in Higher Education, *Electronic Journal of Knowledge Management, 7*(2), 255 -260.

Naylor, S. and Keogh. B. (1999). Constructivism in class-room: Theory and practice. *Journal of Science Teacher Education*, 10(2), 93-106.

Naylor, S., Keogh, B., de Boo, M. and Feasey, R. (2001). Formative assessment using concept cartoons: Initial teacher training in the UK. In R. Duit (Ed.) *Research in Science Education: Past, Present and Future*, pp.137-142. Dordrecht: Kluwer.

Novak, J. D. and A. J. Cañas, *The Theory Underlying Concept Maps and How to Construct and Use Them*, Technical Report IHMC CmapTools 2006-01 Rev 01-2008, Florida Institute for Human and Machine Cognition.

Novak, J. D. (1993). How do we learn our lesson?: Taking students through the process. *The Science Teacher*, 60(3), 50-55.

Peper, R.J. and Mayer, R.E. (1986). Generative Effects of Note-taking during Science Lectures, *Journal of Educational Psychology*, 78(1) 34-38.

Rakes, G. C. (1999, Sept). Teaching visual literacy in a multimedia age, *TechTrends*, 43(4), 14-18.

Ramsden, P. (1992). *Learning to Teach in Higher Education*, London: Routledge.

Ramsden, P. (Ed.), (1988). *Improving Student Learning: New Perspectives*, London: Kogan.

Raney, K. (1999). Visual Literacy and the Art Curriculum', *Journal of Art and Design Education,18*(1), 42-47.

Reeve, J. M. (1996). *Motivating Others, Nurturing Inner Motivational Resources*, Massachusetts: Allyn and Bacon.

Renaud, R.D. and Murray, H.G. (1996). Aging, personality and Teacher effectiveness in academic psychologists. *Research in Higher Education*, 37, 323-340.

Schwartz, L.L. (1980). Criteria for effective University Teaching, *Improving College and University Teaching*, *28*(3), 120-123.

Stevens, D. (2009). How to mind map, available at: http://www.study-habits.com/how-to-mind-map.

Vygotsky, L.S. (1962). *Thought and Language*, Cambridge, MA: MIT Press.

Weick, K. E. (1979). The social psychology of organizing, Reading, Addison Wesley: MA.

Wileman, R.E. (1980) *Exercises in Visual Thinking,* New York:Hastings House.

Wood, J.D. (1983). 'Lecturing: Linking Purpose and Organisation, *Improving College and University Teaching*, 31 (2), 61-64.

Young, S. and Shaw, D.G. (1999). Profiles of Effective College and University Teaching, *The Journal of Higher Education*, *7*(6), 670-686.

Chapter 3

EMBEDDING THRESHOLD CONCEPTS INTO TEACHING THROUGH VISUAL INSTRUCTION

ABSTRACT

Demonstrating to the 21st century design student that the threshold concept of learning the necessary knowledge and skills to recognise a designer's work or a design style and understand colour theory is a challenge for design educators in higher education. Utilizing prototypical design examples and semantic cues to assist students to move beyond the threshold required recognizing a designer's work or design style has many benefits for the learner. This chapter will discuss a variety of methods for teaching threshold concepts to design students in particular in the disciplinary focus of teaching design history and colour theory.

INTRODUCTION

The notion of 'Threshold concepts' introduced by Meyer and Land (2003) and applied to economics by Davies (2003) the same year, offers educators a viable method for describing different levels of understanding of a subject. This approach to categorising learning has been adopted across a variety of disciplinary areas in education. Threshold concepts according to Kiley and Wisker (2009), assist toward identifying core learning outcomes that represent seeing things in a new or transformed way. This chapter will firstly, argue that in order to view design examples in a 'new or transformed way' educators need to utilise design prototypes as part of the curriculum that represent key concepts that need to be learnt. Secondly, this chapter will argue that to assist students to recognise the key points to be learnt of a design prototype, semantic cues should be included in instruction.

This chapter will analysed also how teaching colour theory and in particular discussing various notions about the construct of colour harmony has been problematic for students. It will investigate methods for utilising colour communication design that can be used to assist students to overcome the stumbling blocks of learning threshold concepts required to comprehend colour theory in higher education. It will also be premised that teaching colour theory in particular the constructs of colour harmony is particularly problematic for students and suggestions will be discussed to assist teaching this threshold concept to students in higher education.

There will be a discussion on the role prototypes can play in teaching design history to first year novice students in higher education. 'Prototypes' according to Solso (2003), are utilised in art or design to assist with the recognition of the central visual characteristics of a work. They are the abstractions of stimuli against which patterns are judged. Solso (2003) advocated, that it is also far more economical to store impressions that embody the most frequently experienced features of a class of objects, when learning art or design imagery. To learn a key threshold concept in design history it is argued, students need to be exposed to a number of design prototypes that encapsulate a body of knowledge. Students also need to be provided with learning activities that assist them towards understanding the disciplinary knowledge and language.

One method that educators can adopt to assist the learner with recall is to use retrieval cues in instruction. Evidence has been presented to suggest that these cues should be provided when the material is first presented to the learner (e.g. Perkins and Salomon, 1988; Tulving and Osler, 1968). Semantic cues in particular could be used to direct the viewer's attention to key ideas, which can assist with retrieval of information from long-term memory by linking prior knowledge to the information that needs to be learnt.

According to Cunliffe (1992), "we achieve understanding of the world through actively finding meaning which we test against our existing schemata" (p.143). These semantic cues maybe used to infer a metaphor in art and design and the role of the educator is to use semantic cues to provide better access to the meaning of the work and eliminate confusion and misunderstandings. It is first necessary to define what is meant by a "threshold concept," in order to understand what it is that students need to learn.

WHAT IS MEANT BY A 'THRESHOLD CONCEPT'?

It seems appropriate to begin to consider some views on the idea of a 'concept' in education for there are differing opinions on how to define a 'concept'. In cognitive science for example, concepts are viewed as word-like mental representations (Pinker, 1994). Perkins (2006) stated that, "fundamentally, concepts function as categorisers" (p.41). Dummett (1993) and Brandom (1994) have put forward the view that concepts were abilities. Grasping a 'concept' can also happen intuitively in one discipline whereas in another it could be considered a complex idea to learn. For example an artist may have an "instinct" for color selection that may take an interior designer years to master, so this understanding is for the designer a threshold concept, but for the artist it is intuitive knowledge.

In order to understand what is meant by a 'threshold' concept, it seems also necessary to briefly discuss the five concepts put forward by Meyer and Land (2003) and later apply these to the teaching of design history. According to Meyer and Land (2003), the first characteristic of a threshold concept is that they are core concepts that once understood, transform perception of a given subject. It involves a transformed way of understanding, interpreting or viewing "something," which may happen suddenly or take time. Meyer and Land (2003) described this as "liminality" (the period that precedes the actual crossing), where prior to reaching an understanding of a subject students mimic the language required of them.

Secondly, they should be "irreversible;" for once a learner's perspective is transformed it is believed, they cannot understand in a less conceptually complex manner (Meyer and Land, 2003). In other words, it is often inconceivable that the learner would go back to their previous way of thinking once they have begun to perceive the world in terms of a threshold concept. Thirdly, a threshold concept is 'integrative'; this is where the concept has the capacity to expose the previously hidden interrelatedness or connections of something, according to Meyer and Land (2003). Fourthly, a threshold concept is "bounded," they have borders that when crossed can lead to other conceptual developments and as such they assist in the definition of the boundaries of a subject area.

Threshold concept may also be counter-intuitive, as they may lead to knowledge that for the learner is inherently counter-intuitive. Perkins (2006) added another characteristic to the Meyer and Land (2003) list, stating that a threshold concept could be "troublesome" for they usually required the learner grasping conceptually difficult knowledge. This is exemplified in the many novice learners in higher education who have not studied design history in their secondary education, who find it an extremely complex process to recognise and comprehend key design examples. Expressing an understanding of the key points needed to recognise a design prototype is a "threshold concept" in design history that students need to understand in order to apply the body of knowledge that is design history. This will be discussed in more detail in the next section of this chapter.

THRESHOLD CONCEPTS APPLIED TO LEARNING DESIGN HISTORY

As a teacher of design history in higher education it is useful to consider threshold concepts as described by Meyer and Land (2003, 2005) and Meyer, Land and Davies (2006) in relation to teaching novices some of the distinctive characteristics of a design style or movement. There is considerable debate in the literature by design historians to move away from this approach (see Margolin, 2005) as well as to deter from a focus on a Western design narrative that distract from the broad cultural forces that design history should provide (see Gieben-Gamal, 2005; Cooper and White, 2005). The content of the design history curriculum is forever evolving, what does not change is the fact that learning to differentiate one designer's work from another is a difficult process for novice learners. This requires being able to retrieve key schemas (or building blocks of knowledge) from their long-term memory that encapsulate a whole body of knowledge that they may not yet have acquired. This process involves having an understanding of historical periods, cultural contexts, available materials, stylistic influences, politics to name but a few. In other words understanding the key concepts required to identify a designer's work can unlock (and link to) a whole body of knowledge that is constantly being acquired.

THEORISING HOW DESIGN EDUCATORS CAN SUPPORT THIS LEARNING

To assist in this process design educators can break down the content into manageable 'chunks' to learn and by mapping the content into a learning journey (Refer to Figure 1), which each student visually presents in mind maps. Software can be utilised to assist students to visually graph out their design history learning in an organized systematic way.

One mind map software that is simple to utilise for students is freemind, (http://freemind.sourceforge.net/wiki/index.php/Main_Pagehttp://freemind.sourceforge.net/wiki/index.php/Main_Page). Freeman and Jessup (2004) suggested that graphic organizers are useful in enhancing learning as they assist students in retention and organization of information. On these mind maps students add each week any new themes, theories, concepts, designers etc. as well as their own perspectives, studio focuses and outside interests to encourage interdisciplinary links. To scaffold this learning, educators can use prototypical exemplars and the key concepts learnt as a basis then link these too lesser known examples to provide a wider cultural, political and historical context to assist the learner to view the 'big' picture.

The instructional scaffoldings role towards supporting cognitive function in the learner has been examined by Greene and Land (2000). They found that students were more focused and developed in their course projects when instructor developed guiding questions and procedural scaffolding was provided. It could be argued that learning key concepts of prototypical design examples could assist students towards grasping the basic disciplinary knowledge of design history. This should be followed by learning activities that encourage students to ask questions, debate opinions and critically analyse the examples shown. Mind maps can be used to assist students in scaffolding their own learning process, which can provide a basis for visually displaying their knowledge and to assist them towards answering essay questions.

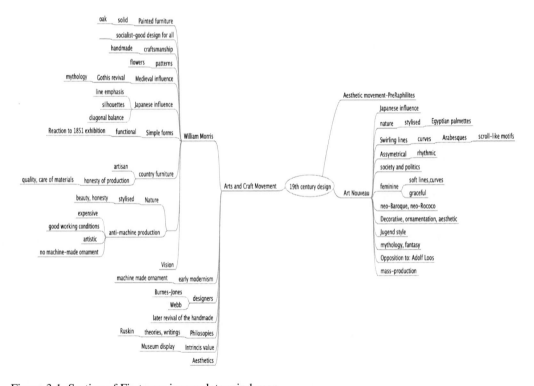

Figure 3.1. Section of First year incomplete mind-map.

These visual maps of students own thought processes can be later discussed by both the teacher and the class. As previously mentioned in Chapter 2, this approach uses the model of procedural scaffolding, a Constructivist learning theory based upon Lev Vygotsky's (1978) idea that "cognitive development can be encouraged through stimulating environments and attention to the role of social factors"(Santrock,2005, p.130), where students learn from each other.

Students also need to be taught how to present using visual material and to link what they are saying to any key concepts or features in a design example. By showing students the key concepts in a design example and identifying how to recognise these concepts in a direct manner, the teacher demonstrates a way of expressing such understanding, which may then assist students in their own presentations. In their future design professions one of the key skills they will need is to be able to clearly communicate understanding of the historical, social, philosophical and political context of design in order to place their own practice in a wider context. Hence being able to identify as well as 'read' the semiotic cues in a design work will assist towards gaining this understanding. This chapter will discuss this further in subsequent pages. Karjalainen (2007) also argues, that students need to be provided with analytical methods to identify designs. "To be better prepared to face the challenges of design practice, design for visual brand recognition is a theme that needs to be embraced by new approaches also in design education" (p.67).

It has also been suggested by Davies and Mangan (2006), that threshold concepts could be embedded into the curriculum first as pedagogical principles then as learning activities, which would break down the complexity of the knowledge to be learned. They stated "if the theory of threshold concepts (Meyer and Land, 2003) is to be useful in guiding teaching and improving student performance, it must be translated into principles that can inform the design of teaching and the curriculum" (Davies and Mangan, 2006, p.2). Students learn the practical application of design elements and principles in their studio classes this knowledge can be utilised in design history classes to develop a student's disciplinary language.

What then needs to be added to this is the acquisition of visual skills that aid the learner to comprehend what they see and the development of a disciplinary language (beyond just understanding elements and principles of design) to assist them to express in words (written or auditory) this understanding to others. For according to Rakes (1999): "Visual literacy skills can expand students' abilities to learn and communicate" (p.17) and it is imperative that educators provide activities that promote the acquisition of visual literacy skills as has been previously argued. Ausburn and Ausburn (1978) suggested that visuals had their own vocabulary, grammar and syntax and that a visually literate person should be able to read and write in a visual language, and should be able to decode (interpret) visual messages successfully and to encode (compose) meaningful visual messages. What also needs to be taken into account is that communicating an understanding of design styles and forms can also be expressed through visual communication. This process also involves developing a deeper conceptual understanding of applying the disciplinary language that goes beyond simple mimicry. In fact it could be argued that acquiring the visual literacy skills and grasping the disciplinary language is the "threshold concept," which once obtained you will visually see the world in a new transformed way that could be described as "irreversible." The learner then acquires a more conceptually complex way of viewing the visual world.

This also fits the 'integrative' characteristic of threshold concepts, as the learner is able to see the connections between design examples and coherently express this link. The 'boundaries' of the threshold concept become apparent when parameters are set, in this case by the knowledge required in order to identify the particular historical design style. However, further conceptual development can occur when the learner questions these boundaries and reinvents new boundaries or parameters that could require developing a new set of threshold concepts. As Davies and Mangan (2006) concurred, "this assumption of 'irreversibility' does not mean that further change is not possible. Acquisition of further threshold concepts will again transform thinking" (p.3). This does not mean however that what has been previously 'grasped' is lost, the learner builds upon their cognitive architecture linking past knowledge to new knowledge as new threshold concepts transform the learner's thinking.

An important factor of threshold concepts is that they can be seen as 'troublesome' for the learner, as they usually require them grasping conceptually difficult knowledge as previously mentioned. Many novice learners find design history visual examples difficult to comprehend particularly as very few have studied design history in high school. An example of this is when teaching Modernism to first year students in design history, the educator would try to illustrate the meaning of various terminologies such as 'form follows function'. Below is Arne Jacobsen's 'Ant' chair (1953) (Refer to: Figure 3.2) that expresses the notion of both 'ergonomics' and 'zoomorphism'. Specifically these terms relate to the shape of the chair with its mouldered double shell plywood seat that is proportioned and shaped to accommodate the human body as well as the fact that its shape curves like the form of an ant. To explain this concept it is important not to overload the learner with superfluous information but instead coherently and concisely explain what needs to be learnt and provide visual examples that do not confuse but reinforce this. This provides a solid foundation that can be built on not only by the teacher in a lecture situation but also by providing class activities that utilise visuals to encourage students to express their own views and understanding.

There has been some valid criticism of Meyer and Land (2003) threshold concept characteristics put forward by Rowbottom (2007) worth considering. Which included his argument that threshold concepts "had been defined in such a way that it becomes almost impossible, even in principle, to empirically isolate them" (Rowbottom, 2007, p. 263).

Figure 3.2. Arne Jacobsen 'Ant' chair (1953) chair owned and photographed by author.

In courses where there are many ways of viewing a topic or theme such as in learning design history where the educators themselves cannot often agree on the boundaries, content and future direction of the discipline, this seams especially pertinent. For according to Doordan (1995), "Design history, like other areas of historical inquiry, is constantly reconfiguring itself, reformulating its subject-matter, and redefining its methods in order to contribute in a vital way to the discussion of contemporary issues and opportunities" (pp. xi-xii).

It was also argued by Rowbottom (2007), that what is a threshold for one learner is not necessarily for another and that "concepts are not reducible to abilities"(p.263). He also suggested that, "acquisition of a given concept may be necessary, but not always sufficient, for the possession of an ability" (p.263). This is something educators have to grapple with as courses in higher education become more accessible to a wider variety of students as electives as a result previous knowledge cannot be assumed. Students also have different learning styles that need to be catered for especially when the economical way of teaching large classes in higher education is via a lecture format. This approach to delivering information does not always encourage active engaged student learning.

There is also the concern that it is difficult to judge whether a concept has been learnt especially in courses where there are many interpretations of a subject and where there is not an exact science or wrong or right answer. As Rowbottom (2007) questioned "how is it possible to test for concepts, rather than abilities?" Educators also need to consider according to Rowbottom that there "is more than one possible conceptual route to the same ability" (p.263). To further discuss Rowbottom's (2007) criticism of threshold concepts this paper has isolated a specific acquisition of knowledge that of identifying a designer's style, however it must again be emphasised that developing visual literacy skills or abilities are imperative and interlinked with the threshold concept as previously discussed. Also it be mentioned that as Hayes (2008) argued, that the "challenge is to accept and understand that the real world is an uncertain place open to interpretation" (p.26) and when teaching disciplinary knowledge teachers need to take this notion into account.

It was also put forward by Rowbottom (2007) that, "concepts are not reducible to abilities" (p.263), however it could be argued for example that these become intrinsically linked when teaching design history to future designers. As Rowbottom's also suggested that: "a threshold for one learner is not necessarily for another" (p.263) is a useful premise when considering a novice learner who is learning new material where it is a question of whether they have or have not grasped the concept. Rowbottom (2007) questioned "how is it possible to test for concepts, rather than abilities?" (p.263), is an interesting question particularly as in the case presented here where 'the concept' and 'the ability' are interlinked. The other question: "how can we tell if there is more than one possible conceptual route to the same ability?" (p.263), is a another significant observation. Particularly in the case presented here, for design and art often have a flexible metaphoric interpretation that allows for the introduction of various viewpoints.

It has been suggested by Hayes (2008) that the "challenge is to accept and understand that the real world is an uncertain place open to interpretation" (p.26), therefore it becomes imperative that educators teach disciplinary knowledge that is transferable to other courses as well as other situations outside the university world. Particularly in the case of teaching design history, students need to be given learning opportunities that assist them to comprehend the relevance of the subject to their future professions as designers. This is particularly pertinent, as many students do not see the link between their studio and design history course content. One method to start teaching novices both the disciplinary knowledge and language and to begin to reinforce the links between design history and studio practice is to utilize typical design prototypes in instruction and classroom activities, which the next section of this chapter will deliberate upon.

USING DESIGN PROTOTYPES TO TEST THE THRESHOLD CONCEPT

Recent research conducted by Rourke and O'Connor, (2009a, 2009b) has demonstrated that first year design students in higher education lack the visual literacy skills needed to identify key characteristics of historic design styles, even after receiving instruction on the material to be learnt (Rourke and O'Connor, 2010). It was recommended by these researchers that students need to be provided with more learning activities in class to develop their visual literacy skills and that instruction should utilize multiple key visual prototypical exemplars which students practice identifying.

Educators could ask students for example, some key questions about design prototypes to identify if they have gained the threshold concepts required to identify a design style or movement or designer. Take the examples below (Refer to Figure: 3.3), the Philippe Starke lemon squeezer, stool and telephone, students could be asked about any key characteristics they see in these designs related to their form, function, materials, influences etc. They should have little trouble answering these questions if they have gained the threshold concepts related to identifying these designs to the designer. Problem-solving strategies are often utilised to teach art and design appreciation and criticism in the classroom that require the student to provide their own solutions to open-ended questions on specific design examples. This learning process is often carried out with little guidance or input from the teacher. Davies, Conneely, Davies and Lynch (2000) have suggested that, "spontaneity is useful for what educationalists call 'discovery learning', in which students generate and internalise their own way of understanding concepts and principles" (p.122).

Figure 3.3. Philippe Starke designs, left: Salif juicer (author's photo); middle: WW stool (1991)(photo reproduced with permission from Vitra (http://www.vitra.com/en-un/home/products); right: OLA phone (1996) (author's photo).

There are advocates particularly in art education who support the premise that discovery learning is an effective learning strategy (Dorn, 1998; Jausovec, 1994). They believe that discovery learning is a reaction against the more 'didactic methods' where facts are given which students memorise. The research basis for supporting the use discovery learning methodology in education to promote worthwhile relevant learning is premissed by some to be largely lacking (Mayer, 2004; Kirschner, Sweller and Clark, 2006; Sweller, Kirschner and Clark, 2007).

Novak and Cañas (2008) also cautioned that "there is the mistaken notion that 'inquiry' studies will assure meaningful learning. The reality is that unless students possess at least a rudimentary *conceptual* understanding of the phenomenon they are investigating, the activity may lead to little or no gain in their relevant knowledge and may be little more than busy work" (p.4). It could be argued that when students have domain specific knowledge, discovery learning is an effective learning strategy. However for students without such knowledge, supplying appropriate worked examples consisting of the visual with a list of significant features could be a more effective method.

The argument for using worked examples in instruction for teaching design history is based on the view that critiquing art and design is a problem-solving activity for novice learners. In order to further explain their purpose, worked examples needs to be defined. A worked example can be defined as: an instructional method that provides a domain specific example to follow and study of a problem that includes a worked-out solution (often in steps). A large number of studies on instructional design have examined learning from worked examples, particularly in the fields of mathematics, physics and computer programming (e.g. Ward and Sweller, 1990; Paas and van Merriënboer, 1994; Carroll, 1994; Tuovinen and Sweller, 1999).

A study by Rourke (2006) tested these methods of instructional design in the area of teaching design history. In a real situational format of lecture followed by tutorial, the effectiveness of worked examples compared to completing problem-solving tasks was tested. This study was divided into three stages conducted over a three-week period of a university semester. Stage one of the experiment was a lecture with prototypical visual examples on five designers from the Art Nouveau or the early Modernist period (approximately 1880-1914) that emphasized key characteristics. In Stage two the class was divided up into two groups (Experimental and Control group) each group was given ten different practice exercises using chair examples. The Experimental group received five worked examples (visual with list of key characteristics) and five practice exercises (applying learnt characteristics to different prototypical examples) and the Control group received ten problem-solving tasks (prototypical examples they wrote about, no information was provided). In Stage three both the Experimental group and the Control group completed a three-page test. The first page of the test asked students to match the designer to the chair, the second page had other design examples (not chairs), and the third page had short answer questions asking about key characteristics of the designs from page two.

In the Stage two practices that used visuals of chairs, the Experimental group scored on average 41.25% better than the Control group after studying worked examples compared to completing problem-solving tasks. In the Stage three test where students were required to match a chair to a designer, the Experimental group scored on average 15.4% better than the Control group. On the second and third page of the three page Stage three test, students were required to match the designers from the practice and page one of the test, to non-chair examples to test their transfer skills. In this section of the Stage three test the Experimental group on average scored 25% better than the Control group and when required to list the characteristics of each design, the Experimental group scored on average 6% better than the Control group. The principle conclusion drawn from this experiment was that novice learners who have a moderate level of visual literacy skill are more successful at identifying a designer's work after studying worked examples compared to novice learners provided with problem-solving tasks.

The premise behind this was that recognising a designer's style required students having an understanding of design prototypes which, as mentioned, is a complex cognitive process that takes deliberate practice, visual literacy skills and disciplinary knowledge to master. By providing students with activities that test their knowledge and understanding of design prototypes educators are able to identify areas of misunderstanding. For as Cousins (2006) suggested, "it is difficult for teachers to gaze backwards across thresholds" (p.5), as a result "they need to hear what the students' misunderstandings and uncertainties are in order to sympathetically engage with them"(p.5).

Another study by Rourke and O'Connor (2010) investigating student's preference for the use of visuals in instruction discovered that a large portion (64%, n: 296) preferred to have relevant features in visual examples pointed out by the lecturer. If students do prefer explicit instruction then it seems imperative that design educators do not presume their students know what to look for in a visual example in order to comprehend it. It then appears appropriate that teachers first let students know what factors of the visual example they need to remember.

Interestingly it was revealed through this study that less than half the participants (46%) preferred visual examples coupled with detailed discussion by the lecturer, suggesting they preferred that only key factors where pointed out. This supports Miller's (1956) suggestion that working memory has a limited capacity for simultaneously holding large amounts of novel information. In particular, it would suggest that as novices lack the necessary schemas (or building blocks of knowledge) in their long-term memory to identify design prototypes, it seems appropriate to limit the amount of information novices are expected to absorb. One method for achieving this and for assisting students towards learning key threshold concepts in design history would be for educators to provide verbal and visual semantic cues that point to key information that needs to be learnt. The use of semantic cues will now be discussed.

The Method of Semantic Cue to Teach Threshold Concepts

In order for educators to use visual exemplars effectively, it "requires sufficient understanding of how the human cognitive systems interact" (Schnotz, 2002:114) with the visual stimuli. A number of studies have ascertained that instructional design that includes both verbal and pictorial information should be presented in a coherent manner with some semantic overlap (e.g. Carney and Levin, 2002; Mayer and Gallini, 1990). Well-designed instructional material should provide interconnection between verbal and visual information so that they enter working memory simultaneously (Schnotz, 2002). According to Koroscik, Short, Stavropoulos and Fortin, (1992), one method that assists with this process is the use of semantic cues, which can facilitate transfer by assisting the viewer in finding connections between the artwork's (or design work's) characteristics and the viewer's prior knowledge.

Semantic cues are 'hints' that assist the viewer to understand the content or meaning of a visual example. Design history teachers can use verbal, written or visual language to draw the learner's attention to these 'hints' to assist them towards an understanding of design history. In design this can often mean understanding symbols that denote or represent something. According to Cunliffe (1992), what "is required when reading and making works of art is to try to understand the visual code that is being used and how this relates to the purpose or function of the work of art" (p.149), could also be applied to comprehending design examples.

Koroscik, Short, Stavropoulos and Fortin (1992) hypothesised that verbal cues might assist students to connect the characteristics of an artwork with their own previously acquired domain specific knowledge. Their study investigated the contextual variables that influenced the comprehension of a work of art. This study utilised the verbal contextual conditions of cues and non-cues to demonstrate whether students required explicit verbal prompts to discover relationships among works of art. Using both a multiple-choice matching test and an open-ended writing task, the results showed that verbal cues prompt students to elaborate on possible art meanings.

Meyer and Land (2003) suggested that one of the characteristics of a threshold concept is that there is a period of "liminality" that precedes the actual crossing where students move from mimicking to understanding a subject. It could be argued that to achieve this aim educators need to provide students with learning activities that allow them to first mimic and practice the disciplinary language as well as link and apply new knowledge to previously acquired knowledge. Students then need to be provided with learning opportunities to acquire the attributes needed to reach a level of critical understanding required to grasp the 'threshold concept'. If educators provide clear indication of the points to be learnt of a prototypical example they also provide the learner with opportunity to acquire the knowledge needed to understand other similar examples.

One method for achieving this is for educators to provide semantic cues that clearly indicate the important points that students need to learn. For example see below the 'Sentence making wall clock' designed by Martí Guixé manufactured by Alessi Factory in Italy. The designer statement on the Alessi website is that, "objects have become tools for perceiving every day, and also for communicating not only with objects, but also with other people through the objects…. (This clock) is based on new typologies revolving around this concepts" (retrieved 23rd December, 2011 from Alessi website: http://www.alessi.com /en/32576/clocks/24h-sentence-maker-wall-clock).Designer statements provide a good basis for opening up class discussion on student's views and ideas of designer objects. This clock is an excellent example to utilise to discuss the difference between Modernist design and recent contemporary design, in particular to discuss how function has become less important than the 'concept' and 'message' in the design alongside social, ethical and environmental concerns. As the study Koroscik *et al.* (1992) discovered, students who were provided with an art context by the teacher, scrutinize the artworks for common features to discover comparative relationships between artworks. They also found that students who were given verbal cues synthesized their ideas better and constructed more elaborate meanings about the artworks, than those who were not cued. The students who were given the verbal cues also had fewer misunderstandings about the artworks. The students who were not given the verbal cues used broader search strategies, which proved to be a less effective approach than the teacher directed method.

Figure 3.4. 24h 'sentence making wall clock' designed by Martí Guixé manufactured by Alessi Factory in Italy, printed with permission from Di Palma Associati International Press Agency for Alessi, http://www.alessi.com/en/3/1415/silver-objects/tea-and-coffee-service.

In this study the teacher verbally directs students to see the works through the teachers eye, it needs to be acknowledged here that students without direction from the teacher may have seen the work from a more personal or broader perspective, which educators should also encourage.

A study by Warren and Horne (1982) had also discovered that students' comprehension of pictures could be influenced by contextual cues. However, in order for learners to make use of their cognitive resources, they need to discover meaningful connections between their existing knowledge and whatever they are attempting to understand (Prawat, 1989). Educators need to provide learning activities that utilise visual examples previously explained in a lecture, to reinforce not only key points to be learnt but also to guide the learner towards 'making sense' of the new material to be learnt. For as Severin (1967) earlier suggested, one of the principles of learning is that "learning is increased as the number of available cues or stimuli is increased" (p.237). Then once the learner has grasped the foundation knowledge of the design period, theme, theory or issue to be learnt then the contextual cues from the teacher could be lessened and replaced by verbal and visual prompts that encourage the learner to explore their own interpretations and ways of viewing design.

One method for further engaging students with the course material who have acquired the threshold concepts to recognise a designer's work is to provide a variety of visual examples of different designs and then separately provide key philosophical statements from the designers. Then ask the students to match the statements to each design then have them explain why they made this choice. This can be done individually or in groups. This is an effective method to utilise to promote class discussion on the connections between a designer's philosophy and their designs and also a useful method for mapping out various historical periods and cultural, social, economic factors etc. that influence each design and designer's philosophy.

Utilizing semantic cues effectively in teaching takes the guesswork out of learning, which could provide an easier path for the learner to master the threshold concept needed in order to identifying designers and design styles in design history. As Cunliffe (1992) states, "finding ways for students to acquire new schemata should be seen as the purpose of art education" (p.145), and providing access to comprehending pictures via semantic cues is one method of demystifying the complex images of art and design which should assist the learner to acquire schemas. Semantic cues can also be utilised in other disciplinary areas where the visual example requires further verbal explanation that cannot be frugally represented by visual form alone.

It must be acknowledged however, that meaning related to specific designs cannot always be reduced to characteristics or design elements in a didactic way, for 'meaning' according to Hodder (1998) can often remain tacit and implicit, not part of conscious analytical thought. As Lave and Wenger (1991) emphasize, learning always involves a process of 'becoming' that is never reducible to a cognitive or technical processes. However as educators we need to consider the multiple ways to simplify or deconstruct many of the complex concepts we teach in higher education to enable students to grasp the essential threshold concepts of the discipline.

Colour Theory: Utilizing Ontology to Teach a Threshold Concept

Teaching a different aspect of design history in tertiary education highlights another approach to 'troublesome' threshold concepts. In this example, teaching colour theory and in particular discussing various notions about the construct 'colour harmony' from different ontological perspectives provides students with the knowledge required to see the construct of 'colour harmony' in a new and transformed way. Specifically, there are a number of different approaches to the notion of colour harmony in the literature and these include a plethora of predictive colour harmony principles, guidelines and formulae, as well as more probabilistic approaches.

All of these different approaches are underpinned by ontological assumptions, which previously had been rarely examined. A key benefit for the student in examining these ontological assumptions is the opportunity to focus on a core concept embedded within the construct of colour harmony which, once understood, transforms perception about this construct forever. As such, this new understanding represents a "new and previously inaccessible way of thinking about something", and provides students with the foundational knowledge to examine and discuss contemporary perspectives on colour theory and application (Meyer and Land, 2003, p1).

Ontological Perspectives on Colour Harmony

It has been suggested that "Colours seen together to produce a pleasing affective response are said to be in harmony" (Burchett, 2002, p. 28). The simplicity of this statement belies the complexity of the interface between colour and aesthetic response, and a plethora of colour harmony theories exist in the literature (Feisner, 2000; Gage, 1995, 2000, 2006). Arnkil (2008) suggests that these theories tend to fall into one of two categorises:

a) Colour harmony based on equilibrium in terms of the balance of contrasting or complementary colour (for example, see Chevreul, 1855; Itten, 1961; Munsell, 1921; Ostwald, 1916);

b) Colour harmony based on similarity (for example, see Hard and Sivik, 2001; Itten, 1961; Munsell, 1921).

The second approach has gained greater currency possibly due to the influence of Itten as suggested by both Feisner (2000) and Gage (1995). Colour harmony based on similarity is evident in school curriculum in Australia prompting the notion that this approach to colour harmony may actually be a learned response (NSWDET, 2005). It behoves the student to examine the assumptions underpinning key colour harmony theories from an ontological perspective in some detail as follows:

- Sir Isaac Newton drew an analogy between colour and music, and suggested that colour harmony relied on the proportional arrangement of colours similar to the mathematical basis underlying musical composition (Newton, 1704).

- Goethe suggested that colour harmony rests on the notion of 'balance' in terms of balancing or neutralising opposing forces – a concept that harks back to Heraclitus and also recurs in the theories of Itten, Munsell and Ostwald (Goethe, 1810).

- Chevreul suggested that "Maximal contrast of the complementaries (are equated) with maximum harmony" (Chevreul, 1855, p. 32). Chevreul (1855) championed a strong link between colour harmony and complementary colours and he extolled this view in *The Law of Harmonious Colouring*, considered to be "the most widely used colour-manual of the 19th century" (Gage, 1995, p173).

- Ostwald declared: "Colour (harmony) is order" (Ostwald, 1916, cited in Gage, 2000, p258). In *Die Harmonie der Farben* (Harmony of colours, 1918) Ostwald provided a number of principles that underpinned his approach to colour harmony: "Only such colours can appear harmonious the attributes of which stand in certain simple relations" defined as follows (Ostwald cited in Spillman, 1985, p. 6):

    – Colours of different hues that exhibit equal levels of whiteness;
    – Colours of different hues that exhibit equal levels of blackness;
    – Colours of different hues that exhibit equal levels of saturation.

- Munsell asserted that "Colors appear to be harmonious or related if their properties are in certain simple relationships" (Munsell cited in Kuehni, 2005, p. 167). Munsell also provided a set of rules and determined that "Colour harmony is attained when any three rules are followed" (Munsell, 1921, cited in Cleland, 1937, p. 19):

    – Use as few hues as possible;
    – Use a high tonal value colour with a low tonal value colour;
    – Use a high level chroma (saturation) with a low level chroma (saturation;
    – "Area is inversely proportional to the product of value times chroma (Munsell, 1921, cited in Cleland, 1937).

- Moon and Spencer devised a formula for colour harmony based on Birkhoff's quantitative aesthetic measure (Birkoff, 1933; Moon and Spencer, 1944a, 1944b):

  $$M = O/C$$

  wherein M represents aesthetic measure; the factor of order *(O)* is represented by the components: colour identity (that is, basic colour identity such as *red* or *green*) as well as hue similarity; and contrast of hue, value and chroma; and finally the factor of complexity *(C)* is represented by:

  C = (No. of colour/s) + (no. of pairs of colour/s with hue difference)
  + (No. of colour pairs with chroma difference)

- While Itten asserted that colour harmony was subjective, he proposed two approaches to colour harmony: Firstly, "(Colour) harmony implies balance; a symmetry of forces" (Itten, 1961, p. 21). Under this approach, balance occurs when neutral grey or 'equilibrium' is achieved in the retina: "(Colour) harmony in our visual apparatus then would signify a psychophysical state of equilibrium in which dissimilation and assimilation of optic substances are equal.
  Neutral grey produces this state. I can mix such a grey from black and white; or from two complementary colours and white; or from several colours provided they contain the three primary colours: yellow, red and blue in suitable proportions" (Itten, 1961, p22).Secondly, Itten suggested that, "the colour combinations called 'harmonious' in common speech usually are composed of closely similar chromas, or else different colors in the same shades.
  They are combinations of colors that meet without sharp contrast. As a rule, the assertion of harmony or discord simply refers to an agreeable-disagreeable or attractive-unattractive scale. Such sentiments are personal sentiments without objective force" (Itten, 1961, p. 21).
- Albers proposed a phenomenological approach to colour harmony based on experience and experimentation. Albers suggested that predictive colour harmony rules, formulae or models are "...worn out. No mechanical colour system is flexible enough to pre-calculate the manifold changing factors...in a single prescribed recipe" (Albers, 1963).
- Hard and Sivik acknowledged that responses to colour are always open to the influence of external factors and, given that the number of colour combinations are "almost infinite", question whether it is possible to devise a prescriptive model of colour harmony (Hard and Sivik, 2001, p. 4).
- Kuehni suggested that, due to the lack of consensus regarding colour harmony in the literature, practitioners should 'create their own harmonies' using a range of tools including colour atlas, colour chips and so on (Kuehni, 2005).
- O'Connor suggested that responses to colour are highly subjective and open to a range of influences and mediating factors, and has devised the following conceptual model:

$$\text{Colour harmony} = f\,(\text{Col}_{1,\,2,\,3...n}) \times (ID+CE+CX+P+T)$$

Under this approach, colour harmony is a function (f) of the interaction between colour (Col1,2,3. . .n) and the factors that influence positive esthetic response to colour: individual differences (ID) such as age, gender, personality, and affective state; cultural experiences (CE), the prevailing context (CX) which includes setting and ambient lighting; intervening perceptual effects (P) and the effects of time (T) such as social or design trends that change over time (O'Connor, 2010).

While each of these approaches is different, each tends to reflect certain ontological assumptions. The process of examining these assumptions provides an opportunity for the student to examine their understanding about colour in general and colour harmony in particular. In doing so, they often cross an intellectual boundary from one perspective on colour harmony to a new perspective that was generally previously inaccessible. In doing so, the student moves through an intellectual portal wherein the notion of colour harmony is transformed and changed forever.

Ontology, which has to do with the fundamental nature of a construct under focus as opposed to its theoretical framework, often acts like a lens through which a research topic is perceived (Crotty, 1998; Moore, 1997). Moore suggests that ontological assumptions exist along a number of continuums and these are described as follows in relation to colour harmony:

a) *Nomothetic-idiographic:* That is, whether colour harmony can be defined and explained in terms of universal laws, rules, and principles that apply to all; or whether such universal laws, rules, and principles are inappropriate due to the influence of individual differences (age, gender, cultural experience, personality, affective state, etc) as well as contextual, perceptual and temporal factors;

b) *Deterministic-random:* That is, whether colour harmony can be defined as a strictly cause-effect phenomenon wherein an irrefutable causal link exists between colour and aesthetic response; or, whether colour harmony can be defined as a more stochastic and randomly determined phenomenon that is less predictable and more probabilistic;

c) *Atomistic-holistic:* That is, whether colour is essentially divisible (that is, can be broken down into discrete, isolated parts and studied as such) and wherein colour harmony can be defined as an isolatable phenomenon effectively existing in a vacuum; or, whether colour harmony is a more holistic phenomenon existing within a state of flux and therefore more than the sum of its parts.

When applying these ontological assumptions to theories about colour harmony including those listed above, it is clear that the majority adopt a nomothetic, deterministic and atomistic approach. This approach, which tends to be the most predominant ontological understanding of colour harmony, has a number of weaknesses. Firstly, it assumes that one-size-fits all colour harmony formulae, rules or principles are appropriate despite numerous studies indicating that a range of factors influence aesthetic response to colour such as individual and cultural differences, and also contextual, perceptual and temporal factors. Secondly, while research exists that propose the existence of a causal link between colour and aesthetic response, the results of these studies may be study-bound and the generalization of such findings to other settings, different contexts or varying population segments is now considered methodologically unsound (Guba and Lincoln, 1994; Moore, 1997; Popper, 1979). In addition, studies evaluating aesthetic response to colour in controlled environments or in time or context-free isolation tend to lack reliability and transferability (Guba and Lincoln, 1994). These weaknesses suggest that attempts to define colour harmony as a universal and deterministic phenomenon renders the construct out-dated from a current theoretical perspective.

In addition, it is estimated that humans can distinguish between 1.8 million and ten million different colours (Gouras, 1991; Judd and Wyszecki, 1975; Pointer and Attridge, 1998). It has also been suggested that, given the huge range of distinguishable colours, the number of possible colour combinations is "almost infinite" (Hard and Sivik, 2001, p. 4). Furthermore, it has recently been asserted that humans are not hard-wired, psychologically or physiologically, to respond in any particular way in regard to colour; and that we all differ in terms of our stimulus screening ability and hence in the way we respond to environmental stimuli (Mehrabian, 1977; Wise, Wise, and Beach, 1988).

In view of this, the proposition that colour harmony principles and formulae have any currency contradicts both logic and recent research.

Students who examine the ontological assumptions embedded within colour harmony theories benefit from an intellectual shift in regard to this construct. This 'troublesome' threshold concept represents an intellectual portal whereby the notion of colour harmony is transformed and changed forever, and as a result students are able to progress in their studies about colour especially in relation to 21st century perspectives.

They are less likely to maintain a universal, deterministic approach to colour and more likely to move to an idiographic, probabilistic approach to colour and acknowledge the various factors that influence the interface between colour and human response such as individual and cultural differences, as well as temporal, perceptual and contextual differences. This in turn changes the way they think about colour and their approach to colour application.

CONCLUSION

This chapter has discussed a variety of methods for teaching threshold concepts to design students in particular in the disciplinary focus of teaching design history and colour theory. The premise advocated is that in order for students to learn a 'threshold concept' in design history in higher education certain skills need to be developed and practiced before these concepts can be learnt.

It has also been argued that students learning about colour theory need to be encouraged to examine the ontological assumptions that underpin the core concept embedded within the construct of colour harmony which, once understood, transforms perception about this construct forever.

Threshold concept research involves educators delving closely into their discipline and identifying areas that students find difficult to understand and formulating the best method for teaching and learning 'troublesome' knowledge. The contribution threshold concepts has made to the teaching and learning literature ultimately is to encourage educators to continuously reflect on their teaching and maintain the enthusiasm to examine and adopt new and exciting methods for promoting learning.

REFERENCES

Albers, J. (1963). *The interaction of color*. New Haven, NY: Yale University Press.

Ausburn, L. and Ausburn, F. (1978). Visual literacy: Background, theory and practice. *PLET*, *15* (40), 291-297.

Birkoff, G. D. (1933). *Aesthetic measure*. Cambridge, MA: Harvard University Press.

Brandom, R. (1994).*Making it explicit: Reasoning, representing, and discursive commitment*. Cambridge, MA: Harvard University Press.

Burchett, K. E. (2002). Color harmony. *Color Research and Application, 27*(1), 28-31.

Carney, R.N. and Levin, J.R. (2002). Pictorial illustrations still improve student's learning from text. *Educational Psychology Review, 14*(1), March, 5-26.

Carroll, W. M. (1994). Using worked examples as an instructional support in the algebra classroom. *Journal of Educational Psychology, 86*(3) 360-367.

Chevreul, M. E. (1855). *The principles of harmony and the contrast of colours: And their applications to the arts (Facsimile edition; Trans. C Martel)*. Whitefish, MT: Kessinger Publishing.

Cleland, T. M. (1937). *A practical description of the Munsell color system*. Baltimore: Munsell Color Co.

Cooper, R. and White, D. (2005). Teaching transculturation: pedagogical processes. *Journal of Design History, 18*(3), 285-292.

Cousins, G. (2006).An introduction to threshold concepts. *Planet, 17*, 4-5.

Crotty, M. (1998). *Foundations of social research: Meaning and perspective in the research process*. Sydney: Allen and Unwin.

Cunliffe, L. (1992). Why a theory of symbols is necessary for teaching art. *Journal of Art and Design Education, 11* (2), 143-153.

Davies, P. and Mangan, J. (2006). Embedding Threshold Concepts: from theory to pedagogical principles to learning activities, *Threshold Concepts within the discipline Symposium*, 30th August-1st September, Glasgow.

Davies, P., Conneely, J., Davies, R. and Lynch, D. (2000). Imaginative ideas for teaching and learning. In Booth, A. and Hyland, P. (Eds.). *The Practice of University History Teaching*. Manchester and New York: Manchester University Press.

Davis, D. (2003).Barriers to reflective practice. *Active Learning in Higher Education*, 4(3), 243-255.

Doordan, D. (1995), (Ed.). *Design History, An anthology*. Cambridge: The MIT press.

Dorn, C.M. (1998). *Mind in art: cognitive foundations in art education*. Mahwah, N.J.: Erlbaum.

Dummett, M. (1993). *The seas of language*. Oxford: Oxford University Press.

Feisner, E. A. (2000). *Colour: How to use colour in art and design*. London: Laurence King.

Freeman, L.A. and Jessup, L.M. (2004). The power and benefit of concept mapping: measuring use, usefulness, ease of use and satisfaction. *International Journal of Science Education, 26*(2), pp.151-169.

Gage, J. (1995). *Colour and culture*. London: Thames and Hudson.

Gage, J. (2000). *Colour and meaning: Art, science and symbolism*. London: Thames and Hudson.

Gage, J. (2006). *Color in art*. London: Thames and Hudson.

Gieben-Gamal, E. (2005). Diversifying the design history curriculum: A review of recent resources. *Journal of Design History, 18*(3), 293-297.

Goethe, J. W. (1810). *Zur Farbenlehre (Theory of colours; English translation, 1970)* (C. L. Eastlake, Trans.). Cambridge: MIT Press.

Gouras, P. (1991). Cortical mechanisms of colour vision. In P. Gouras (Ed.), *Vision and visual dysfunction* (Vol. 6, pp. 179-197). London: Macmillan.

Greene, B. A. and Land, S.M. (2000). A qualitative analysis of scaffolding used in a resource-based learning environment involving the World Wide Web. *Journal of Educational Computing Research, 23*(2), 151.

Guba, E. G., and Lincoln, Y. S. (1994). Competing paradigms in qualitative research. In N. K. Denzin and Y. S. Lincoln (Eds.), *Handbook of Qualitative Research*. Thousand Oaks, CA: Sage.

Hard, A., and Sivik, L. (2001). A theory of colors in combination: A descriptive model related to the NCS color-order system. *Color Research and Application, 26*(1), 4-28.

Hayes, J.M. (2008). Thresholds and transformation. *European Journal of Management, 8*(3), 24-46.

Hodder, I. (1998). The interpretation of documents and material culture.Denzin, Norman K. and Lincoln, Yvonna S. (Eds.), *Collecting and interpreting qualitative materials*, (pp.110-129). Thousand Oaks: SAGE Publications.

Itten, J. (1961). *The art of color (Revised edition, 1973)*. New York: John Wiley.

Jausovec, N. (1994). Problem finding and empathy in art. In M.A. Runco, (Ed.), *Problem-finding, problem-solving and creativity*. Norwood, N.J.: Albex.

Judd, D. B., and Wyszecki, G. (1975). *Color in business, science and industry*. New York: Wiley.

Karjalainen, T. M. (2007). It looks like a Toyota: Educational approaches to designing for visual brand recognition. *International Journal of Design, 1*(1), 67-81.

Kiley, M. and Wisker, G. (2009). Threshold concepts in research education and evidence of threshold crossing. *Higher Education Research and Development, 28*(4), 431-441.

Kirschner, P.A., Sweller, J. and Clark, R. E. (2006). Why minimal guidance during instruction does not work: an analysis of the failure of constructivist, discovery, problem-based, experiential, and inquiry-based teaching. *Educational Psychologist, 41*(2), 75-86.

Koroscik, J.S., Short, G., Stavropoulos, C. and Fortin, S. (1992). Framework for understanding art: The function of comparative art context and verbal cues. *Studies in Art Education, 33* (3), 154-164.

Kuehni, R. G. (2005). *Color: An introduction to practice and principles (2nd ed.)*. New York: John Wiley and Sons.

Lave, J. and Wenger, E. (1991). *Situated learning: legitimate peripheral participation*. Cambridge: Cambridge University Press.

Margolin,V. (2005). A world history of design and the history of the world. *Journal of Design History, 18*(3), 235-243.

Mayer, R. E. (2004). Should There Be a Three-Strikes Rule Against Pure Discovery Learning? The Case for Guided Methods of Instruction. *American Psychologist, 59*(1), 14-19.

Mayer, R.E. and Gallini, J. (1990). When is an illustration worth ten thousand words? *Journal of Educational Psychology, 82*(4), 715-726.

Mehrabian, A. (1977). Individual differences in stimulus screening and arousability. *Journal of Personality, 45*, 237-250.

Meyer, J. and Land, R. (2003). *Threshold concepts and Troublesome knowledge (1): linkage to ways of thinking and practicing within the disciplines, Improving student learning – Ten years on.* Oxford: OCSLD.

Meyer, J. H. F., and Land, R. (2003). *Threshold concepts and troublesome knowledge: Linkages to ways of thinking and practising within the disciplines (Occasional Report 4).* Edinburgh: ETL Project: Universities of Edinburgh, Coventry and Durham.

Meyer, J.H.F. and Land, R. (2005). Threshold concepts and troublesome knowledge (2): epistemological considerations and a conceptual framework for teaching and learning. *Higher Education, 49*(3), 373-388.

Meyer, J.H.F., Land, R. and Davies, P. (2006). Implications of threshold concepts for course design and evaluation. In J.H.F. Meyer, and R. Land, (Eds.), *Overcoming Barriers to Student Understanding: threshold concepts and troublesome knowledge*, (pp.195–206). London and New York: Routledge.

Miller, G.A. (1956). The magical number seven, plus or minus two: some limits on our capacity for processing information. *Psychological Review, 63*, 81-97.

Moon, P., and Spencer, D. E. (1944a). Aesthetic measure applied to color harmony. *Journal of the Optical Society of America, 34*, 234-242.

Moon, P., and Spencer, D. E. (1944b).Geometric formulation of classical colour harmony. *Journal of the Optical Society of America, 34*, 46-59.

Moore, G. T. (1997). *Toward environment-behaviour theories of the middle range II: The analysis and evaluation of environment-behaviour theories.* Paper presented at the Environment-Behaviour Studies for the 21st Century: Proceedings of the MERA97 International Conference, Tokyo.

Munsell, A. H. (1921). A grammar of color. Retrieved 20 October 2003, from http:/www.gretamacbeth.com/Source/Solutions/munsell/index.asp.

Newton, I. (1704). Opticks: A treatise of the reflections, refractions, inflections and colours of light (4th ed.). Retrieved 30 March 2010, from http://books.google.com/books?id=Gn AFAAAAQAAJ

NSWDET. (2005). Professional support and curriculum, Creative Arts, Stage 2 units of work. Retrieved 27 June 2005, from http://www.curriculumsupport.nsw.edu.au/CreativeArts

O'Connor, Z. (2010). Colour harmony revisited. *Color Research and Application, 35*(4), 267-273.

Ostwald, W. (1916). *Die Farbenfibel (The colour primer). Cited in Gage, J. (2000) Colour and meaning - Art, science and symbolism.* London: Thames and Hudson.

Paas, F. and van Merriënboer, J. (1994). Variability of worked examples and transfer of geometrical problem-solving skills: A cognitive-load approach. *Journal of Educational Psychology, 86*(1) 122-133.

Perkins, D. (1999). The many facets of constructivism. *Educational Leadership, 57*(3), 25-37.

Perkins, D. (2006). Constructivism and troublesome knowledge. In J.H.F. Meyer, and R. Land, (Eds.), *Overcoming Barriers to Student Understanding: threshold concepts and troublesome knowledge*, (pp.195–206). London and New York: Routledge.

Perkins, D.N. and Salomon, G (1988). Teaching for transfer. *Educational Leadership*, *46*(1), 22-32.

Pinker, S. (1994).*The language instinct: The new science of language and mind.* London: Penguin.

Pointer, M. R., and Attridge, G. G. (1998).The number of discernable colours. *Color Research and Application, 23*, 52-54.

Popper, K., R. (1979). *Objective knowledge: An evolutionary approach.* Oxford: Clarendon Press.

Prawat, R.S. (1989). Promoting access to knowledge strategies and disposition in students: A research synthesis. *Review of Educational Research, 59* (1), 1-41.

Rakes, G. C. (1999, Sept.). Teaching visual literacy in a multimedia age, *Tech Trends*, 43(4), 14-18.

Rourke, A, J. (2006). *Cognitive load theory and the use of worked examples in design history to teach novice learners to recognise the distinctive characteristics of a designer's work.* EdD thesis, Kensington: The University of New South Wales.

Rourke, A. (2012). Embedding threshold concepts into first year design history: Can we transform students understanding and way of seeing? *ACCESS: Critical perspectives on Communication, Culture and Policy Studies*, Thresholds and Transformations, *30*(2).

Rourke, A. and O'Connor, Z. (2010). Visual literacy levels and predominant learning modalities among first year design students: The influence of teacher intervention, *Design Principles and Practices: An International Journal, 4*(1), 347-360.

Rourke, A. and O'Connor. Z. (2009a). Look before you leap: testing assumptions on visual literacy and predominate learning style modalities of undergraduate design students in Australia and New Zealand, *International Journal of Learning, 16*(8), 33-46.

Rourke, A.J. and O'Connor, Z. (2009b). Investigating visual literacy levels and predominant learning modality among undergraduate design students in Australia: preliminary findings. *Design Principles and Practices: An International Journal, 3*(2), 17-28.

Rowbottom, D. P. (2007). Demystifying threshold concepts. *Journal of the Philosophy of Education, 41*(2), 263 -270.

Santrock, J.W. (2005). *Adolescence*, 10th Edition, University of Texas. McGraw Hill, New York.

Schnotz, W. (2002). Towards an integrated view of learning from text and visual display.*Educational Psychology Review, 14*(1), March, 101-120.

Severin, W.J. (1967). *Cue summation in multiple channel communication.* Doctoral dissertation, University of Wisconsin.

Solso, R.L. (2003). *The psychology of art and the evolution of the conscious brain.* Cambridge: MIT Press.

Spillman, W. (1985). Color order systems and architectural color design. *Color Research and Application, 10*(1), 5-11.

Spillman, W. (1985). Color order systems and architectural color design. *Color Research and Application, 10*(1), 5-11.

Sweller, J., Kirschner, P.A. and Clark, R.E. (2007). Why Minimally Guided Teaching Techniques Do Not Work: A Reply to Commentaries. *Educational Psychologists*, *42*(2). 115-121.

Sweller, J., Kirschner, P.A. and Clark, R.E. (2007). Why Minimally Guided Teaching Techniques Do Not Work: A Reply to Commentaries. *Educational Psychologists*, *42*(2). 115-121.

Tulving, E. and Osler, S. (1968). Effectiveness of retrieval cues in memory for words. *Journal of Experimental Psychology*, *77*, 593-601.

Tuovinen, J. and Sweller, J. (1999). A comparison of cognitive load associated with discovery learning and worked examples. *Journal of Educational Psychology*. *91*(2) 334-341.

Vygotsky, L.S. (1978). *Mind and Society: The development of higher psychological processes*. Cambridge, MA: Harvard University Press. Sections of this chapter have been published in:

Ward, M. and Sweller, J. (1990). Structuring effective worked examples. *Cognition and Instruction*, *7*(1) 1-39.

Warren, L.R. and Horne, J.W. (1982). What does naming a picture do? Effects of prior picture naming on recognition of identical and same-name alternatives, *Memory and Cognition*, *10*(2), 167-175.

Wise, B. K., Wise, J. A., and Beach, L. R. (1988). *The human factors of color in environmental design: A critical review. NASA Grant No. NCC 2-404*. Moffett Field, CA: NASA Ames Research Centre.

Chapter 4

LEARNING STYLE MODALITIES
AND VISUAL LITERACY

ABSTRACT

Learning is a complex and highly individual process that differs for every learner irrespective of age, gender or culture. Each individual has their own preferred way of gathering, organising and considering new concepts presented to them in a learning context. In addition, levels of visual literacy varies and, as Rakes (1999) notes, in the e-learning world of the 21st century it is imperative that we are able to think critically, manipulate and effectively process visual information so that we can interpret and draw reliable meaning from such information. Educators have a responsibility to ensure that a close match exists between their teaching approach and support materials, and the range of possible learning styles. In addition, educators can play a key role in assisting students to develop their visual literacy skills to meet the challenges and demands of the visually cluttered digital era.

LEARNING STYLE MODALITIES

Learning is a complex human process and a range of theories and related models exist that attempt to describe and explain the mechanics of this process. The term learning style, which is generally considered to comprise cognitive styles, instructional preferences and learning strategies, has been defined as "an individual's characteristic and preferred ways of gathering, organising, and thinking about information" (Fleming, 2001, p. 1). Knowledge about different learning characteristics and preferences is imperative in the design of teaching materials and effective visual communications.

Gardner's (1983) theory of multiple intelligences suggests that a range of influences and factors impact on the learning experience, and the complexity of leaning is reflected in the diversity of learning theories and models (Gardner, 1983). A systematic review of learning style models identified 71 learning style models, which have evolved in the UK, USA and Western Europe (Coffield, Moseley, Hall, and Ecclestone, 2004). These models, which emerged across diverse fields including psychology, education, sociology and business studies, can be further categorised as pedagogical, theoretical and commercial. Underpinning each learning style model is a marginally different set of assumptions as well as varying definitions of key constructs, prompting Coffield *et al* (2004) to note that a unified definition of learning style is lacking within the literature. Sub-categories of learning style models include the following.

a) Learning styles related to genetic or constitutionally based factors;
b) Learning styles linked to cognitive features and structures;
c) Learning styles as a component of stable personality types;
d) Learning styles that reflect flexibly stable learning preferences;
e) Learning approaches, strategies and orientations (Coffield *et al*, 2004).

Within each of these sub-categories, learning style models tend to have a different focus with some resting on ideas relating to cognitive functioning while others focuson personality traits or intellectual abilities. Learning style models also tend to vary in terms of predicted stability; that is, whether the learning style remains fixed over time or whether it evolves and changes. While an individual's learning strategies are linked to their learning preferences within their overall learning style, these characteristics are not necessarily stable over time. An indication of the way these characteristics inter-relate is as follows (Curry, 1983).

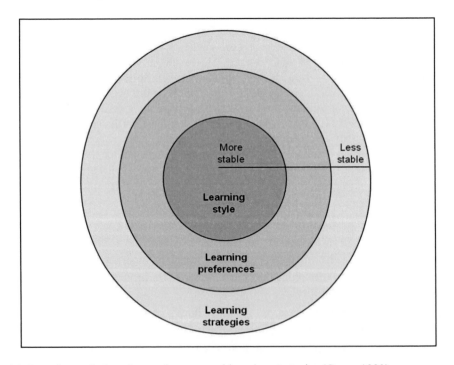

Figure 4.1. Learning style, learning preferences and learning strategies (Curry, 1983).

KEY LEARNING STYLE MODELS

Thirteen of the 71 learning style models reviewed by Coffield *et al* (2004) have been identified as key learning style models. These met specific selection criteria that included whether the learning style model was influential or potentially influential; whether the inherent claims were supported by empirical evidence; whether the link between learning style model and students' learning was supported by empirical evidence and whether the model had broad implications for pedagogy. The key learning style models identified by Coffield *et al* (2004) are as follows.

a) *Genetic and constitutionally based factors learning style models:*
   - Gregorc's mind styles model and style delineator;
   - The Dunn and Dunn model;
b) *Cognitive structures based learning style models:*
   - Riding's model of cognitive style and Cognitive Styles Analysis (CSA);
c) *Stable personality types:*
   - The Myers-Briggs Type Indicator (MBTI);
   - Apter's reversal theory of motivational styles and the Motivational Style Profile (MSP);
   - Jackson's Learning Style Profiler (LSP);
d) *Flexibly stable learning preferences:*
   - Kolb's Learning Style Inventory (LSI);
   - Honey and Mumford's Learning Style Questionnaire (LSQ);
   - The Hermann 'whole brain' model and the Hermann Brain Dominance Instrument (HBDI);
   - Allinson and Hayes' Cognitive Style Index (CSI);
e) *Learning approaches and strategies:*
   - Entwistle's approaches and study skills inventory for students (ASSIST);
   - Vermunt's frameworks for classifying learning styles and his Inventory of Learning Styles (ILS);
   - Sternberg's theory of thinking styles and Thinking Styles Inventory (TSI).

In addition to providing a theoretical framework of the learning process, each of the key learning style models feature an assessment or measurement instrument that includes various learning style descriptors, measures and assessment outcomes. In their comprehensive review of key learning style models, Coffield *et al* (2004) provided a thorough examination of each of these measurement instruments which includes an assessment of the measurement instrument and assessment process in terms of reliability and validity as well as empirical evidence of pedagogical impact. Zywno and Waalen suggest that, of the many learning style models, the most widely used include Kolb's model; the Dunn and Dunn model; the Herman Brain Dominance model and the VARK model (Zywno and Waalen, 2002). It is possible that the widespread use of these models may be due to the ease of application of the associated measurement instruments.

VAK and VARK Learning Modality-Specific Models

In addition to the assessment instruments of the thirteen key learning style models discussed above, a number of modality-specific questionnaires exist. These focus on assessing or measuring modality-specific strengths and weakness in terms of visual, auditory and kinaesthetic processing that are considered to influence the learning process (Coffield *et al*, 2004; Rourke *et al*, 2002). Developed by Fleming (2001) , the VARK questionnaire provides a measure of visual, auditory, read/write and kinaesthetic modalities. The additional category of read/write refers to learners who prefer to absorb information via the process of reading and writing essays, reports, definitions, lists, manuals, and so on. Fleming's research suggests that 41% of participants (who completed the questionnaire online) have single style preferences; 27% two preferences, 9% three and 21% had a preference for all styles.

The VAK test "deals with perceptual modes. It focused on the different ways we take in and give out information. The only perceptual modes, or senses, it does not address are taste and smell" (Hawk and Shah, 2007, p.6). This self-administered test, devised by Chislett and Chapman (2005), has been used to assess students' predominant learning style in terms of three modalities: visual, auditory and kinaesthetic, as follows:

- Visual: A preference for the transfer of information via seen or observed things including images, illustrations, diagrams, demonstrations, displays, hand-outs, notes, films, etc. Predominantly visual learners tend to prefer to observe and take notes in a learning situation;
- Auditory: A preference for the transfer of information via listening to lectures, audio tapes, the spoken word, etc. Predominantly auditory learners tend to listen but not necessarily take notes in a learning situation.
- Kinaesthetic: A preference for the transfer of information via physical experiences, demonstrations, hands-on experiences, practical exercises, etc. Predominantly kinaesthetic learners prefer to take an active role in learning.

Recent research conducted with higher education design students used the VAK test because this particular test was self-administered thereby providing students with the opportunity to discover their own learning preferences (Rourke and O'Connor, 2008, 2009a, 2009b, 2010b). This approach was taken because a key element of learning styles and instructional preferences "lies in the individual becoming aware of her or his preferred style. This depends upon the opportunity being made available for an individual to learn about their own style, but also the predisposition of the learner to be motivated to become self-aware and to behave in flexible and different ways when circumstances demand it" (p.407) (Sadler-Smith and Smith, 2004, p. 407).

Findings from recent research indicate that courses that have a strong visually-based curriculum do not always attract visual learners. In addition, predominant learning modality is not necessarily fixed and may change over time. For example, a study conducted at the College of Fine Art (University of New South Wales) involved 296 first year design students. Data was collected before and after teaching intervention during their first year at university. In regard to Cohort A (Before teaching intervention), 40.8% of students identified their predominant learning modality as visual; 24.7% as auditory and 34.5% as kinaesthetic. In respect to Cohort B (After teaching intervention), 57.6% of students identified themselves as visual learners; 10.2% as auditory learners and 32.2% as kinaesthetic learners as illustrated in the following Figure (Rourke and O'Connor, 2010c).

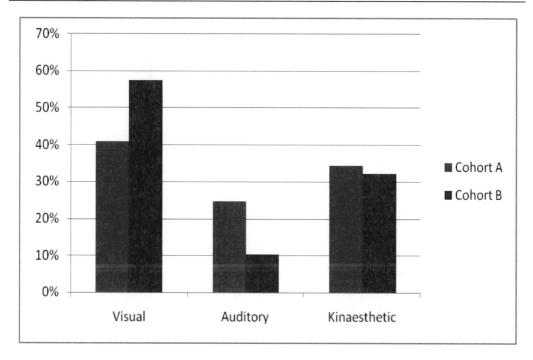

Figure 4.2. Predominant learning modality of 296 design students.

In this study, Cohort A and B received an identical series of twelve auditory lectures supported with the same range of visual materials. However, the auditory lectures delivered to Cohort B included additional instructions and keywords that repeatedly highlighted specific features in the visual materials with the defined purposed of imposing these features on the memories of the learners. In this way, the learning experience was specifically used to manipulate and/or improve the visual literacy of higher education design students.

Recent research argues against the sole use of text-based learning materials in an e-learning environment and findings indicate the following preferences for undergraduates (Willems, 2007):

Information processing:	Active	56%
	Reflective	44%
Information perception:	Sensing	62%
	Intuitive	38%
Information reception:	Visual	88%
	Verbal	12%
Information understanding:	Sequential	56%
	Global	44%

These findings indicate that e-learning content should include opportunities for both active and reflective information processing plus the strong preference for visual information reception (88%) over verbal/aural information reception (12%) appears to provide support for the continued use of PowerPoint slides or similar.

Learning Style Models: Implications for Educators and Learners

An understanding about students' learning styles is critical for educators in terms of developing learning programs that are productive and effective for all students. However, during the design and development of learning programs, educators often make the "assumption that learners exhibit uniformity in the ways in which they process and organise information (cognitive styles), in their predispositions towards particular learning formats and media (instructional preferences) and the conscious actions employed to deal with demands of specific learning situations (learning strategies)" (Sadler-Smith, 2004, p395).

An understanding about individual learning styles is also crucial from the learner's perspective as research indicates that high student performance occurs in learning activities that match student's learning style (Fleming, 2001). According to Sadler-Smith and Smith (2004), a key element in the learning process "lies in the individual becoming aware of her or his preferred style. This depends upon the opportunity being made available for an individual to learn about their own style, but also the predisposition of the learner to be motivated to become self-aware and to behave in flexible and different ways when circumstances demand it" (Sadler-Smith and Smith, 2004, p407).

A number of objections have been raised in regard to learning styles and the first of these has to do with criticism of specific aspects or features of learning style models and/or measurement instruments. Another key objection relates to the quantitative nature of learning style models and measurement instruments, with detractors suggesting that a quantitative approach is inappropriate and espousing a qualitative approach instead. The commercialisation of some learning style models and measurement instruments has also provided cause for objection, as has the prominence accorded to learning style models by some practitioners. Despite these objections, learning style models and measurement instruments provide a useful insight for educators when developing teaching and learning programmes.

Learning Styles: Implications for the Design of Visual Materials

Learning style models and measurement instruments provide useful insight for educators when developing teaching and learning programmes in general and visual learning materials in particular. Educators are faced with a balancing act between the visual, verbal and text-based while also providing sufficient opportunity for refection and active participation. However, in the design of visual materials, it is imperative to ensure that such materials are clear, concise and highly legible to improve the information-transfer process for learners who may be predominantly auditory or kinaesthetic learners rather than visual learners.

Given the known variations in learning style preferences, it is recommended that the design of learning materials also includes the following:

a) Text, images, illustrations, diagrams, demonstrations, displays, hand-outs, notes, films, etc, to suit students who are predominantly visual learners and tend to prefer to observe and take notes in a learning situation;

b) Lectures (spoken word), audio tapes, etc, for students who are predominantly auditory learners and who tend to listen in a learning situation;

c) Physical exercises, demonstrations, hands-on experiences, practical exercises, etc, for students who are predominantly kinaesthetic learners and who prefer to take an active role in a learning situation.

To improve the effectiveness of visual materials, it is also recommended that the content, style and layout of visual materials are designed in such a way as to present information in a clear and unambiguous manner. In doing so, the information presented will not disadvantage learners who are not visually orientated and who may be categorised as auditory or kinaesthetic learners.

VISUAL LITERACY

Visual literacy has been defined as the ability to read visuals and it is considered to be a universal attribute that is developed through the acquisition of a set of principles used for reading visual form (Boughton, 1986). The International Visual Literacy Association, an organization dedicated to the research, study and publication of visual literacy material, use the following extract from Fransecky and Debes, (1972) to define visual literacy:

> "…a group of vision competencies a human being can develop by seeing and at the same time having and integrating other sensory experiences. The development of these competencies is fundamental to normal human learning. When developed, they enable a visually literate person to discriminate and interpret the visual actions, objects, and/or symbols, natural or man-made, that are [encountered] in [the] environment. Through the creative use of these competencies, [we are] able to communicate with others. Through the appreciative use of these competencies, [we are] able to comprehend and enjoy the masterworks of visual communications" (Fransecky and Debes, 1972, p. 7).

To be visually literate, one has to develop the ability to 'read' and comprehend what is seen plus have the ability to generate visual material that can be seen and understood. This implies the "ability to construct meaning from visual images" (Giorgis, Johnson, Bonomo, and Colbert, 1999, p. 146)(p.146). However, for the observer to find meaning in an art image or design object for example, they need to comprehend the basic elements of a universal visual language; a language that may vary across different academic disciplines.

In terms of memory and retention, earlier research indicates that memory for a picture-word combination is superior to memory for words alone or pictures alone (Adams and Chambers, 1962; Haber and Myers, 1982). Although these insights now seem dated it could be argued that very little has changed despite the information revolution: visual information is recognized and remembered for longer durations than verbal information alone (Levie, 1987; Mayer, 1989; Peeck, 1987). In addition, memory for pictures is considered superior to memory for words (Branch and Bloom, 1995; Paivio, 1979). It has also been suggested that the effectiveness of visual representation is dependent on the learner's ability to independently and accurately decipher these images (Downy, 1980).

Braden and Hortin (1982) define visual literacy as "the ability to understand and use images, including the ability to think, learn and express oneself in terms of images" (Braden and Hortin, 1982, p41). This definition implies a relatively high level of cognitive processing and analysis, and it has been suggested that visual literacy is actually a "learned ability to interpret visual messages accurately", thereby suggesting that visual literacy skills are not innate and that teaching-instruction plays a role in the acquisition of the ability (Heinrich, Molenda, and Russell, 1982, p62). Taking these views into consideration it seems imperative that educators equip students with the skills needed to comprehend the visual material that is utilised in teaching, for it has been argued that students tend to be visual learners as their world is rich in visual stimuli (Owston, 1997). To this end, it has been suggested that in order to become a visually literate person one needs to have developed the ability to access, analyse, evaluate and communicate information in any variety of forms that engages the cognitive processing of visual images (Hobbs, 1997). Hence, to be visually literate one has to develop not only higher order thinking skills but also the ability to recognize what one sees and to accurately link this to previous knowledge becomes paramount.

Visual Literacy: Its Role in Education

It is widely accepted that visual materials play a key role in education and that retention of learning is often better if visuals accompany auditory and written information particularly in the case of novice learners (Chandler, 1997; Mayer, Bove, Bryman, Mars, and Tapangco, 1996; Swetmon, 1998). It has also been suggested that visual images often allow learners to see what might not be evident in textual explanation (Smith and Blankinship, 2000).

Visuals are often used in education to support or replace text, and it is imperative that the encoding and decoding of information in visual form is unambiguous. Demystifying the process of comprehending visual images relies heavily on the educator's ability to explain each element or symbol represented and, for both educator and learner alike, it is necessary for a visually literate person to have "a working knowledge of symbols" that is relevant to their area of study (Cunliffe, 1992, p. 149). An early study suggested that the visual presentation of words (typeface, size, colour etc) does not influence the meaning which the words convey, and it was found that readers generally remembered semantic meaning not structural information such as presentation of the text (Lockhart, Craik, and Jacoby, 1976). Similar to verbal language, visual forms are also coded in syntax, roughly equivalent to spoken communication (Boughton, 1986). Dondis (1973) took basic elements such as the dot, line, shape, direction, tone, colour, texture, dimension, scale and movement and compared these to linguistic grammar and syntax to provide a similarity (Dondis, 1973).

The purpose of comparing visual elements to language structures is an attempt to make visual communication transparent and easy to comprehend. Instructional design should follow this 'user friendly' philosophy breaking down the process of understanding the visual material by providing information on a 'need to know' basis scaffolding the learning process so that simple concepts are dealt with first, repeated, then practiced and tested before moving on to more complex issues.

Visual Literacy: Expert-Novice Differences

The use of the term 'literacy' in visual literacy suggests that comprehending visual material is an active process that takes time. For example, it takes time, visual literacy skills and domain specific knowledge, to develop the expertise required to fully understand and appreciate the visual arts.

In order to develop expertise, educators need to firstly assist students to acquire the skills needed to identify and comprehend relevant examples in any given field. Educators should provide learning opportunities that assist learners to assimilate their prior knowledge to any new knowledge in order to promote schema acquisition that can assist with comprehension. Studies in the area of art education have found that comprehension of art is reliant on both the nature of the visual stimulus and the viewer's cognitive structures or existing knowledge (Koroscik, 1982; Koroscik, Desmond, and Brandon, 1985). Koroscik, Desmond and Brandon (1985), have suggested that comprehending art involves a complex interplay between encoding its formal qualities and its semantic characteristics.

In reference to art education, it has been suggested that there are three kinds of visual literacy (Raney, 1999). The first identified was 'perceptual sensitivity' which is the perception all sighted people have which can be sharpened by education. A second kind of visual literacy was identified by Raney (1999) as 'cultural habit', where people are predisposed to see in certain ways; ways which vary according to what they have been exposed to.

The third kind of visual literacy, which has to do with 'critical knowledge', includes "knowledge of the ways the visual images have been used throughout history, awareness of different kind of intentionality, of how an image, object or event is put together to offer a particular experience" (Raney, 1999, p. 45).

An art expert can comprehend most art without difficulty, as they have developed a high level of perceptual sensitivities, have had direct experience with a variety of art within a variety of contexts and they have acquired critical knowledge of art history and theory.

Prawat (1989) suggested that it was important that educators consider both the structure of the discipline as well as the cognitive structure of expert learners in that particular discipline. Students should be provided with the concepts and principles that are most likely to promote domain-specific expert competence (Prawat, 1989).

Under this approach, expert performance is acquired gradually and, in order for students to improve their performance in a discipline, they will depend on the teacher's ability to provide a series of simple training tasks that the students can successfully master by repetition, while being provided with feedback and instruction (Ericsson, Krampe, and Tesch-Romer, 1993).

Novices tend to have fairly low visual literacy levels and a limited grasp of the disciplinary language required to describe a visual example (Koroscik, Short, Stavropoulos, and Fortin, 1992). They can however recognize the formal (structural) qualities of a visual image which is expressed using basic descriptive language (Koroscik, 1982).

These learners have difficulty comprehending visual subtleties or as Raney (1999) would suggest lack 'perceptual sensitivity' hence they provide superficial answers to questions as well as irrelevant observational points about visual examples.

Learners with a low level of visual literacy have difficulty decoding or interpreting visual messages successfully in order to encode or compose meaningful visual messages that visual literate persons are able to do (Ausburn and Ausburn, 1978). They tend to require longer viewing time to study visual materials and often require repeat focused instruction about the visual image in order to improve their visual comprehension skills.

Identifying Visual Literacy Levels and Predominant Learning Modality

A recent study focused on two key aims: to examine levels of visual literacy among undergraduate design students; and to identify predominant learning modalities among undergraduate design students in relation to the categories of visual learners, auditory learners and kinaesthetic learners (Rourke and O'Connor, 2010a). The occurrence of high visual literacy levels among undergraduate design students is a reasonable assumption but remains an untested hypothesis. In addition, a preponderance of visually inclined learners among undergraduate design students also seems a reasonable assumption but is also hypothetical. Gaining an understanding of visual literacy levels and predominant learning styles among undergraduate design students will provide teachers with the opportunity to modify and match their teaching strategies to the learning environment.

In this study, quasi-experimental research techniques were applied, and qualitative procedures were coupled with quantitative analysis. Two separate qualitative procedures, the F-sort and Q-sort techniques, were used in a controlled classroom situation and the results were quantitatively analysed. The test was kept specifically short in duration for a number of reasons. Firstly, the length and duration of testing procedures are considered to impact the reliability and veracity of test outcomes, and the maximum recommended number of questions or evaluations within a given questionnaire should be around fifty (Heise, 1970). Measurement instruments that include more than fifty questions are considered to contribute to participant-fatigue, thereby impacting negatively on the reliability of results.

To identify predominant learning modality, the self-administered VAK test devised by Chislett and Chapman (2005) was used to assess participant's predominant learning style by assessing their strengths and weaknesses in relation to visual, auditory and kinaesthetic modalities. This test was selected as it could be self-administered and scored by participants, thereby providing data for this study as well as useful information for participants regarding their predominant learning modality. In addition, the VAK test is of relatively short duration and was applied in an attempt to minimise and/or avoid participant-fatigue.

Q-sort and F-sort procedures were used to assess visual literacy levels among the participant group. The Q-sort technique, developed by Stephenson in the 1930s, elicits perceptions and judgments of a subjective nature by directing participants to sort visual stimuli using categories defined by the researcher (Amin, 2000; Stephenson, 1953).

The F-sort technique is a modification of the Q-sort technique and allows participants to define their own categories without direction from the researcher when sorting visual stimuli (Miller, Wiley, and Wolfe, 1986). This methodology combines a qualitative approach with quantitative data analysis and is considered an effective tool for capturing patterns of subjective responses to a set of visual stimuli (Amin, 2000; Brown, 1986).

The visual stimulus sampling approach used in this study involved collecting a large set of digital photographic images that illustrated examples of the historical design styles of the Arts and Crafts movement, Art Nouveau, Art Deco and Bauhaus (Schroeder, 1988; Wohlwill, 1977).

Studies investigating the use of visuals in learning have expressed the importance of testing participants using: 1) material similar to their course material, and 2) that links into the course objectives (Szabo, Dwyer, and De Melo, 1981). The visual stimulus used in this study meets both of these criteria. A total of 62 images were collected and these were assessed using the nominal group consensus technique using the evaluation criteria below.

- The photograph featured an example of the built environment, textile design, or furniture design copyright cleared and available for use in the research project;
- The image represented one of the four selected historical design styles (Art and Crafts movement, Art Nouveau, Art Deco and Bauhaus);
- The image was of good photographic quality with clear and unimpeded features and a simple white (or colour consistent) background;
- The image could be manipulated using computer software to remove distracting elements; maintain and/or adjust consistency of ambient lighting across all images; and to maintain and/or adjust consistency of background colour and effect across all images.

In reference to the selection of images for the study, the nominal group consensus approach was applied. This technique is one of a number of techniques used to gain consensus in respect to research materials and visual stimuli. Unlike the Delphi technique, which uses a panel of experts, the nominal group consensus technique comprises a group of people considered to have relevant knowledge or experience specific to the aims of a research study (Campbell and Cantrill, 2001; Keeney, Hasson, and McKenna, 2001). This technique was selected over the Delphi technique due to convenience and the nominal group, which included the two primary researchers of this study each of whom held doctoral qualifications in design, selected a final set of 12 digital photographic images for use in the study.

In terms of procedure, all students who participated in the study were provided with a questionnaire and a set of visual stimuli in a well-lit classroom situation and were directed to self-administer the questionnaire. The questionnaire included a 'Participant Information' section; an 'F-sort' section and a 'Q-sort' section, and participants were directed to complete each section in serial order. The study proceeded under the supervision of the researchers and the resulting data was collected and bundled for subsequent data analysis.

The Participant Information questionnaire included questions relating to a limited range of personal information such as age, gender and previous education. The F-sort questionnaire required participants to sort through the visual stimuli and arrange the images into groupings according to their own categories. Once sorted, participants were then required to record the sorted visual stimuli, using code numbers, under their own category headings on the instruction form. The participants were then directed to complete the Q-sort questionnaire. This questionnaire required participants to sort the visual stimuli again and group them under the headings of *Arts and Crafts movement*, *Art Nouveau*, *Art Deco* and *Bauhaus*.

The total sample size was 178 and participants for this study were drawn from first year undergraduate design students from the College of Fine Art (The University of New South Wales). Of the sample group, 71% were between 17 and 20 years of age; 26% were between 21 and 30 years of age and 3% were aged 30 or more of these participants 72% were female and 28% were male. Of the sample group, 62% had studied Art at high school level and 13% had studied Design and Technology at high school level. The remaining 25% had not studied Art or Design related subjects at high school level.

The data collected from the study was input into statistical software in two large batches and the results were analysed using descriptive statistics as follows. The F-sort task required participants to sort the visual stimuli into categories using headings that they created themselves. Just over half the participant group (51.4%) categorised the images using object type descriptors (such as "furniture, textile, building"). Of the remaining participants, 17.7% created categories based on relatively common design category descriptors (such as "Modern; Post-modern" or "Modern, Medieval, Organic, Oriental"). Almost 10% (9.7%) formulated categories based on shape, pattern and/or colour descriptors (such as "Geometric, Floral, Green, Grey"). Nearly 9% (8.6%) of the participant group sorted the images using categories that represented a mixture of object type/design category descriptors such as "Chairs, Exteriors, Art" and "Postmodern, Brown organic, Modern geometric, Old-fashioned, Intricate patterns".

A small group of participants (8.0%) created groups of images but did not provide any form of category headings or descriptions; while a smaller group (1.7) categorised the images into a large range of multiple groups with multiple headings. Finally, only 2.9% of participants sorted the images into categories that matched the categories devised by the researchers. Results of the F-sort task are illustrated in the following Figure.

In terms of the Q-sort task, a relatively small percentage (5.6%) of the participant group achieved a '4 of 4 correct' score' by correctly identified all twelve images representing the four design styles used in the study (Arts and Crafts, Art Nouveau, Art Deco and Bauhaus). A smaller group (3.4%) achieved a '3 of 4 correct' score by correctly identifying all images within three of the four design styles, and 10.7% scored '2 of 4 correct' by correctly identifying images within two of the four design styles.

Of the remaining participants, 21.3% achieved a '1 of 4 correct' score and over half of the participant group (57.3%) were unable to correctly sort the images into any of the four design styles. A small group of participants (2.2%) indicated on their questionnaires that they were not familiar at all with the design style categories used in this study and were not able to sort the images at all. The results are illustrated in the following Figure.

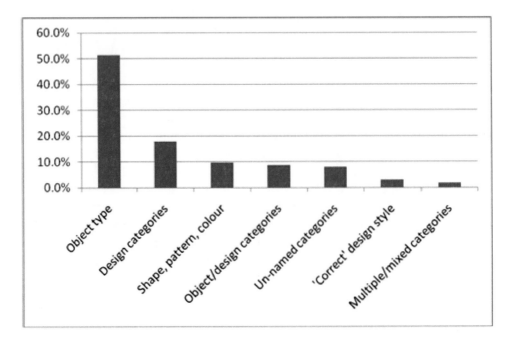

Figure 4.3. F-sort results.

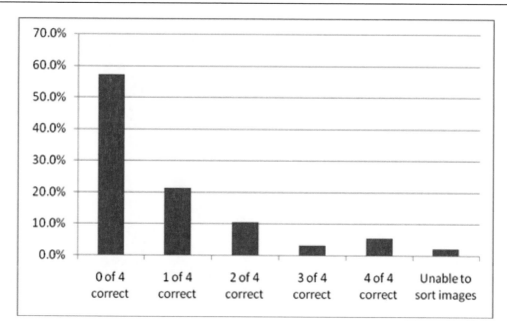

Figure 4.4. Q-sort results.

Of the images correctly identified by 5.6% of the participant group, the Art Deco style achieved the highest correctly-sorted score (26.4%), followed by the Bauhaus style (18.0%) and the Art Nouveau style (17.8%). The Arts and Crafts Movement style achieved the least correctly-sorted score (15.7%). These results indicate that visual literacy levels among undergraduate design students was found to be low with only 2.9% achieving a high score on the F-sort task and 5.6% achieving a high score on the Q-sort task. Levels of stability in visual literacy levels among undergraduate design students will be determined in subsequent studies.

In respect to predominant learning style modality, 40.8% of the participant group identified themselves as visual learners; 24.7% as auditory and 34.5% as kinaesthetic as per the following Figure. Over 90% of the participant group indicated mixed preferences and not a single style preference. While the visual learning modality scores were high, the scores for the kinaesthetic and auditory learning modalities were also relatively high with the visual learning modality only 15% higher than scores for the kinaesthetic learning modality.

The following Figure illustrates patterns of similarity and difference between visual literacy levels and predominant learning modality of the participant group. Among those participants who achieved a 100% correct score in the key Q-sort visual literacy test, visual learners were only marginally above auditory and kinaesthetic learners. No pattern or trend emerged that indicated that any of the predominant learning modalities were any better or worse in terms of visual literacy; except that a surprisingly large proportion of predominantly visual learners scored poorly in the Q-sort visual literacy test compared with auditory and kinaesthetic learners.

The results from this study provide evidence to support the recommendation that teachers in higher education should not take for granted that just because they are teaching a visually-dominant discipline to predominately visual learners, that these learners will necessarily have the visual literacy skills needed to comprehend visual examples used in instruction.

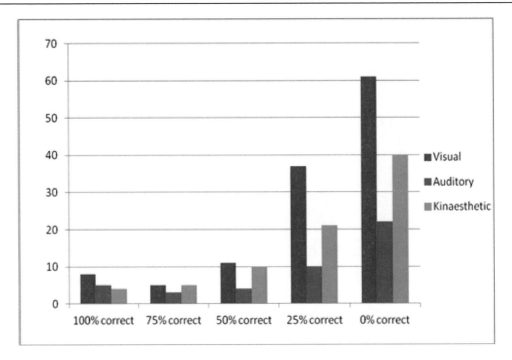

Figure 4.5. Patterns of learning style and visual literacy among the participant group.

As previously mentioned, it is essential that educators provide assistance to help students develop their ability to create meaning from visual materials. In the majority of cases, the participants in this study lacked the ability to 'read' the visual clues evident in the visual materials and, as this study has demonstrated, even predominately visual learners experience difficulty comprehending the link between a visual example and the associated language that needs to be learnt.

As Schnotz (2002) proposes, "it is not enough that learners possess the cognitive schemata of everyday knowledge required for understanding pictorial illustrations" (Schnotz, 2002, p. 116). Students also need to have acquired domain specific prior knowledge and the skills to apply it. Superficial observational points were received from students lacking visual literacy skills and these students tended to rely on visual type-form (recognition schemata) rather than associations that identify individual representations that required having the skill to recognize relevancy and the prior knowledge to put what they had identified into appropriate language.

Visual Literacy: Implications for the Design of Visual Materials

It has been suggested that there are times when 'good pictures fail' primarily because they are often viewed as 'easy' material and hence learners may only examine them superficially (Weidenmann, 1989). However, studies that extensively investigated the usefulness of adjunct illustrations to text found that this method was an effective tool for facilitating students' understanding of scientific explanation (Mayer, 1989; Mayer and Gallini, 1990). It has also been suggested that the more complex the text the more useful illustrations become (Levin and Mayer, 1993).

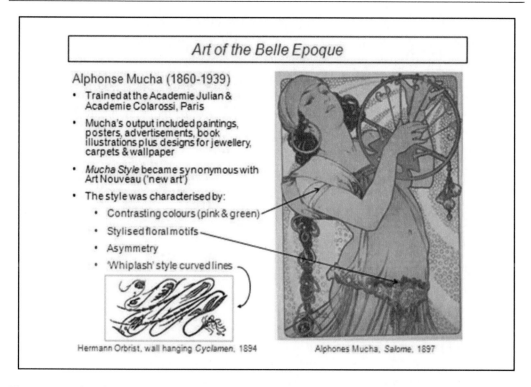

Figure 4.6. Using visual cues such as arrows and colour differentiation to highlight key information.

In addition, where learners are inexperienced in the content domain, illustrations have been found to be an effective tool for learning difficult material (Mayer and Gallini, 1990).

It is recommended that care is taken in the design of visual materials to ensure that text and illustrations provide high quality support to lectures and tutorial activities. The economic use of well placed symbols, colours or codes can combine multiple disconnected visual elements into one clear and concise informational chunk. This can serve to reduce the cognitive load for the less experienced learners and provide critical visual cues to key information for novice learners and those who are not visual learners.

It is recommended that educators actively help students to develop their ability to decipher the visual subtleties imbedded in visual images, graphs, tables, maps or any other visual material being used in teaching. It is often these visual subtleties that provide meaning to the image and assist in explaining specific themes, issues or concepts that need to be learnt. For example, the auditory learner can be trained to efficiently and effectively pick up these visual subtleties through engaged focused listening. Instructors can assist with this objective by sign-posting important points for the auditory learner through vocal emphasis and changes in tone and level of voice.

Repetition of semantic cues in conjunction with contemplation time can improve the effectiveness of visual materials. Semantic cues, which can be delivered via auditory, visual or kinaesthetic techniques, support the notion that "learning is increased as the number of available cues or stimuli is increased" (Severin, 1967, p. 237). Similarly, effective use of pauses and 'contemplation time' can encourage students to think further about the points being raised in respect to visual materials.

In addition, recapping and repetition of the main points in respect to visual materials can assist learners across all the learning styles. For predominantly auditory learners, this provides reinforcement of the main points to be learnt; for kinaesthetic learners, the action of note-taking keeps them engaged and physically active; and for visual learners, repetition assists them in recording accurate notes for later study as well as providing the opportunity to add appropriate visual emphasis to their notes such as arrows, highlighting, underlining and circling key phrases.

REFERENCES

Adams, J. and Chambers, R. (1962). Response to simul- taneous stimulus of two sense modalities. *Journal of Experimental Psychology, 63,* 125–198.

Amin, Z. (2000). Q methodology - A journey into the subjectivity of the human mind. *Singapore Medical Journal, 41,* 410-414.

Ausburn, L., and Ausburn, F. (1978). Visual literacy: Background, theory and practice. *PLET, 15*(40), 291-297.

Boughton, D. (1986). Visual literacy: Implications for cultural understanding through Art education. *Journal of Art and Design Education, 5*(1), 125-142.

Braden, R. A., and Hortin, J. A. (1982). Identifying the theoretical foundations of visual literacy. *Journal of Visual/Verbal Languaging, 2,* 37-42.

Branch, R. C., and Bloom, J. R. (1995).The role of graphic elements in the accurate portrayal of instructional design. In D. G. Beauchamp, R. A. Braden and R. E. Griffin (Eds.), *Imagery and Visual Literacy.* Broken Arrow, OK: The International Visual Literacy Association.

Brown, S. R. (1986). Q technique and method: Principles and procedures. In W. B. Berry and M. S. Lewis-Beck (Eds.), *New tools for social scientists: Advances and applications in research methods.* Newbury Park, CA: Sage.

Campbell, S. M., and Cantrill, J. A. (2001). Consensus methods in prescribing research. *Journal of Clinical Pharmacology and Therapeutics, 26*(5-14).

Chandler, L. (1997). The effects of verbal elaboration and visual elaboration on student learning. *Instructional Journal of Instructional Media, 24*(4), 333-339.

Chislett, V. and Chapman, A. (2005) VAK learning styles self-assessment questionnaire. Available from www.businessballs.com. Accessed on 10 February 2010.

Coffield, F., Moseley, D., Hall, E., and Ecclestone, K. (2004).*Learning styles and pedagogy in post-16 learning: A systematic and critical review.* London: Learning and Skills Research Centre.

Cunliffe, L. (1992). Why a theory of symbols is necessary for treaching art. *Journal of Art and Design Education, 11*(2), 143-153.

Curry, L. (1983). *An organisation of learning styles theory and constructs*: ERIC Document Retrieval Service, TM 830554.

Dondis, D. A. (1973). *A primer of visual literacy.* Cambridge: MIT Press.

Downy, M. T. (1980). Pictures as teaching aids: Using pictures in history textbooks. *Social Education, 44*(2), 93-99.

Ericsson, K. A., Krampe, R. T. H., and Tesch-Romer, C. (1993). The role of deliberate practice in the acquisition of expert performance. *Psychological Review, 100*(3), 363-406.

Fleming, N. D. (2001). *Teaching and learning styles: VARK strategies.* Christchurch, NZ: ND Fleming.

Fransecky, R. B., and Debes, J. L. (1972). *Visual literacy: A way to teach; A way to learn.* Washington: Association for Educational Communication and Technology.

Gardner, H. (1983). *Frames of mind: Theory of multiple intelligences.* New York: Basic Books.

Giorgis, C., Johnson, N. J., Bonomo, A., and Colbert, C. (1999). Visual literacy. *Reading Teacher, 53*(2), 146-153.

Haber, R. N. and Myers, B. L. (1982). Memory for pic-to-grams, pictures, and words separately and all mixed up. *Perception, 11,* 57–64.

Hawk, T.F. and Shah, A.J. (2007) Using learning style instruments to enhance student learning, *Decision Sciences Journal of Innovative Education, 5*(1), 1-18.

Heinrich, R., Molenda, M., and Russell, J. (1982). *Instructional media and the new technologies of instruction.* New York: John Wiley and Sons.

Heise, D. R. (1970).The semantic differential and attitude research.In G. Summers (Ed.), *Attitude measurement.* Chicago: Rand McNally.

Hobbs, R. (1997). Literacy for the information age. In J. Flood, S. Brice-Heath and D. Lapp (Eds.), *The handbook of research on teaching literacy through the communicative and visual arts* (pp. 7-14). New York: John Wiley and Sons.

Keeney, S., Hasson, F., and McKenna, H. P. (2001).A critical review of the Delphi technique as a research methodology. *International Journal of Nursing Studies, 38,* 195-200.

Koroscik, J. S. (1982). The effects of prior knowledge, presentation time and task demands on visual processing. *Studies in Art Education, 23*(3), 13-22.

Koroscik, J. S., Desmond, K. K., and Brandon, S. M. (1985). The effects of verbal contextual information in processing visual arts. *Studies in Art Education, 27*(1), 12-33.

Koroscik, J. S., Short, G., Stavropoulos, C., and Fortin, S. (1992). Framwork for understanding art: The function of comparative art context and verbal cues. *Studies in Art Education, 33*(3), 154-164.

Levie, W. H. (1987). Research on pictures: A guide to literature. In D. A. Houghton and E. M. Willows (Eds.), *The psychology of illustration: Instructional issues (Vol 2)* (pp. 1-50). New York: Springer-Verlag.

Levin, J. R., and Mayer, R. E. (1993). Understanding illustrations in text. In B. K. Britton, A. Woodward and M. Brinkley (Eds.), *Learning from textbooks* (pp. 95-113). Hillsdale, NJ: Erlbaum.

Lockhart, R. S., Craik, F. I. M., and Jacoby, L. (1976). Depth processing, recognition and recall. In B. K. Britton, A. Woodward and M. Brinkley (Eds.), *The arts, cognition and basic skills.* St Louis: Cemrel.

Mayer, R. E. (1989). Systematic thinking fostered by illustrations in scientific text. *Journal of Educational Psychology, 81*(2), 240-246.

Mayer, R. E., and Gallini, J. (1990). When is an illustration worth ten thousand words? *Journal of Educational Psychology, 82*(4), 715-726.

Mayer, R. E., Bove, W., Bryman, A., Mars, R., and Tapangco, L. (1996). When less is more: Meaningful learning from visual and verbal summaries of science textbook lessons. *Journal of Educational Psychology, 88*(1), 64-73.

Miller, D. M., Wiley, D. E., and Wolfe, R. G. (1986). Categorisation methodology: An approach to the collection and analysis of certain classes of qualitative information. *Multivariate Behavioral Research, 21*(2), 135-167.

Owston, R. D. (1997). The world wide web: A technology to enhance teaching and learning. *Educational Research, 26*(2), 27-33.

Paivio, A. (1979). *Imagery and verbal processes.* Hillsdale, NJ: Lawrence Erlbaum Associates.

Peeck, J. (1987). The role of illustrations in processing and remembering illustrated text. In D. A. Houghton and E. M. Willows (Eds.), *The psychology of illustration: Basic research* (Vol. 1, pp. 115-151). New York: Springer-Verlag.

Prawat, R. S. (1989). Promoting access to knowledge strategies and disposition in students: A research synthesis. *Review of Educational Research, 59*(1), 1-41.

Rakes, G. C. (1999, Sept.). Teaching visual literacy in a multimedia age, *TechTrends, 43*(4), 14-18.

Raney, K. (1999). Visual literacy and the art curriculum. *Journal of Art and Design Education, 18*(1), 42-47.

Rourke, A. J., and O'Connor, Z. (2008). I can see it but I don't understand it! Investigating visual literacy skills and learning styles in higher education design history curriculum. *International Journal of the Humanities, 6*(6), 19-26.

Rourke, A. J., and O'Connor, Z. (2009a). Investigating visual literacy and predominant learning modality among undergraduate design students in Australia: Preliminary findings. *Design Principles and Practice, 3*(2), 17-28.

Rourke, A. J., and O'Connor, Z. (2009b). Look before you leap: Testing some assumptions on visual literacy and predominant learning modalities of undergraduate design students in Australia and New Zealand. *International Journal of Learning, 16*(8), 33-45.

Rourke, A. J., and O'Connor, Z. (2010a). Examining ways to improve visual teaching materiala: The role of visual literacy and predominant learning modality. In M. L. Albertson (Ed.), *Developments in higher education* (pp. 1-37). New York: Nova Science.

Rourke, A. J., and O'Connor, Z. (2010b). *The expectations-reality interface: Visual literacy levels, predominant learning modalities and preferences among first year design students.* Paper presented at the 13th Pacific Rim First Year in Higher Education Conference 2010.

Rourke, A. J., and O'Connor, Z. (2010c). Visual literacy levels and predominant learning modality among first year design students: The influence of teaching intervention. *Design Principles and Practice, 4*(1), 347-360.

Sadler-Smith, E., and Smith, P. J. (2004).Strategies for accommodating individuals' styles and preferences in flexible learning programmes. *British Journal of Educational Technology, 35*(4), 395-412.

Schnotz, W. (2002). Towards an integrated view of learning from text and visual display.*Educational Psychology Review, 14*(1), 101-120.

Schroeder, H. W. (1988). Visual impact of hillside development: Comparison of measurements derived from aerial and ground-level photographs. *Landscape and Urban Planning, 15*, 119-126.

Severin, W. J. (1967). *Cue summation in multiple channel communication.* Unpublished Doctoral dissertation, University of Wisconsin.

Smith, B. K., and Blankinship, E. (2000). Justifying imagery: Multimedia support for learning through explanation. *IM Systems Journal, 39*(3/4), 749-767.

Stephenson, W. (1953). *The study of behavior: Q-technique and its methodology.* Chicago: University of Chicago Press.

Swetmon, B. R. (1998). *Communication skills for the 21st century: How to understand and be understood.* Plano, Texas: Skill-Speak Press.

Szabo, M., Dwyer, F. M., and De Melo, H. (1981). Visual testing: Visual literacy's second dimension. *Educational Communication and Technology Journal, 29,* 177-187.

Weidenmann, B. (1989). When good pictures fail: An information-processing approach to the effect of illustrations. In H. Mandl and J. R. Levin (Eds.), *Knowledge acquisition from text and pictures* (pp. 157-171). Amsterdam: Elsevier.

Willems, J. (2007). Does style matter? Considering the impact of learning styles in e-learning, ICT: Providing choices for learners and learning. Proceedings of ASCILITE Singapore 2007 Available from http://www.ascilite.org.au/conferences/singapore07/procs/willems-poster.pdf.

Wohlwill, J. F. (1977). *Visual assessment of urban riverfront.*Unpublished manuscript.

Zywno, M. S., and Waalen, J. K. (2002). The effect of individual learnign styles on student outcomes in technology-enabled education. *Global Journal of Engineering Education, 6*(1), 35-44.

Chapter 5

EFFECTIVE USE OF VISUAL CUES TO SCAFFOLD ONLINE COURSES

ABSTRACT

This chapter discusses online learning and teaching in higher education specifically focusing on how educators' can develop new engaging spaces through digital scaffolding that can provide the needed bridge for supporting students in the online learning process (Rourke and Coleman, 2010a). There will be a discussion on how visual cues were utilised in an online Postgraduate course to scaffold student learning and to promote active learner engagement and collaboration. It will be argued that educators should employ in their online course design assessment that not only enhances the learning experiences of students but also that engages them in real-world authentic tasks. This fully online course was developed with the goal of having clear alignment between the learning outcomes, the assessment as well as method and materials of instruction. The aim in the learning design was to develop a model for learning where students were explicitly scaffolded using colour coding, cues and concept maps to enable learning research and writing skills that would culminate in a research paper directed by individual student interests.

INTRODUCTION

Personalized online learning spaces have emerged in recent years as an important factor when developing content and designing the learning in Learning Management Systems (LMS). The 'one size fits all' approach to presenting content and providing learning activities and assessment in the LMS does not always take into account students' individual differences or preferences for learning. Learning styles in higher educational settings have become more important to the learning and teaching of students as universities seek to implement outcome-based assessment and develop authentic programs for an increasingly diverse student background with varying prior learning experiences. Stewart and Felicetti (1992) define learning styles as "those educational conditions under which a student is most likely to learn" (p.15). Learning styles are not concerned with what is learned but rather how a student learns (Stewart and Felicetti, 1992; Davis, Misra and Van Auken, 2000). Graff (2003), who recommended that web developers and educational designers design and develop online learning environments to match not only the expectations of students but also their cognitive style, concurs with this view. This chapter seeks to present how important it is for visual arts and design students to engage in holistic right brain visual eLearning and have access to interactive visual interfaces versus the sequentially organized left-brain corporate models used in many learning management systems.

This case study presents a project that builds upon previous work in LMS and the acquired knowledge and experiences of online learning and teaching. In order to actively engage predominantly visual spatial learners, the design of the LMS should use emerging adaptive technologies to support student's learning styles and preferences where appropriate. The learning design that establishes the visualization of learning for students in this Postgraduate higher education course was created as a graphic representation of the learning content.

The aim was to design a LMS interface that advances one step further than the typical approach to personalization in eLearning. Previously the authors were involved in an upgrade of an existing online course that was designed to teach Postgraduate students how to write a research paper in arts administration after the course was migrated from Web CT Vista to Blackboard early in 2010. This shift provided an opportunity for those involved to reassess how best to improve the site for the specific learning needs of the student cohort. As these students were at the end of their Masters degree in Arts Administration and the fact that many had completed their undergraduate degree in art related disciplines it was envisaged that the online site would benefit from emphasizing visually the links between the course materials.

An important aspect of the learning design was the fact that the course throughout scaffolds the learning in each aspect of the assessment. Scaffolding students learning is viewed as a worthwhile approach to assist with promoting thinking particularly as our brains organize knowledge in hierarchical frameworks. As such learning approaches that assist towards facilitating this process should be utilised in education (Bransford, and Cocking, 1999; Tsien, (2007). To further assist students in their engagement with the process the author's needed to examine ways of effectively utilising color, icons and simple charts and to reduce text. Mind maps were also utilized in order to assist students to visualize their way through the process of writing the research paper. Visual elements not only helped with the structuring of the course, they also assisted with providing links between related material, sign posting what was important as well as providing multiple entry points to material that catered for individual preferences for navigating the site. In order to consider learner's individual preferences and approaches to learning, the role learning styles play in the design of LMS needed to be considered.

Considering Learning Styles Online

In developing this online course, we went back to ground the learning design in educational theory to build a pedagogically sound LMS. Initially, Kolb's (1984) learning styles inventory (1984) was investigated. It identified different orientations to learning, and related these to the model for experiential learning. In this Kolb (1984), differentiated learners according to which aspect of the experiential learning cycle they prefer (refer to Figure 5.1) concrete experience, active experimentation, reflective observation, or abstract conceptualization.

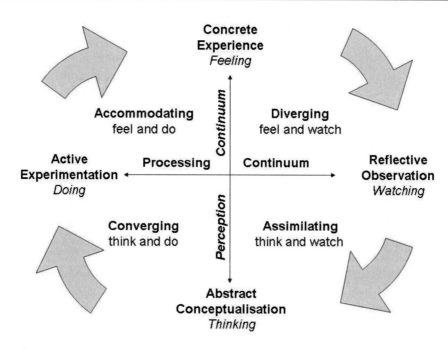

Figure 5.1. Experiential Learning cycle (1984) from Clark (2004).

This learning process as Kolb (1984) describes was developed to "ensure that teaching and tutoring activities give full value to each stage of the process. This may mean that for the tutor or mentor, a major task is to 'chase' the learner round the cycle, asking questions which encourage reflection, conceptualization, and ways of testing the ideas" (Atherton, 2010, NPN). Gardner's theory of multiple intelligences (1983) was also examined in developing the scaffolding for the learning object and site. Gardner's work has been criticized in the past for lacking in empirical evidence, however, it is accepted by educational theorists and practitioners that the provision of a range of material and activities rather than a narrowly focused text-based approach (i.e. assimilation of text followed by text-based analysis/synthesis) can accommodate a broader range of learning styles and assist most learners (Stahl, 1999). It seemed likely that the students in the current cohort would be responsive to both visual media and activities oriented towards their disciplinary preference.

From a pedagogical perspective, we also believed that it was important that students felt that their individual learning styles and preferences were taken into account as in the face-to-face classroom. To address this, other developers Liu and Chen (2008) created a personalized e-learning management system that automatically selected appropriate learning content and methods for each learners individual learning style. Felder and Silverman (1988) recommended however, that an educator always tailoring materials to students was a flawed pedagogical approach. This, they reasoned was because students should be taught to learn using a variety of tools, not just those most efficient to a particular cognitive style. When used appropriately with this in mind, LMS have the opportunity to provide this as web 2.0 has facilitated more scope of learning and teaching tools for educators. Following this we believe that it is imperative that LMS are designed to clearly communicate the pathway to learning by whatever method best communicates the course content and learning activities. Scaffolding is one method that can be adopted towards achieving this end.

Scaffolding a Learner Support System in Art Administration

Postgraduate coursework students have used online learning and teaching tools for some years in the Master of Art Administration (M.Art Admin.). Students enrolled for ten years have used a number of LMS as well as web 2.0 tools for reflective blogging and e-portfolios for assessment as learning (Rourke and Coleman, 2009b). The MArt Admin.is a f2f (face-to face) coursework Masters; however a core component toward completion of the degree is the completion of the fully online Research paper course. Students write a 10,000 word situated learning (Herrington, Reeves and Oliver, 2010) paper modeled on their practice and experience in art administration. Many students are simultaneously completing the industry based learning 240-hour Internship placement in the art industry as a component of an authentic program. A cognitive and social constructivist learning approach was cultivated through the development of the digitized scaffold to support the student's needs in an environment that was as authentic as it could be. It was crucial in the design of this course that visual strategies were utilized to emphasis links between teaching material, student's knowledge, assessment tasks and learning activities so that students were motivated to complete each task.

Rakes suggested that, "Constructivist learning paradigms emphasize connections. Using visuals can be an effective means for creating some of those unique connections between text elements and connections with past knowledge, especially in the Information Age" (p.18). During the last four years, the strengths and weaknesses of the assessment as learning in this course have been evaluated (Rourke, Mendelssohn and Coleman, 2008; Rourke, Mendelssohn, Coleman and Allen, 2008; Rourke and Coleman, 2009a; 2010a; 2010b; Coleman, Rourke and Allen, 2011), critically reflected upon and adjusted as evaluations, student needs and the LMS have changed. As Young (1993) suggested, "assessment can no longer be viewed as an add-on to an instructional design or simply as separate stages in a linear process of pre-test, instruction, post-test; rather assessment must become an integrated, ongoing, and seamless part of the learning environment" (p.48). From the outset, it has been imperative that the students 'learn to learn' online through both procedural and instructional scaffolding for assessment as learning. It was also important for the learning to be an authentic learning experience to further enable the 'cognitive apprenticeship model' (Collins, Brown and Newman, 1989). Through this model, the skills of collaboration and peer review that have been a hallmark of this degree have been both facilitated and enhanced by a community of practice.

The digital scaffolding used in the LMS is instructional and procedural for "sequencing of lessons so students have a chance to apply a set of skills in constructing an interesting problem solution before they are required to generate or remember those skills. This requires some form of scaffolding" (Collins, Brown and Newman, 1989, p.485). At the completion of the integrated three-staged sequenced learning model, the students are more independent and self regulated learners. An important aspect of the scaffold used to teach these students how to research and write a research paper is to start with a strongly supported structure and remove this gradually over the Semester as students become more confident and independent in their learning. If course designers also take into account students previous knowledge and experience and apply this to authentic tasks that have future relevance then the chances are students will be more engaged and invest time and effort into the learning process.

'Authentic' tasks are those that are contextualized in real-life experiences and in the professional domain of the discipline. These tasks should also support critical thinking and learning and enable the learner to apply their developed capabilities to new contexts (Herrington and Oliver, 2000; Stein, Isaacs, and Andrews, 2004). Scaffolding in this context is a method that can support the student to extend their learning through sequential steps. Scaffolding is a form of assistance provided to a learner by a more capable teacher or peer that helps learners perform a task that would normally not be possible to accomplish by working independently (McLoughlin and Marshall, 2000). Scaffolds can also incorporate resources to be independently accessed and used by the learner, as well as regular multi-dimensional feedback (Herrington and Oliver, 2000).

Scaffolding the Course Design

According to McKenzie (1999) the eight characteristics of web-based educational scaffolding include that scaffolding: provides clear directions, clarifies purpose, keep student on task and offers assessment to clarify expectations. Scaffolding also point's students to worthy sources, reduces uncertainty, surprise and disappointment, delivers efficiency and finally creates momentum (McKenzie, 1999). Greene and Land (2000) went further and examined instructional scaffoldings role in supporting cognitive function. They discovered that guiding questions that were instructor developed with procedural scaffolding further assisted students to focus and develop their course projects. An important aspect of procedural scaffolding is that it provides a framework where students can work at their own pace while being guided by verbal, visual and written instruction in the LMS. As Schum (1995) suggested, self-pacing was an important characteristic of online learning. He discovered that students appreciated being able to move through their courses at their own pace. There are various methods that can be utilized in the LMS to achieve this including using color coding and iconography to direct the learners' attention to important content materials, as the learners requires it in each stage of the learning process.

As students move through the course they work through each scaffolded learning task, which is later submitted to the discussion forum for self and peer review. The course content is also scaffolded so that students build on each section of their paper in incremental stages. The course was designed so that the assessment was driven by the students and was based around their individual interests in the profession this was in order to provide an authentic context for learning. Here as Herrington, Reeves and Oliver (2010) suggested, the scenario is created by the student. An important aspect that was considered was that these students were located in a 'community of practice' in the art world that required practicing and mastering certain skills one of which was their ability to be both pro-active and collaborative. These students will ultimately work as art administrators, art curators, gallery managers and educationalists. Therefore, the Research paper must have an authentic context for relevance in their future careers, where as Collins, Brown and Newman (1989) concur, "drawing students into a culture of expert practice in cognitive domains involves teaching them how to 'think like experts'" (p. 488).

These experts in their fields offer peer-to-peer collaboration and review throughout the task, where the scaffold provides the framework for them to facilitate and share their knowledge. The online material is structured to support the development process for learners through modeling and visual cues to indicate stages and activities in the learning process.

To provide social presence and an immediate visual component for learners to relate to, a course welcome from the lecturer, with a photograph, appears on the first screen of the course (Refer to Figure 5.2).

Welcome from Dr Arianne Rourke

Dear RP Students,
Welcome to the SAHT9116 Research paper site I hope you will find the peer review process, activities and other information useful for you in your journey towards writing a research paper. Please always email me at a.rourke@unsw.edu.au if you need a quick response I will only be answering questions here once a week. You may find it also useful to ask your fellow students for advice as they are also going though the same process as you to research and write their papers. Also as Postgraduate students you all come to your studies with already a wealth of knowledge and experience that it would be worthwhile for all if you could share it here. We have students who are interstate and overseas doing this course, in the past these students have always really appreciated having the collaboration and collegiality of communicating online with their fellow students as they do not have the class contact local students have as they work through writing their papers. So please use the discussion forums frequently this will help you stay motivated and on track and to meet deadlines as you write your research paper. Finally, best of luck to all of you writing and researching your paper.

Regards,
Arianne

Figure 5.2. Welcome and introduction to the LMS.

Scaffolding of the course is approached as follows:

1. *Scaffold the learning task.* The learning task is structured as three distinct stages with a submission required for each. Each stage is linked to exemplars and templates to guide the submission process.
2. *Scaffold the course content and information.* Content and information is clearly linked at each relevant stage of the courses learning task. For each stage three distinct categories of content are available: instructions for completing the submission, resources and exemplars to guide development of the submission, and templates to guide the format of content for the submission.
3. *Scaffold the feedback.* At each stage peer review provides structured feedback, and evaluation of review performance, which supports learners in assessing their developing review skills.

The development of the task takes into consideration immediately the objectives of the course and positions all of the assessment components in what the students will have learned by completing the task. The teachers' **first scaffolding role is important for ensuring that** students do not feel completely overwhelmed by the task. This is accomplished by trying to avoid limiting this to narrow outcomes that do not support the intended learning. The task is developed through three assessable stages (McKenzie, 1999). Therefore, a "critical element in fostering learning is to have students carry out tasks and solve problems in an environment that reflects the multiple uses to which their knowledge will be put in the future" (Collins, Brown and Newman, 1989, p. 487). All stages of the process and assignments completed at the end of the process become part of the chaptered research paper. By the use of simple steps that build in complexity and by providing authentic examples demonstrating how each exercise could be completed, it is envisaged that students will not feel completely overwhelmed by the task, an important aspect to scaffolding an online course according to McKenzie (1999). One method that assisted with this goal was to include in the course design colour coding and iconography. This was in order to simplify instruction, guide students to what was important and to aid towards scaffolding the course material and student learning, which the next section of this chapter will discuss.

Colour Coding and Iconography

Crutsinger, Knight and Kinley (2005) recommended that: "the application of the elements and principles of design is imperative in creating web activities that generate interest, create smooth transitions and emphasize important course material"(p.273). Colour-coding and iconography in particular can assist towards maximizing students learning if carefully utilized. Colour if effectively used, could also assist with personalizing the online space, which can often appear bland, uninspiring and uniform. Colour in LMS can provide a visual emphasis on important material that needs to be learnt. If used effectively colour can be utilized to 'draw the eye' of the learner to the links they need to make between the course material, while reducing the need for lengthy detailed written explanation. Simple iconography can also assist with this, as well as sign-posting where to look for information in an economical, easy-to-follow manner.

There are also other advantages to utilizing these visual approaches for according to Rakes (1999), "Visual strategies can be motivational and can reinforce other basic skills. They can encourage organizational skills along with creative and analytical thinking" (p.18). Colour can be utilized to organize material into manageable blocks that is less likely to overload the learner's working memory as it would if trying to cope with simultaneously comprehending large blocks of black text on a white page.

The authors believe that it is important that online courses do not overwhelm students with information, instead course material should be provided in the most effective, efficient manner, be this visual, written, verbal or a combination of these. However caution must be taken when utilizing more than one of these mechanisms to communicate the same information as this could cause the online learner to become disengaged with the learning process. In particular for the more expert learner who had previous knowledge of the material, the elimination of redundant text rather than the integration of the text with diagrams could promote learning. The redundancy effect occurs when redundant material is eliminated which results in a better performance than when the redundant material is retained (e.g. Chandler and Sweller, 1991; 1996; Mayer, Bove, Bryman, Mars, and Tapangco, 1996). Colour-coding and iconography if cleverly utilized can not only reduce the overuse of text but also provide a powerful visual stimulant that could encourage the online learner to engage further with the learning material.

According to McLoughlin and Krakowski (2001): "Computer visuals and simulation tools provide objects and representation, to model and activate cognitive processes. Primarily, these representations are visual, ie symbols, pictures, graphics, simulations and animations" (p.5); colour can play an important role to assist these mechanism towards facilitating learning.

Each stage of the course has been colour-coded making it clear to the learner what resources and activities are aligned to each stage of the task. On the main course page showing what each stage contains, the use of colour and photographs provides a more engaging and readable interface than a simple text list (Refer to Figure 5.3). Colour-coding was initially developed to match the entry points. It was later discovered that using the multiple entry points offered students other advantages; through color-coding they could visually locate areas of information they needed to navigate the online space.

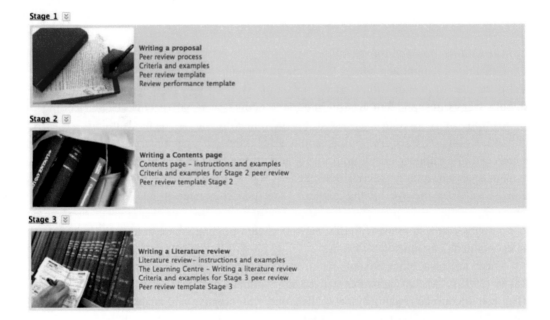

Figure 5.3. Colour-coded course entry.

Icons are also utilized to identify the type of resources or activities embedded in each stages instructions, mind map, peer review, review performance. The writing of a research paper has been broken down into three assessable tasks which are peer reviewed, which include: Stage 1: Writing a proposal, Stage 2: Writing a contents page and Stage 3: Writing a literature review, all these components become part of the final paper. Once the online stages are completed and the full paper is written, a paper draft is emailed to a supervisor who reads and comments on areas that could be improved. Once students have adapted their papers based on their supervisors comments a bound hard copy is submitted for marking by an examiner who was not their supervisor. During this process students produce mind maps that are updated as they move through each stage of writing a research paper, this will be discussed in detail in the next section of this chapter.

Use of Mind Maps to Promote Learning Online

One possible method for reaching the visual learner is by providing visual diagrams that summarize the linkages between the learning content (Maal, 2004; Sword, 2004). Visual learners according to Castellino and Schuster (2002) learn more effectively when linkages are provided for a holistic view, as it is important for these learners to see not only the 'big picture' but also the connections between topics to be learnt. Buzan (1991) suggested that diagrams should be created and later studied in a form that best resembles the brain's memory process.

A visual in the form of mind map or diagram is a useful tool for conceptualizing thoughts, ideas and knowledge as on the whole visual images are not limited by words or a sequential ordering (Williams, 1998). According to Ruffini (2008) a "mind map makes information more meaningful than if it were just memorized, because, like concept maps it takes the information in the context of existing knowledge" (p.56).

It is important when designing online content and activities that educators not just provide information but consider methods for engaging students in the learning process that link new information to previously acquired knowledge and understanding. When it comes to learning, Vygotsky (1962) also suggested that visual graphics containing key ideas and information was easier to remember than extended text, whether the text was visual or verbal. He put forward also that the use of both visual and verbal language to create graphic organizers could result in active learning.

It has also been suggested that creating graphic organizers to illustrate the organization of ideas and information aids comprehension and learning (Flood and Lapp, 1988).

In the online course students develop mind maps to visually conceptualize their research and generate their own model of learning. Mind maps were selected as a visual tool to assist students to link as well as see the 'big picture' of the literature, their ideas and argument in relation to their topic focus and research question. Zanting, Verloop and Vermunt (2003) suggested that mind maps or visual summaries were most effective for abstract topics, they were not as useful for verbally orientated concrete information.

In this online course learners incrementally develop their own mind maps relating to the process of developing a research paper as they progress through the learning task, engaging them in the development of a visual representation of their understanding.

This method of representing knowledge and understanding can be effective as Jonassen (1996) suggested, students demonstrate some of their best thinking when they attempt to represent something graphically, and thinking is a necessary condition of learning. Hence it is imperative that educators when designing courses in LMS they consider ways of encouraging students to think deeply about the course material.

Mind maps as a learning tool offer an effective method to assist towards promoting higher order thinking skills as well they provide the opportunity to engage in a creative process that many visual learners enjoy.

According to Novak and Cañas (2008), "one of the reasons concept mapping is so powerful for the facilitation of meaningful learning is that it serves as a kind of template or scaffold to help to organize knowledge and to structure it, even though the structure must be built up piece by piece with small units of interacting concept and propositional frameworks" (p.7).

A sample mind map is provided in the Research paper online course to scaffold student's engagement in the learning process. The example was provided in the LMS to assist students to understand what is meant by a 'mind map' and also to help them to create their own mind map, or if they choose they can develop their own from scratch (Refer to Figure 5.4).

According to Freeman and Jessup (2004) graphic organisers are useful in enhancing learning they also assist students in retention and organization of information.

The next section of this chapter will discuss how other graphic organisers were utilised in this online course to enhance student learning.

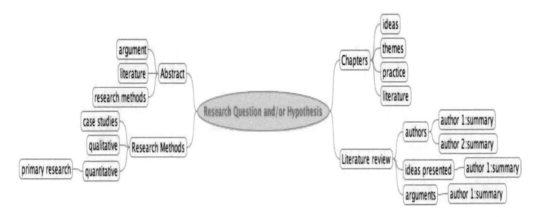

Figure 5.4. Mind map example from the LMS.

Sign Posting, Worked Examples and Multiple Entry Points

In order for active learning to take place, educators can consider utilising simple iconography to sign post important information, as well as appropriate 'meaning' charged visuals and graphically presented content lists. This approach to designing the VLE (Virtual Learning Environment) is specifically appropriate for the visual learner as it draws their attention to what is really important to engage with and learn from. Many believe that the key to memory lies in providing a visual depiction of the material (Barbe and Milone, 1981; Mayer, Heiser and Lonn, 2001). Visual learners in particular learn more effectively through sight, hence pictorial depictions of the materials become central to memory (Higgins, 1994). As Barbe and Milone (1981) suggested, visual learners have difficulty retaining information that is not graphically illustrated. As it has been put forward that the brains memory power primarily works when key concepts are interrelated, or linked in some manner (Higgins, 1994). For visual learners in particular, a well-chosen visual can communicate a wealth of knowledge. For these learners it is also imperative that VLE's do not overload their working memory with excess written detail as they have a learning preference for illustrated instruction. As Mayer, Heiser and Lonn (2001) advocated, adding excessive text to visual learning material can overload the learners working memory, causing learners to split attention between two sources which can cause lowering the effectiveness of learning.

In the VLE it is also important to maximize the effect of using different modes of learning that are appropriate to get the message across. When attempting to engage the learner particularly from predominately visual disciplines in the VLE, economy of words and limited duplication between visual and text information also becomes imperative. When designing VLE's educators should consider choosing the most effective tool for communicating the material to be learnt and activities to be engaged in. A well-designed eLearning platform as previously mentioned, uses the best method be it visual, written or auditory, to engage the learner efficiently and effectively in active not passive learning when designing authentic learning materials and assessment. Nunes and MacPherson (2006) put forward that "learning activities must be authentic...embedded in realistic and relevant contexts" (p.4). As with learning in the f2f classroom, the VLE should 'build' upon student's knowledge and skills rather than just being an information provider that is not 'tailored made' to engage the various learning styles of the student cohort.

Worked examples are particularly useful for students solving relatively unfamiliar problems. They direct student's attention towards understanding the steps needed to complete a task. Worked examples can be also be utilized to take the 'guess work' out of problem-solving by supplying both the working steps and answers, this assists in overcoming the limited processing capacity of short-term memory. By reducing the use of problem-solving activities and replacing this time with studying worked examples and practicing the skills demonstrated, it is believed that novices will begin to acquire the schemas to perform effectively and efficiently (Paas and van Merriënboer, 1994; Ward and Sweller, 1990). Worked examples can be accessed through hyper-links from the home page color-coded learning object flow chart.

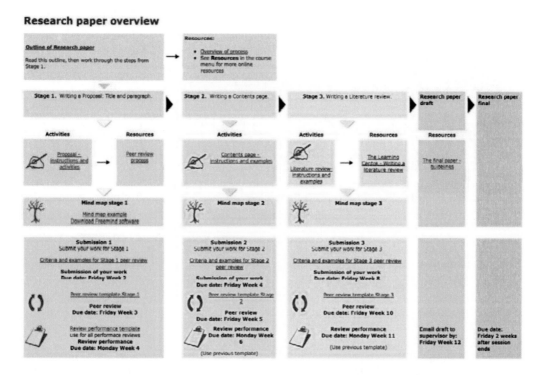

Figure 5.5. Learning Object.

The student can navigate to each stage of the course from this course homepage learning object, the course menu or they can access an online planner that scaffolds the entire course – an overview of the writing process, as well as links to all instructions, resources and templates from the color coded flow chart (Refer to Figure 5.5).

Column colors indicate the stage of the process, and icons sign post the different resources and activities within each stage, many of which as mentioned link to a worked example that students use as a model to guide their work. The use of sign posting allowed students to enter at different spaces within the course and develop site knowledge in the learning process. Each underlined blue text offered a hyperlink to the related documents that could be downloaded onto the desktop, some of which can be typed into then uploaded into the Discussion forum for peer review. Another addition to the existing site was to include the use of metaphors for visual enhancement to further personalize the space.

Using Metaphor to Personalize the Online Learning Environment

Metaphors can be used as analytical devices that assist with the understanding of an unknown situation in terms of a familiar one (Lakoff, 1993; Ortony, 1991). Researchers coming from an organizational science perspective suggest that metaphors "guide our perceptions and interpretations of reality and help us formulate our vision and goal" (Cornelissen, Oswick, Christensen and Phillips, 2008, p.8).

Organizational researchers (Grant and Oswick, 1996; Palmer and Dunford, 1996) have made a distinction between 'deductive' metaphors, which are imposed on or applied to situations and metaphors, which are 'inductively' derived from talk and interactions. According to Tsoukas (1991) the 'deductive' use of metaphors can assist more with the theory building process.

Stage 3. Writing a Literature review.

The Literature Review Tree

This tree could be considered a metaphor for encapsulating the stages of your thinking process when you search the literature, process your ideas and write your literature review. The roots of the tree are the foundation ideas that underpin your hypothesis or argument, which is the trunk of the tree. The roots need nourishing this can be achieved by spending time reading, writing and revising your ideas on your topic. These foundation ideas become the sub-heading topics in your literature review which structure it and provide links between the hypothesis (trunk) and main literature (main branches) which you group your authors together on which are the leaves. The tree grows as you add further ideas (roots), links (small branches) and leaves (authors). Research is an ongoing process that requires dedication (the water, that keeps the tree alive), skills (the earth that nourishes the tree) and time (the sun that helps the tree grow) as well as knowledge and understanding (the air that it needs to survive). It is up to you to decide how much or little you use these resources and how you go about getting help to improve the trees chance of survival. You are not on your own as the tree is in a forest, collaborate with your online class and contribute to their learning as they will to yours and seek help from wiser trees of knowledge when you feel your tree has become stunted in its growth.

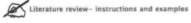 Literature review– instructions and examples

Attached Files
📄 3_Lit.Review.pdf (94.486 KB)
📄 Writing a Literature Review.ppt (868.5 KB)

Writing a literature review – resources from The Learning Centre
Getting Started on your Literature Review

Stage 3 Mindmap

Figure 5.6. Metaphors and Imagery.

The use of a well-selected metaphoric image can be a particularly useful method in eLearning for encapsulating complex concepts that would take an overload of text to explain. This method is particularly useful in domains where students are used to learning via visual images. These images should be directly related to the concept or principle being explained. In some cases it maybe necessary for the instructor to provide a brief descriptive analysis that provides the relationship and links between the visual image and the content being explained. This is in order that the student can clearly visualize the steps, stages or layers the image is trying to communicate. For according to McLoughlin and Krakowski (2001) "visual forms of representation are important, not just as heuristic and pedagogical tools, but as legitimate aspects of reasoning and learning" (p.2). They believe that, "technologies can offer visual experiences which foster higher order cognition" (McLoughlin and Krakowski (2001, p.2), as previously discussed.

For students unfamiliar with the conceptual process of writing, but familiar with visual communication, a visual metaphor is a powerful tool to induct and engage students in the learning process. The use of a 'tree' metaphor assists towards simplifying this complex process, as it provides a visualization of the organic thought process of researching and writing a research paper. The visual resemblance of the mind map that they develop reinforces the metaphor (Refer to Figure 5.6). The use of metaphors in the learning design was imperative for visual and kinesthetic learners to feel connected to the physicality of the tree when approaching their literature review. Writing a literature review is a difficult task for students who have had little experience previously developing these concepts.

EVALUATION

Assessment of student learning outcomes, course feedback and assessment results demonstrate that students found the process of writing a research paper less overwhelming and stressful than expected as the whole process was broken down into manageable and easily visually identifiable stages. Students also indicated that they appreciated having a number of deadlines as this forced them to start writing much earlier than they would normally have if left on their own to meet only a final deadline. Smedley (2005) recommended that this is an important factor of online courses where learner "motivation plays an important role in learners completing their e-courses. Sometimes this can be external but the strongest motivation comes from an internal desire to complete the learning journey once it has commenced" (p.81). The design of the online course received positive comments from students who found it easy to navigate because of the color-coding and icons offering them a clear visual link to related course material. In particular student's commented that they found the color coded flow chart useful as it offered a 'one stop shop' for resources and course material as well as providing a visual display of the journey they would take towards completing their research papers.

CONCLUSION

It has been acknowledged in the literature that when instructional methods take into account student's learning styles they not only learn more but also retain information longer, some even as a result develop a more positive attitude towards the subject (Stewart and Felicetti, 1992; Felder and Henriques, 1995). Researchers agree that when instructional content is provided through a visual context it can facilitate richer and broader associations while providing the 'big picture', which offers many opportunities for effective learning (Buzan, 1991; Adkins and Brown-Syed, 2002). As Collins, Brown and Newman (1989) confer, the "cognitive apprenticeship, as we envision it, differs from traditional apprenticeship in that the tasks and problems are chosen to illustrate the power of certain techniques or methods, to give students practice in applying these methods in diverse settings, and to increase the complexity of tasks slowly, so that component skills and models can be integrated" (p. 459).

The nature of this authentic task is as Herrington, Reeves and Oliver (2010) would suggest, has provided collaboration and a real world integration that supported the collegial peer review process within the assessment and situated learning task. This has provided opportunities for the students to become effective performers in cooperation and collaboration with their peers. As a community of practice these students have developed their problem solving skills, engaged in reflective learning, and developed more effective communication skills within a socially cohesive environment that they could further develop in their future professions in the art world.

As online learning and teaching is the direction of higher education in the future and educators' continue to develop new engaging spaces, digital scaffolding can provide the needed bridge for students to be supported in the online learning process (Rourke and Coleman, 2010a). Reflective practice enables educators' to learn from their experiences and develop curriculum and learning experiences that cater to the needs of their students. As reflective practitioners, we continue to better the Research Paper course, developing a new scaffold environment grounded in the methodology of a learner support system with each new cohort. The pedagogical goals as linked to the concept of scaffolding as a model in online learning and teaching discussed in this chapter provides a reflection on the scaffolding process as the University of New South Wales (UNSW) continues to move into a new era of LMS and VLE. The aim was to develop and design an interface that advances one step further than the typical approach to personalization in eLearning and can be disseminated across disciplinary in an honors project. Future research will investigate methods of data collection to ascertain whether the learning outcomes have from the student's perspective met their needs of an authentic assessment task that links to their future careers in Art administration.

REFERENCES

Adkins, D. and Brown-Syed, C. (2002, August). Accommodating all learners: Critical inquiry and learning styles in the LIS classroom. *Paper presented at the 68th IFLA Council and General Conference,* Glasgow, Scotland.

Atherton, J.S. (2010). Learning and Teaching; Experiential Learning [On-line] UK: Available: http://www.learningandteaching.info/learning/experience.htm

Barbe, W.B., and Milone, M. N. (1981, February). What we know about modality strengths. Educational Leadership, 378-380.

Bransford, J., Brown, A. L., and Cocking, R. R. (Eds.). (1999). *How people learn: Brain, mind, experience, and school.* Washington, D.C.: National Academy Press.

Buzan, T. (1991). *Use both sides of your brain.* New York: Plume.

Castellino, A. R. and Schuster, P.M. (2002). Evaluation of outcomes in nursing students using clinical concept map care plans. *Nurse Educator, 27,* 149-150.

Chandler, P. and Sweller, J. (1991). Cognitive load theory and the format of instruction. *Cognition and Instruction*, 8(4) 293-332.

Chandler, P. and Sweller, J. (1996). Cognitive load while learning to use a computer program. *Applied Cognitive Psychology*, 10, 151-170.

Clark, D. R. (2004).Kolb's Experiential Learning cycle. The Art and Science of Leadership. Retrieved December 20, 2011 from: http://nwlink.com/~donclark/leader/leader.html

Collins, A., Brown, J. S., and Newman, S. E. (1989). Cognitive apprenticeship: Teaching the crafts of reading, writing, and mathematics. In L. B. Resnick (Ed.), *Knowing, learning, and instruction: Essays in honor of Robert Glaser* (pp. 453-494). Hillsdale, NJ: Lawrence Erlbaum Associates.

Cornelissen, J.P., Oswick, C., Christensen, L. T. and Phillips, N. (2008). *Metaphor in Organizational Research: Context, Modalities and Implications for Research – Introduction, Organization Studies*, 29(1) 7-22.

Crutsinger, Knight and Kinley (2005). Learning style preferences: Implications for web-based instruction, *Clothing and Textile Research Journal*, 266-278.

Davis, R. Misra, S., and Van Auken, S. (2000). Relating pedagogical preference of marketing seniors and alumni to attitudes towards the major. *Journal of Marketing Education*, 22, 147-154.

Felder, R.M. and Henriques, E.R. (1995). Learning and teaching styles in foreign and second language education. *Foreign Language Annuals*, 28, 21-31.

Felder, R.M. and Silverman, L.K. (1988). Learning and Teaching Styles in Engineering Education, *Engineer Education*, 78(7), 674-681.

Flood, J. L. and Lapp, D. (1988).Conceptual mapping strategies for understanding information texts, *The Reading Teacher*, 41, 780-783.

Freeman, L.A. and Jessup, L.M. (2004). The power and benefit of concept mapping: measuring use, usefulness, ease of use and satisfaction, *International Journal of ScienceEducation, 26(2), 151-169.*

Gardner, H. (1983). *Frames of Mind: The Theory of Multiple Intelligences*. New York: Basic Books.

Graf, S., and Kinshuk (2007). Providing adaptive courses in learning management systems with respect to learning styles. In G. Richards (Ed.), *Proceedings of the world conference on E-learning in corporate, government, healthcare, and higher education* (E-learn)(pp. 2576–2583). Chesapeake, VA: AACE Press.

Graff, M. (2003). Learning from web-based instructional systems and cognitive styles. *British Journal of Educational Technology*, 34(4), 407-418.

Grant, D. and Oswick, C. (1996). *Metaphor and Organization*, London: Sage.

Greene, B. A. and Land, S.M. (2000). A qualitative analysis of scaffolding used in a resource-based learning environment involving the World Wide Web. *Journal of Educational Computing Research*, 23(2), 151-180.

Herrington, J., and Oliver, R. (2000). An instructional design framework for authentic learning environments. *Educational Technology Research and Development*, 48 (3), 23-48.

Higgins, J. M. (1994). *Creating creativity. Training and Development*, 48(11), 11-16.

Jonassen, D.H. (1996). Computers as mind tools for schools: engaging critical thinking, Englewood Cliffs, NJ: Merrill.

Kolb, D.A. (1984). *Experiential Learning*. Englewood Cliffs, NJ: Prentice-Hall.

Lakoff, G. (1993). The Contemporary Theory of Metaphor. In A. Ortony (Ed.). *Metaphor and Thought,* (pp.202-251), Cambridge: Cambridge University Press.

Liu, M. and Chen, L. (2008). *Personalized learning systems based on Solomon learning style.* Computer Science and Software Engineering International Conference.

Maal, N. (2004).*Learning via multi sensory engagement.* Association Management, 56 (11), 61.

Mayer, R., Bove, W., Bryman, A., Mars, R. and Tapangco, L. (1996). When less is more: Meaningful learning from visual and verbal summaries of science textbook lessons. *Journal of Educational Psychology*, 88(1), 64-73.

Mayer, R. E., Heiser, J. and Lonn, S. (2001). Cognitive constraints on multimedia learning: When presenting more material results in less understanding. *Journal of Educational Psychology,* 93(1), 187-198.

Mayer, R.E. and Massa, L.J. (2003). Three Facets of Visual and Verbal Learners: Cognitive Ability, Cognitive Style, and Learning Preference. *Journal of Educational Psychology*, 95(4), 833–846.

McKenzie, J. (1999). Scaffolding for Success, Beyond Technology: Questioning, Research and the information Literate School Community, The Educational Technology Journal, 9(4). Available URLhttp://emifyes.iserver.net/fromnow/dec99/scaffold.html,

McLoughlin, C. and Krakowski, K. (2001, Sept.). Technical tools for visual thinking: what does the research tell? Paper presented at the: Apple University Consortium Academic and Development Conference, James Cook University, Townsville, 23-26.

McLoughlin, C. and Marshall, L. (2000). Scaffolding: A model for learner support in an online teaching environment. In A. Herrmann and M.M. Kulski (Eds), *Flexible Futures in Tertiary Teaching.* Proceedings of the 9th Annual Teaching Learning Forum, 2-4 February 2000. Perth: Curtin University of Technology. http://lsn.curtin.edu.au/tlf/tlf2000/mcloughlin2.html

Novak, J. D. and Cañas, A. J. (2008). The Theory Underlying Concept Maps and How to Construct and Use Them, Technical Report IHMC CmapTools 2006-01 Rev 01-2008, Florida Institute for Human and Machine Cognition. Available at: http://cmap.ihmc.us/Publications/ResearchPapers/TheoryUnderlyingConceptMaps.pdf

Nunes, M. and McPherson, M. (2006). Learning support in online constructivist environments in information systems.*HEA-ICS Electronic Journal*, 5(2). 1-11.

Ortony, A. (1991). *Metaphor and Thought.* Cambridge University Press: New York.

Paas, F., and Van Merriënboer, J. J. G. (1994). Instructional control of cognitive load in the training of complex cognitive tasks. *Educational Psychology Review,* 6,51-71.

Palmer, I. and Dunford, R. (1996). Conflicting uses of metaphors: Reconceptualizing their use in the field of organizational change, *Academy of Management Review*, 21, 691-717.

Rakes, G. C. (1999, Sept.). Teaching visual literacy in a multimedia age, *Tech Trends*, 43(4), 14-18.

Rourke, A. J., Coleman, K. and Allen, B. (2011). Actively Engaging Visual Learner's Online, *The International Journal of Technology*, Knowledge and Society, 7.

Rourke, A. J. and Coleman, K. (2010a). A learner support system: Scaffolding to enhance digital learning, *The International Journal of Technology, Knowledge and Society*, 6(1), 55-70.

Rourke, A.J. and Coleman, K.S. (2010b). Knowledge building in 21st Century: learners, learning and educational practice. Curriculum, Technology and Transformation for an Unknown Future.The 27th ASCILITE annual conference, University of Technology, Sydney, 5-8 December 2010.

Rourke, A. and Coleman, K. (2009a). Interactive and Collaborative Learning in an e-learning environment: Using the peer review process to teach writing and research skills to Postgraduate students. *The International Journal of Technology, Knowledge and Society*, 5(1), 169-182.

Rourke, A. J. and Coleman, K. (2009b). *An emancipating space: reflective and collaborative blogging,* ASCILITE, University of Auckland, New Zealand, 888-897.

Rourke, A .J. Mendelssohn, J. and Coleman, K. S. (2008). Peer Review and the Coursework Postgraduate student: Two case Studies from the Master of Art Administration at COFA, UNSW, *The International Journal of Learning*, 14(12), 7-12.

Rourke, A.; Coleman, K. S.; Mendelssohn, J. and Allen, B. (2008). Did I tell you its anonymous? *The triumphs and pitfalls of online peer review.* ASCILITE, 1-11.

Ruffini, M. F. (2008). Using E-Maps to Organize and Navigate Online Content. *EDUCAUSE Quarterly*, 31(1), 56-61.

Schum, L. (1995). Online course: What have we learnt? *Paper presented at the World Conference on Computers in Education*, Birmington, UK.

Smedley, J. (2005). Working with Blended Learning. In *Enhancing teaching in Higher Education: New Approaches for Improving student Learning.* Routledge Falmer: New York.

Stahl, S. A. (1999). Different Strokes for Different Folks?: *A Critique of Learning Styles, American Educator.* Fall, 27-31.

Stewart, K. L. and Felicetti, L. A. (1992). Learning styles of marketing majors. *Educational Research Quarterly*, 15(2), 15-23.

Stein, S.J., Isaacs, G. and Andrews, T (2004). Incorporating authentic learning experiences within a university course. *Studies in Higher Education*, 29, 2, 239-258.

Sword, L. (2004). I think in pictures you teach in words: The gifted visual special learner. http://www.nswagtc.org.au/oz.gifted/conferece/swordsvisualspacial.html

Tsien, J. Z. (2007). *The Memory. Scientific American*, July, 52-59.

Tsoukas, H. (1991).The missing link: A transformational view of metaphors in organizational science, *Academy of Management Review*, 16, 566-585.

Vygotsky, L.S. (1962). *Thought and Language*, Cambridge, MA: MIT Press.

Young, M.F. (1993). Instructional design for situated learning, *Educational Technology Research and Development*, 41(1), 43-58.

Ward, M. and Sweller, J. (1990). Structuring effective worked examples. *Cognition and Instruction,* 7(1), 1–39.

Willems, J. (2007). Flexible learning: Implications of "when-ever, "where-ever" and "what-ever". *Distance Education*, 26 (3), 429−435.

Williams, V.S. (1998). Visual learning and technology: A mutual support system. *College and University Media Review*, 5, 85-95.

Zanting, A. Verloop N. and Vermunt. J. D. (2003). Using interviews and concept maps to access mentor teachers' practical knowledge, *Higher Education*, 46, 195-214.

Sections of this chapter were published by Common Ground Publishing as:Rourke, A. J., Coleman, K. and Allen, B. (2011). Actively Engaging Visual Learner's Online, The International Journal of Technology, Knowledge and Society, 7.

Chapter 6

VISUAL LITERACY AND VISUAL MEMORY

ABSTRACT

This chapter discusses what is visual literacy and defines the skills students need to develop in order to learn from visual material presented in lectures and other course material. It is argued that it is important that teachers in higher education provide learning activities to promote visual literacy skills to assist students towards fully comprehending the many visual images utilised as teaching and learning aids. Specifically this chapter provides discussion on how to promote visual literacy skills with art and design students that could be adapted for teaching other disciplines in higher education. How we cognitively understand visual material will also be analysed in terms of how we use our visual memory to assist in reasoning how best to utilise visuals in education to promote meaningful learning.

WHAT IS VISUAL LITERACY?

In general terms visual literacy is the ability to 'read' visuals, that is, to understand the meaning of what one sees. Visual literacy is a broad attribute that may be developed by acquiring a set of principles for reading visual form as previously mentioned (Boughton, 1986). It is a semantics branch of linguistics concerned with meaning and the reading of visual forms, "visual literacy is the ability to 'read' visual material with skill, and to write with visual means, expressing oneself effectively and appropriately" (Elwell and Hess, 1979, p.28).

The visually literate has the knowledge and skill required for deciphering visual codes and reading qualitative syntaxes. This knowledge and skill assists the student towards demystifying (or decoding) the visual world around them and interpreting this knowledge into visual, auditory and written form as part of the learning process. "Persons who are visually literate develop the competencies for visual literacy in the proper environment, and are then able to use it to interpret future actions, objects and symbols" (Kintgen, 1988, p.158). To be visually literate requires not only obtainment of competency required to 'read' visuals but also an ability to transfer this knowledge onto accessible verbal or visual communication. Frederick (2000) reasoned that students were motivated by visuals because they could more easily understand and remember a concept if they saw it. However, in order to utilise their visual learning students need to be taught how to 'read' visual text as rigorously as printed text. Particularly as it has been suggested that to be visually literate the viewer has to have "awareness of the conventions through which the meanings of visual images are created" (Messaris and Moriarty, 2005, p.481), these conventions are not derived at intuitively they need to be taught.

In order to 'read' forms, such as words, numbers, movements, images and patterns, it requires an understanding of their rules, their context and their syntactical structures (Eisner, 1989). The concept of literacy involves not only representing but also recovering meanings of visual forms. Literacy is connected with graphic symbolic systems, which lend themselves to an affiliation with the visual. The concept of literacy is metaphorically associated with 'reading and writing' rather than pictorial form. Allen (1994) identified two problems with the term: 'visual literacy' in relation to art. Firstly, the definition is somewhat 'hazy', so the visual educator does not feel inclined to debate it's meaning and use. Secondly, visual literacy is usually located squarely within the practice of reading images, and this concerns 'visual perception'. As a consequence, Allen (1994) suggests that as educators, we may need to extend our concept of visual education to embrace other disciplines rather than assuming that visual literacy is simply the product of art or design education. As well students need to develop critical as well as visual literacies.

Visual literates not only have to develop skills to distinguish visual subtleties through critical analysis, they also have to acquire the ability to 'read' sequences of visuals that represent a process, an abstract idea, emotion or fictional narrative (Kintgen, 1988). John Debes is well known in the field of visual literacy, in 1972 he outlined the characteristics of visual literacy, listing the skills that needed to be developed before one becomes visually literate:

- To read visuals with skill.
- To write with visuals expressing oneself effectively.
- To know the grammar and syntax of visual language and be able to apply them.
- To be familiar with the tools of visual literacy and their use.
- To appreciate the masterworks of visual literacy.
- To be able to translate from visual language to verbal language and vice versa
  (Kintgen quotes John Debes, 1988, p.159).

There is some worthwhile constructive criticism of Debes characteristics of the visual literate in this report in the transcript of an interview with an academic member of staff who teaches studio practical classes to Applied Arts students. This lecturer pointed out how difficult it would be to apply this theory to the practice of educating vision.

Boughton in 1986 described two types of visual literacy, visual (artistic) literacy where the focus is confined to the study of art, and visual (aesthetic) literacy: the study of the visual world through the framework of various theories of aesthetics where "objects of all types can be considered in the analysis of aesthetic response. This includes both art and non-art objects" (p.138). He stressed the importance of educating students towards understanding visuals, which in turn will increase visual literacy levels. By describing the practical application of teaching visual literacy skills, one can work towards developing criteria for defining the essence of visual literacy. Broughton (1986) also suggested that teacher training should focus more clearly on the production of the 'literate' teacher.

The skills required to becoming a visual literate need to be conceivable in practice, relative to the visual world not only within an elite cultural art context but also within daily life. "The visual world may indeed be composed of signs, but the aim of visual literacy is not merely to explain the workings of the semiotic systems that provide it with meaning; it is to enable people to use those systems for effective communication, to provide a rhetoric of visuality in addition to a grammar of it." (Kintgen, 1988, p.160). The visuals shown in lectures can be used to familiarise students with what Kintgen (1988) called: "a particular tradition and technology of visual representation" (p.61). To understand the visual representations of the designer for example, the skill of decoding qualitative syntax needs to be explored and understood. Visual forms are like verbal language, they are also coded into a kind of syntax that is roughly equivalent (Boughton, 1986).

Visual literacy also includes interpreting body language, which is a means by which we can communicate processes, ideas, narratives and feelings. Through the positive reinforcing factors of body language students can be encouraged to learn visual forms. The adoption of positive body language communicates enthusiasm for a subject to students, which can have a positive effect on student learning. "If the student is motivated by the lecturer's approach to a subject then he or she is likely to become self-motivated and the lecture will have an influence long after the content has been forgotten" (Brown and Atkins, 1988, p.23).

Visual education is concerned with communication. Through the process of educating vision, skills for developing visually literate individuals can be encouraged. The "need to develop visual literacy in pupils...obviously touches on the need for them to be fluent in the use of symbols for demonstrating understanding as they evaluate and make art" (Cunliffe, 1992, p.146). In the teaching of the history and theory of design or art in higher education artefacts are usually represented through two-dimensional visual forms, following the principle that "images are more precise and richer than literature" (Berger, 1972, p.10). These images in the visual world can be 'read' and design in particular can be 'read' by its syntaxes or codes, these syntaxes are the grammatical arrangements of words specifically 'qualitative syntaxes'.

When the visual syntax of the designer or artist is understood, a defined path becomes apparent to access the work and hence to decode the visual messages, which results in obtaining a higher level of visual literacy, that of understanding and comprehending the design. When an inappropriate set of expectations (codes) are used to decipher images the viewer could fail to find the meaning in the design, which means that the viewer has not learnt to 'read' the syntax of the designer (Boughton, 1986). If students can be taught to understand these qualitative syntaxes then they have access to not only a design work but also access to other visual messages outside the realm of design and visual arts.

Suzanne Langer wrote back in 1957 that artistic mode of knowledge was a non-discursive form of expression that is present immediately in 'sensuous forms of feeling'. Langer (1957) claimed that the visual arts differed from the discursive modes of knowledge which are systematic, rational and propositional "ideas are progressively revealed over time and in this sense are temporal" (Boughton, quotes Langer, 1986, p.131). Langer's theory relates to the notions of creativity, design as a discipline sits between, taking on both a discursive and non-discursive form of expression, it is both a rational and creative activity. Design and art history, theory and criticism involves students in acquiring the language to communicate both in written, verbal and visual form not only the systematic, objective quantitative aspects of art or design, but also the subjective qualitative issues that allow them to express their feelings, opinions and ideas. According to Raney (1999) the notions of creativity should be entwined into the idea of 'being critical', to avoid a rigid divide between reason and unreason and critical understanding, this is a type of visual literacy that usually requires directed study and discussion.

It has been said that the visually literate through creative use of visual competencies are effective communicators (Boughton, 1986). This communication, according to Feinstein (1982) could also involve representing an image pictorially and in order to achieve this one must have "some knowledge of the visual symbol systems, its vocabulary, concept, conventions, and some technical skills to manipulate art material" (p.46). All this acquired knowledge and experience combines together in the visually literate individual, one of the roles of the art and design educator is to teach the skill and knowledge of reading visuals as well as producing visual images. One way of achieving this is too reduce the complexity of visual images and provide easy access to the language. Visuals can also provide a stimulus for directing the production of art and design.

Edmund Feldman wrote in 1986 that a passive viewer cannot react to visual images with critical understanding and "to be visually illiterate is to be 'un-free' in the sense that the individual is a victim of the persuasive devices, or rhetoric of visual communication". (Boughton quotes Feldman, 1986, p.135). Hamblen (1986) discussed the interconnection between aesthetic literacy and knowledgeable appreciation of art. In order to successfully link these dichotomies it would mean bringing to awareness, already present, taken-for-granted definitions of and attitudes towards art for purposes of examination, refinement, and elaboration (Hamblen, 1986, p.68). For it could be argued that learning to read visuals should not only include learning the preconceived constructs for decoding images, it should also include understanding aesthetic literacy through knowledge and personal vision.

When viewing the world we utilise visual thinking, to express this understanding to others we utilize visual literacy skills to record this cognitive process, however these can be viewed as not separate activities but as intrinsically interconnected. According to McLoughlin and Krakowski (2001) visual thinking has three distinct features, which include:

> "First, visual thinking is part of the way we reason, such as when we extract information from a map, chart or table and represent and express it in language. Second, visual thinking can be integral to problem solving, as when we need to use a diagram to explain, document, calculate or show the steps involved in reaching a solution. Third, visual representation can play a role in communication, for instance using diagrammatic and visual forms to communicate information, represent data and show relationships" (p.1).

These aspects of visual thinking, that of reasoning, problem solving and communication are all important attributes to develop and improve in students in higher education across all disciplines, which the next section of this chapter will argue.

David Sless wrote back in 1977 that art has failed to educate vision, one of the reasons could be that the "visual literacy movement....has demanded a breakage of the traditional links between art and visual education" (p.5). In the ten years or so with the introduction of the internet and elearning into higher education it could be said that these links have been reaffirmed. However even though students are now given the opportunity to enhance and improve their visual literacy skills not only in the areas of design and art criticism, art/design appreciation and aesthetics but through experience with the design and art making processes have they improved?

Chapter 4 discussed a study that's findings affirm those of Sless of more than thirty years ago. For the logic as well as creative process of design is now taught so that students not only develop an understanding of its form and content, they are also taught to 'read' (or look) for meaning through an understanding of semiotics, for example. The next section of this chapter endeavors to elaborate on the practicalities of effectively using visuals in design history as well as other disciplinary areas to improve student's visual literacy skills.

TEACHING VISUAL LITERACY SKILLS

This section will specifically focuses on teaching visual literacy skills to art and design students, many of the methods discussed could also be appropriate for teaching in other disciplines. For envisaging knowledge is an important factor of learning in most disciplines. As Tufte (1990) theorised, as humans we need to visualise information in order to reason about it, communicate, document and remember it. Particularly as nowadays there is so much ambiguity in the messages visuals transmit even more so with the availability of an avalanche of images from the World Wide Web, there has been much debate in the literature about the importance of developing visual literacy skills, according to Mohler (2000). For as Steels (1994) concurs as previously mentioned, visual literacy amalgamates personal experience and imagination with social experience, technology and aesthetics as such it is a worthwhile attribute to develop in students in higher education.

Diezmann (1997), research into mathematics teaching discovered that the use of diagrammatic explanation assisted student's comprehension. According to Gleick (1987) and Klotz (1991), scientists and mathematicians have had great success using visualization to not only present but also to further understand their research. Hence even for experts in their field developing visual literacy skills is an important attribute to assist towards further exploring their field of study as well as to represent their disciplines in a new and innovative way.

Visual education in particular, is concerned with visual communication that is developed through learning how to appreciate and critique art as well as through the practice of art making. Through the process of educating vision, skills for developing visually literate individuals can be encouraged. The "need to develop visual literacy in pupils...obviously touches on the need for them to be fluent in the use of symbols for demonstrating understanding as they evaluate and make art" (Cunliffe, 1992, p.146).

Berger (1972), writer of the popular art text 'Ways of Seeing', stated that: "images are more precise and richer than literature" (p.10) and as such images in the visual world could be 'read', once one learns various 'ways of seeing'. Teaching visual literacy involves students learning the 'language' of art as well as developing skills for deciphering visual syntaxes or codes in the visual world. However, this broad unfocused approach to learning visual material does not direct the viewer's attention towards what needs to be learnt. As previously discussed in Chapter 3, utilising semantic cues is one method for directing the learner's attention to important aspects of an art or design work to promote what Müller (2008)calls 'visual perception competence'.

Müller (2008)suggested that visual perception competence relates to an individuals' as well as groups' ability to comprehend visuals. She stated that: "Age, gender, experience, and social as well as cultural factors influence the way in which visuals are perceived" (p.103). Hence it is imperative that educators provide learning activities in the classroom that utilize visual material that promote discussion and debate where multiple interpretations are explored. Asking students their subjective responses to visual material can be a useful method for promoting classroom discussion with novice learners who often have little background knowledge to contribute. Müller (2008)advices that to "be visually competent does not just mean to 'recognise' the depiction, but to put this visual into context, and to grasp the hidden meaning levels as well as to assess the type of visual and its production and reception context" (p. 105). This is a complex cognitive process that takes time to acquire, to begin to understand this process it is important for educators to understand how the learner retrieves information from visuals.

According to McLoughlin and Krakowski (2001) visual and pictorial forms of representation offers some advantages over text-based resources including that they display special relationships; demonstrate proportional relationships within objects and assist towards facilitation perceptual inference such as providing the relative size of an object. They argued that, "visual forms of representation are important, not just as heuristic and pedagogical tools, but as legitimate aspects of reasoning and learning" (p.2).

There has been a number of studies that have examined the encoding and retrieval of information from pictures (Friedman and Bourne, 1976; Kunen, Green and Waterman, 1979; Mandler and Johnson, 1976; Mandler and Ritchey, 1977). The results from these studies are not easily generalised to visual art processing according to Koroscik (1982), who has studied the complexities of visual art processing specifically in relation to the characteristics of pictorial information processing. Koroscik (1982) discovered that prior knowledge, the amount of time allocated to studying the artwork, and the level of the task demanded, all affect student's ability to learn visual material.

Koroscik, (1982) proposed that: "individuals with prior knowledge of visual art process more information than those who lack such information" (p.21). Students with specific knowledge of art have the schemas that allow them to process more information in working memory. As previously mentioned, the learner's level of expertise can have an effect on their ability to solve problems in mathematics, similarly, the problem-solving strategy of art critiquing can be a problem for the novice learner who lacks the schemas to effectively analyse a work of art.

Koroscik (1982) study also found that remembering information was influenced by the length of time that was spent viewing the art examples, as other studies indicate (Craik and Lockhart, 1972). Koroscik (1982) claims that participants who had 4.5 minutes to respond to an artwork remembered significantly more than those given 1.5 minutes. This result may seam obvious, but what was interesting was that the type of information that was remembered did not differ significantly, with structural information remembered before semantic information. Research by Koroscik, Desmond and Brandon (1985) suggested that comprehension of art involves a complex interaction between encoding its structure (or formal qualities) and its meaning (or semantic characteristics).

The elemental structure of the artwork is usually the first aspect that the viewer can identify whereas semantic information requires a more indepth reading of the work. Koroscik (1982) suggested that as a result of the need to provide longer viewing times for effective learning, that "one might question the traditional practice of displaying large collections of artworks to students in slide presentations. Students might be better served if classroom viewing activities provided for the detailed examination of a smaller number of artworks" (p.21).

As previously mentioned, art appreciation and criticism in the classroom is usually taught using problem-solving strategies that require the student to provide their own solution to open-ended questions on specific art examples, with little guidance or input from the teacher during this process. Some advocates in art education support the theory that discovery learning is an effective learning strategy (Dorn, 1998; Jausovec, 1994). According to Davies, Conneely, Davies and Lynch (2000), 'discovery learning', provides students with the learning opportunity to "generate and internalise their own way of understanding concepts and principles" (p.122). In order for meaningful learning to take place however as previously mentioned students have to want to learn and educators have to be knowledgeable and proactive by adopting whichever teaching method works best to facilitate this learning.

Novak and Cañas (2008) caution however that both, "direct presentation and discovery teaching methods can lead to highly rote or highly meaningful learning by the learner, depending on the disposition of the learner and the organization of the instructional materials" (p.4). They believe that there is a misconception that, "inquiry studies will assure meaningful learning" (p.4). As previously discussed, there are many variables that educators need to consider when deciding on which teaching and learning methodology to adopt. Including that students learn at different paces; use various learning styles; they bring to the learning process different levels of understanding; and they differ enormously in their levels of motivation to want to learn.

Another method to motivate students to want to learn and towards becoming active not passive learners that is advocated by some educators is to utilise questioning to promote discussion and debate. A study by Adler (1993) discovered that asking students 'why' or 'what' questions about pictures was useful, this study did not use the more complex visual images of art so may not have the same results in this discipline. In Adler's (1993) experiment participants were given different directions to assist them in processing representational pictures of water safety and rescue in order to examine their affects on student's recall of text information. In this study Adler (1993) found that participants who were asked to elaborate via 'what' and 'why' questioning on the representational pictures had a better recall of the text information than participants given no explicit directions at all, some explicit directions (e.g. 'How many objects are in the picture?') and semantic elaboration (e.g. 'Specifically, how does the picture relate to the text').

In contrast, in the discipline of science, Iding (1997) discovered that asking students questions on scientific diagrams in a textbook was not beneficial to learning. In this study questions were either used to replace the figure captions on the illustrations or were placed directly into the text. Iding (1997) placed her findings in cognitive load theory terms stating that: "questions about illustrations might cause cognitive resources to be unnecessarily and deleteriously expended in the text-diagram integration process" (p.22).

Cognitive load theory (e.g. Paas, Renkl and Sweller, 2003; 2004; Sweller, 1988; 1989; 2003), has contributed widely to the fields of education and training. This theory takes into account human cognitive architecture and its role in processing information in short-term and long-term memory. In particular it addresses the importance of designing instructional material that considers the limitations of human working memory. "The fundamental tenet of cognitive load theory is that the quality of instructional design will be raised if greater consideration is given to the role and limitations, of working memory" (Cooper, 1998, p.1). Cognitive load theory suggests ways of improving instructional design in order to assist the learner in acquiring schemas so that the information that has been learnt can be permanently stored and automatically retrieved from long-term memory. Schemas or information networks consist of concepts that are building blocks of knowledge in a hierarchical network of lower order or less complex information units to higher order or more complex information units.

Cognitive load theory assumes that some learning environments impose a higher information processing load on limited working memory resources because they do not take into account its limited capacity for storing, processing and retrieving information (Sweller, 2003). Cognitive load theory suggests that many instructional procedures impose a heavy cognitive load not because of the intrinsic nature of the material being learnt but because of the way the material is presented or activities that are required of the learner (Bobis, Sweller and Cooper, 1993).

The way visuals are presented for example in textbooks can cause a heavy cognitive load particularly for novice learners as they often contain superfluous information that can overload the capacity of working memory. However visuals can be effectively utilised to explain complex textual information as some studies have demonstrated (Levin and Mayer, 1993). However as Weidenmann (1989) argued, 'good pictures fail' for pictures are often viewed as 'easy' material in textbooks so learners usually only examine them superficially. Hence studies such as those conducted by Mayer (1989), Mayer and Gallini (1990) and Mayer, Steinhoff, Bower and Mars (1995) have investigated extensively the usefulness of adjunct illustrations to text and found that this method was an effective tool for facilitating students' understanding of scientific explanation. Levin and Mayer (1993) found that the more complex the text the more useful illustrations become. The result from these studies were based on a Constructivist theory of learning interpretation, which argues that learning entails constructing interrelationships between auditory and visual delineation of a system. However as Jeung, Chandler and Sweller (1977) argued taking on the premise of cognitive load theory, that audiovisual factors would enhance learning only if cognitive resources were not required to relate audio to visual resources.

Mayer and Gallini (1990) have also suggested that where learners were inexperienced in the content domain, illustrations were an effective tool for learning difficult material. The aforementioned studies do not directly address the teaching of visual literacy however they are still significant in addressing the question of how best to use visuals in instructional material. An important part of teaching visual literacy, regardless of the content is the context in which visuals are presented.

Within the context of art and design education, the use of well designed worked examples that integrate the appropriate written knowledge with the relevant visual example as has been argued, can effectively focus the learners attention on the important aspects of the work that needs to be learnt. Via this method, students have access to information that provides an appropriate interpretation of the main features of the work. This allows students to distinguish between superficially irrelevant information and real and valuable knowledge of the artwork. Ausburn and Ausburn (1978) found that the "superficiality of pupils' comprehension of much of what they view, suggests that higher order visual literacy skills do not develop unless they are identified and taught" (p.288).

Once the visual syntax of the artist is understood a defined path becomes apparent to access the work and hence to decode the visual message and reach a level of understanding and comprehension. When an inappropriate set of expectations (codes) are used to decipher images the viewer could fail to find meaning in the artwork, for they have not learnt to 'read' the syntax of the artist (Boughton, 1986). If students can be taught to understand these qualitative syntaxes in a more specific manner through focused art study, then they can interpret art as well as have access to decoding other visual messages outside the realm of the visual arts. "What is required when reading and making works of art is to try to understand the visual code that is being used and how this relates to the purpose or function of the work of art" (Cunliffe, 1992, p.149).

In order to represent an image pictorially one must have "some knowledge of the visual symbol systems, its vocabulary, concept, conventions, and some technical skills to manipulate art material" (Feinstein, 1982, p.46). All this acquired knowledge and experience combines together in the visually literate individual. One of the roles of the art and design educator is to teach the skill and knowledge of reading visual images. One way of achieving this is too reduce the complexity of visual images and provide easy access to the language. The objective of developing in students visual competencies required to analyse art and design knowledge will more likely be fostered when instructional design avoids extraneous cognitive load by removing ambiguous unnecessary detailed information from the curriculum.

Feldman (1986) as previously mentioned emphasised that a passive viewer cannot react to visual images with critical understanding and "to be visually illiterate is to be 'un-free' in the sense that the individual is a victim of the persuasive devices, or rhetoric of visual communication" (Boughton quotes Feldman, 1986, p.135). As argued previously, learning to read visuals should not only include learning the preconceived constructs for decoding images, it should also include understanding aesthetic literacy through knowledge and personal vision. "Aesthetic literacy involves the knowledgeable appreciation of art. This means bringing to awareness already present, taken-for-granted definitions of and attitudes towards art for purposes of examination, refinement, and elaboration" (Hamblen, 1986, p.68).

Sless (1977) as previously discussed suggested that art has failed to educate vision, and one of the reasons could be that the "visual literacy movement.... has demanded a break of the traditional links between art and visual education" (Sless, 1977, p.5). Though Sless's comments are dated, they still can be applied to teaching art and design history in the 21st Century. For visual literacy skills obtained through developing ability in art criticism, art appreciation, aesthetic awareness and experience with the art making process can also lead to improvement in general visual literacy communication. As art logic can be understood in form and content, visuals communicate meaning and this form of visual communication has a grammar that can be learnt. Students should be provided with experiences in education to promote visual literacy skills so that the messages in visual culture can be critically read and understood. There is the belief that pictures are "surpassing text in their ability to record, transmit, and create new knowledge" (Blystone, 1992, p.1).

Research has found that writing outline planning strategies can reduce cognitive load during writing (Galbraith, 1992; Flower, 1994). As with writing, key point summary lists beside the visual images can also be used as an effective teaching tool if appropriately used to direct the learner's attention towards what needs to be learnt about the visual image. "Cognitive load theory suggests that effective instructional material facilitates learning by directing cognitive resources towards activities that are relevant to learning" (Chandler and

Sweller, 1991, p.293). Effective instructional material should not only focus the learner's attention on the content that needs to be learnt but if appropriately designed, also on transferable skills that can be applied to future learning enterprises.

When a student writes down the list of key points provided with the visual image they have combined and recorded multiple interactive elements, which means that this information no longer needs to be held in working memory. This allows the student to then concentrate on studying other aspects of the visual image because their attention has been directed to the relevant facts of this image so they no longer have to hold extraneous or irrelevant information in their limited working memory.

Visual literacy in art and design education can be problematic to teach as Raney (1999) suggested, for in "Western culture, vision is associated with reason, logic, knowledge and control on the one hand, and on the other hand with mobilisation of fantasies, primitive desires and unconscious forces beyond our control. Thus visual representation has a double identity: it is both rational and amendable to analysis, and irrational and resistant to analysis" (pp.46-47). This study takes on board the former premise that visual literacy skills and in particular design history knowledge has a logic that can be learnt via effective worked examples. As has been discussed previously, Cognitive load theory uses our knowledge of our cognitive architecture to devise instructional methods for improving student learning. The next section also examines an aspect of our cognition architecture, specifically visual memory.

VISUAL LITERACY AND MEMORY

Early studies by Sperling, (1960; 1963) and Shepard, (1967) have supported the notion that humans have a remarkable ability to recall images. According to (Rieber, 1995) historical accounts of scientific invention and discovery have demonstrated how visualisation can be a powerful cognitive tool. Visualisation means to form and manipulate mental images, it is crucial for problem solving and spatial reasoning as visualisation allows humans to use a concrete means for dealing with abstract images. (McLoughlin and Krakowski, 2001).

Visual memory systems consist of visual short-term memory (VSTM) and long-term memory (LTM). In the early 1970's there were many ground breaking studies of VSTM such as Cermak, (1971); Phillips, (1974) and Phillips and Baddeley (1971). Many researchers such as Luck and Vogel (1997) have investigated the capacity limits of VSTM. There have also been a number of studies investigating the fact that an enormous amount of information is seen however very little of this is remembered (Crick and Koch, 1990; Lamme, 2003, 2006)

More recent research by Sligte, Scholte, and Lamme (2009) has provided evidence to support the existence of an intermediate visual store that has characteristics of both iconic memory and VSTM. According to Sperling (1960) iconic memory is believed to be of a high capacity but rapidly decaying form of visual memory. It is like an internal snapshot of what is just viewed. They proposed that this intermediate store had a high capacity of storing up to fifteen items and up to a four second prolonged memory trace duration. They discovered this intermediate visual store coexisted with VSTM but unlike visual stimuli it could overwrite the contents of its visual store.

Relating this phenomenon to perceiving art and design works, according to Solso (2003) the first stage in perceiving art is largely independent of conscious control and we all 'see' essentially the same elements of shapes, colours, and patterns as well as organization of forms. The second stage in comprehending art is 'directed perception' where one's personal history and knowledge provides an insight into the artwork. Schnotz (2002) has stated that picture comprehension was "based on a specific interplay between visual perception and higher order cognitive processing" (p.110).

According to Schnotz (2002), in picture comprehension the viewer "constructs multiple mental representations" (p.105). These include a 'surface structure' representation that corresponds to the visual image of the picture in the viewer's mind. Then the viewer constructs through semantic processing a 'mental model' that represents the content seen in the picture on the basis of common structural characteristics between the picture and its referential content. Mental models are not attached to specific sensory modalities, they are essentially indistinguishable from schemas. A mental model from a picture is abstracted, so it contains less information than the corresponding visual image and irrelevant pictorial details included in the visual image are omitted from the mental model.

Mental models of course can contain more information than the corresponding visual image as it includes prior knowledge not included in the visual perception. According to Arnheim, (1969) visual "knowledge acquired in the past helps not only in detecting the nature of an object or action appearing in a visual field; it also assigns the present object a place in the system of things" (p.90).

Another mental representation that the viewer constructs for comprehension of a picture that Schnotz (2002) suggested is the 'propositional' or descriptive representation. Propositional representations include information that is read from the model, which is encoded in the format of symbolic representation or descriptions in language form (Chafe, 1994). According to Baddeley, (1992; 2001) there is a continuous interaction between the propositional representation and the mental model. Another mental representation constructed by the viewer to assist with visual comprehension is the 'communication level', which represents the practical context of the pictorial communication and finally the 'genre level' represents knowledge about the class of pictures and their corresponding functions (Schnotz, 2002).

Schnotz (2002) stated that the perceptual images created in picture comprehension are sensory specific because they link to visual modality and semantic processing is needed to understand a picture as opposed to just perceiving it. According to Kosslyn (1994) the proximity of these images to perception relates to the notion that visual images and visual perceptions are based on the same cognitive mechanism. Ullman (1984) stated that in perceptual processing, domain specific information is selected from cognitive schemata, which is then visually organized through automated visual routines. A number of studies have investigated 'visual sketchpads', which are the viewer's mental representation of a visual perception of a picture in the imagery part of working memory (e.g. Baddeley, 1992, Sims and Hegarty, 1997).

Schnotz (2002) argued that when text processing occurs first before visual processing, most of the capacity of working memory is used leaving little capacity for processing the related pictures. Schnotz (2002) also suggested that a visual image or mental model constructed only from text is likely to differ from the picture presented afterwards, which can interfere with the comprehension of the picture. So according to Schnotz (2002) processing the picture first requires little space in working memory, thus leaving enough capacity for processing text.

Schnotz's (2002) theory could not be applied to the visually complex images of art and design, hence simplifying and physically combining visuals and text as previously discussed, would be a more effective method. For mentally combining multiple pieces of information can result in less efficient attainment of information than if the learner was presented the same material in a physically integrated form (Mousavi, Low and Sweller, 1995). There is also the argument that working memory capacity may be extended by a dual mode presentation of information. It is easier to learn information, according to Cooper (1998) "when some of the information is presented visually and the remainder of the information is presented auditorily than it is when all of the information is presented through a single sense" (p.5).

Potter (1976; 1993) suggested that when many visuals are shown in rapid continuous presentation, unrelated pictures are momentarily comprehended then immediately forgotten. Potter (1993) argued that although pictures are 'grasped', conceptual processing initiated by the next new picture in the sequence interrupts consolidation in memory. Potter (1993) hypothesised that when a stimulus is identified, it's meaning is rapidly activated and maintained briefly in conceptual short-term memory. CSTM is a processing and memory system that is, according to Potter (1993), different from visual (iconic) memory, conventional short-term memory and long-term memory in three respects: firstly, the rapidity with which the stimuli reaches a meaningful level of representation; secondly, the rapid structuring of these representations and thirdly, immediate forgetting of information that is not structured or otherwise consolidated.

Structuring in CSTM ranges from grouping of visuals based on meaning to the more complex semantic interpretation. "Organizing or structuring of new stimuli enhances memory of them" (Potter, 1999, p.13). Intraub (1999) conducted a series of experiments that tested recognition memory under a variety of time limits. She discovered that as long as viewers were given some time between pictorial presentations, there was good recognition memory for briefly glimpsed pictures. The aforementioned studies provide evidence to support the objective that in art education when multiple pictures are presented adequate time should be provided so that the viewer has sufficient time to absorb the pictorial detail.

As previously mentioned, according to Solso (2003) 'prototypes' can be used in art to assist with the recognition of the central visual characteristics of the work. He suggested that to conceptualise art and understand the classification of art periods and individual artists' styles, the process of forming cognitive categories in the form of both personal and knowledge schemata is the predominate way art knowledge is stored in long-term memory. According to Solso (2003), from the experience of viewing a typical exemplar of an art period, the viewer forms a general impression of the style, so when another work of the period is viewed it can be immediately 'recognized' as belonging to the same period as the 'prototype'.

Solso (2003) stated that: "the formation of a prototypical memory is accomplished through perception of features that are recombined in memory" (p.233). In other disciplines prototypical exempla's can be utilised to represent key concepts, which can reduce the amount of information that needs to be verbally communicated as well as processed in memory. This can assist in reducing the cognitive load on working memory and in doing so can assist in promoting student learning.

There has been a number of studies which have asserted that instructional design that includes both verbal and pictorial information should be presented in a coherent manner with some semantic overlap (e.g. Carney and Levin, 2002; Mayer and Gallini, 1990). Well-designed instructional material should provide interconnection between verbal and visual information so that they enter working memory simultaneously (Schnotz, 2002). One method that assists with this process is the use of semantic cues as discussed in Chapter 3, which can facilitate transfer by assisting the viewer towards finding connections between the artwork's characteristics and the viewer's prior knowledge (Koroscik, Short, Stavropoulos and Fortin, 1992).

CONCLUSION

It has been premised that in order for educators to use visual exemplars effectively, it "requires sufficient understanding of how the human cognitive systems interacts" (Schnotz, 2002, p.114) with the visual stimuli. For as McLoughlin and Krakowski, (2001) argued: "Increasingly, learning must take into account the range of symbolic and visual forms that enable construction, analysis and refinement of ideas" (p.9) as a result educators need to place more value and efforts towards promoting the acquisition of visual literacy skills and themselves use visuals appropriately as discussed to promote meaningful learning.

Feldman (1976) recognised the complexity and ambiguity of images when he stated that: "more than one valid reading of an image is possible. However there is a family resemblance among several readings that a single image is capable of supporting" (p.198). The notion behind Feldman's observation is that because of the limited capacity of working memory, the novice learner in particular could benefit from instruction that takes this into account by reducing extraneous information not necessary for learning the required concept. With this in mind it is imperative that educators choose the most efficient and economical method for communicating knowledge to students and it has been argued, that selecting appropriate well designed visual material that takes into account the limited capacity of working memory will assist towards this end.

Educators need to teach students to look more deeply into visual images and also provide more learning activities that explore reading the messages that visuals communicate. For once students learn to comprehend the main features of an image that relate to the information to be learnt, they have obtained a base knowledge that can be built upon in other learning enterprises. As Carroll (1994) suggested, the learner needs to "look beyond the surface features of the problem to the underlying structural similarities, a process that would facilitate construction of a base schema" (p.365). Carroll (1994) was discussing teaching mathematics, this same basic premise can also be applied to other disciplines. It has been argued that educators need to understand the cognitive process involved in learning in order to comprehend how they might best go about facilitating the acquisition of knowledge and understanding in their students. As has been premised, one method to assist with this aim is to understand what visual literacy is and how visual memory works and educators should use this knowledge when using visuals in their teaching to promote the best possible learning outcome.

As Schnotz (2002) has stated, "semantic processing is required to understand a picture as opposed to merely perceiving it" (p.110) and in order to process written and pictorial information in working memory without overloading its limited capacity, prior knowledge of the relevant subject-matter needs to be present. As has been discussed, when students lack both prior knowledge and visual literacy skills, they have great difficulty processing the visual material used in teaching.

Many students tend to rely on visual type-form (recognition schemata) rather than associations that identify individual representations that require having the skill to recognize relevancy and the prior knowledge to put what they have identified into appropriate language. Hence it is imperative it has been argued, that educators provide learning activities to promote this skill as well as being aware themselves of how to most effectively utilise visual materials to promote the long-term retention of learning.

REFERENCES

Adler, C. (1993). Directed picture processing: The effects for learners on recall of related text. *PhD,* University of South Florida.

Allen, D. (1994) 'Teaching Visual Literacy – Some Reflection on the Term', *Journal of Art and Design Education*, Blackwell: Oxford, 13(2), 133-143.

Arnheim, R. (1969). *Visual Thinking*, London: University of California Press.

Ausburn, L. and Ausburn, F. (1978). Visual literacy: Background, theory and practice. *PLET*, *15* (40), 291-297.

Berger, J. (1972). *Ways of Seeing*. London: British Broadcasting Corporation.

Baddeley, A.D. (1992). Working Memory. *Science, 255*, 556-559.

Baddeley, A.D. (2001). Is working memory still working. *American Psychologist, 56* (11), 851-64.

Blystone, R. (1992). Visual Literacy. *The National Teaching and Learning Forum, 1*(3), 1-3.

Bobis, J., Sweller, J. and Cooper, M. (1993). Cognitive load effects in primary -school geometry task. *Learning and Instruction, 3*(1), 1-21.

Boughton, D. (1986). Visual Literacy: Implications for cultural understanding through Art Education. *Journal of Art and Design Education, 5*(1and2), 125-142.

Brown, G. and Atkins, M. (1988). *Effective teaching in Higher Education*, London: Methuen.

Carroll, W. M. (1994). Using worked examples as an instructional support in the algebra classroom. *Journal of Educational Psychology, 86*(3), 360-367.

Carney, R.N. and Levin, J.R. (2002). Pictorial illustrations still improve student's learning from text. *Educational Psychology Review, 14*(1), March, 5-26.

Cermak, G.W. (1971). *Short-term recognition memory for complex free-form figures. Psychonomic Science, 25*(4), 209–211.

Chafe, W.L. (1994). *Discourse, Consciousness, and Time*. University of Chicago Press: Chicago.

Chandler, P. and Sweller, J. (1991). Cognitive load theory and the format of instruction. *Cognition and Instruction, 8* (4) 293-332.

Cooper, G. (1998). *Research into Cognitive Load Theory and Instructional Design at UNSW.*<http://www.arts.unsw.edu.au/education/CLT-NET-AUG-97.HTML>1-28.

Craik, F.I.M. and Lockhart, R.S. (1972). Levels of processing: A framework for memory research. *Journal of Verbal Learning and Verbal Behavior, 11* (6), 671-684.

Crick, F. and Koch, C . (1990). Some reflections on visual awareness. *Quarterly Biology,* 55, 953–962.

Cunliffe, L. (1992). Why a Theory of Symbols is Necessary for Teaching Art. *Journal of Art and Design Education, 11* (2), 143-153

Davies, P., Conneely, J., Davies, R. and Lynch, D. (2000). Imaginative ideas for teaching and learning. In Booth, A. and Hyland, P. (Eds.). *The Practice of University History Teaching,* Manchester University Press: Manchester and New York.

Diezmann,C. (1997). *Effective problem solving: a study of the importance of visual representation and visual thinking,* Seventh International Conference on Thinking, Singapore.

Dorn, C.M. (1998). *Mind in art: cognitive foundations in art education,* Mahwah, N.J.:Erlbaum.

Eisner, E. (1989). Structure and Magic in Discipline-Based Art Education. In Thistlewood, D (Ed.) *Critical Studies in Art and Design Education,* London: Longman/ NSEAD.

Elwell, W.C. and Hess, M. (1979). Visual Literacy and the Social Studies. *The Social Studies, 70* (1), 27-31.

Feinstein, H. (1982). Meaning and Visual Metaphor. *Studies in Art Education,23* (2), 45-55.

Feldman, E.B. (1976). Visual literacy. *Journal of Aesthetic Education, 10* (3/4), 197-200.

Flower, L. S. (1994).*The Construction of negotiated meaning: A social cognitive theory of writing.* South Illinois University Press: Carbondale.

Frederick P, J. (2000) 'Motivating students by active learning in the history classroom', Chapter 8, in Booth, A., and Hyland, P. (Ed.) *The Practice of University History Teaching,* (pp.102-112), Manchester: Manchester University Press.

Friedman, A. and Bourne, L.E. (1976). Encoding the levels of information in pictures and words. *Journal of Educational Psychology: General, 105* (2), 169-190.

Galbraith, D. (1992). Conditions for discovery through writing.*Instructional Science,* 21 (1/3), 45-72.

Gleick, J. (1987). *Chaos. Making a new science,* London: Sphere Books.

Hamblen, K.A. (1986). Exploring contested concepts for aesthetic literacy. *Journal of Aesthetic Education, 20* (2), 67-76.

Iding, M.K. (1997). Can questions facilitate learning from illustrated science texts? *Reading Psychology, 18,* 1-29.

Intraub, H. (1999). Understanding and remembering briefly glimpsed pictures. In Coltheart, V. (Ed.), *Fleeting Memories, Cognition of Brief Visual Stimuli,* (pp.47-70). Bradford, MIT Press: Cambridge, Massachusetts, London.

Jausovec, N. (1994). Problem finding and empathy in art. In Runco, M.A. (Ed.), *Problem-finding, problem-solving and creativity,* Albex: Norwood, N.J.

Jeung, H. J. Chandler, P. and Sweller, J. (1977).The role of visual indicators in dual sensory mode instruction*, Educational Psychology, 17*(3) 329-344.

Kintgen, E. (1988). Literacy, Literacy. *Visible Language, 22*(2/3), 149-168.

Klotz E. A. (1991). *Visualisation in geometry: a case study of a multimedia mathematics education project* in W. Zimmerman and S. Cunningham (Eds.) *Visualisation in teaching and learning mathematics,* pp.95-104. USA: Mathematics Association of America.

Koroscik, J.S., Short, G., Stavropoulos, C. and Fortin, S. (1992). Framework for Understanding Art: The Function of Comparative Art Context and Verbal Cues. *Studies in Art Education, 33* (3), 154-164.

Koroscik, J.S., Desmond K.K. and Brandon, S. M. (1985). The effects of verbal contextual information in processing visual arts. *Studies in Art Education, 27* (1), 12-33.

Koroscik, J.S. (1982). The effects of prior knowledge, presentation time and task demands on visual processing. *Studies in Art Education, 23* (3), 13-22.

Kosslyn, S.M. (1994). *Image and Brain, the resolution of imagery debate.* Cambridge, M.A.: MIT Press.

Kunen, S., Green, D. and Waterman, D. (1979). Spread of encoding effects within the nonverbal visual domain. *Journal of Educational Psychology: Human Learning and Memory,5* (6), 574-584.

Lamme V.A.F. (2003). Why visual attention and awareness are different. *Trends Cognitive Scienc*e, 7, 12–18.

Lamme, V.A.F. (2006). Towards a true neural stance on consciousness. *Trends Cognitive Science,* 10, 494 –501.

Levin, J.R. and Mayer, R.E. (1993). Understanding illustrations in text. In Britton, B.K., Woodward, A. and Brinkley, M. (Eds.), *Learning from Textbooks* (pp. 95-113), Erlbaum: Hillsdale, N.J.

Luck, S.J., and Vogel, E.K. (1997).The capacity of visual working memory for features and conjunctions.*Nature*, 390, 279–281.

Mandler, J.M. and Johnson, N.S. (1976). Some of the thousand words a picture is worth. *Journal of Educational Psychology: Human Learning and Memory*, 2 (5), 529-540.

Mandler, J.M. and Ritchey, G.H. (1977). Long-term memory for pictures. *Journal of Educational Psychology: Human Learning and Memory, 3* (4), 386-396.

Mayer, R.E. (1989). Systematic thinking fostered by illustrations in scientific text. *Journal of Educational Psychology, 81* (2), 240-246.

Mayer, R.E. and Gallini, J. (1990). When is an illustration worth ten thousand words? *Journal of Educational Psychology, 82* (4), 715-726.

Mayer R. E., Steinhoff K., Bower, G. and Mars, R. (1995). *A generative theory of textbook design: using annotated illustrations to foster meaningful learning of science text* Educational Technology, Research and Developmen*t, 43*(1), 41–43.

McLoughlin, C. and Krakowski, K. (2001, Sept.). Technical tools for visual thinking: what does the research tell? Paper presented at the: *Apple University Consortium Academic and Development Conference*, James Cook University, Townsville, 23-26.

Messaris, P., and S. Moriarty. (2005). Visual literacy theory. K. Smith, S. Moriarty, G. Barbatsis and K. Kenney (Eds.). *Handbook of visual communication: Theory, methods, and media*, Mahwah, NJ: Lawrence Erlbau Publishers.

Mohler J. L. (2000) *Desktop virtual reality for the enhancement of visualisation skills. Journal of Educational Multimedia and Hypermedia*, 9(2), 151–165.

Mousavi, S.Y., Low, R. and Sweller, J. (1995). Reducing cognitive load by mixing auditory and visual presentation modes. *Journal of Educational Psychology, 87* (2),319-334.

Müller, M.G. (2008). Visual competence: a new paradigm for studying visuals in the social sciences?, *Visual Studies, 23*(2), 101-112.

Novak, J. D. and A. J. Cañas, *The Theory Underlying Concept Maps and How to Construct and Use Them*, Technical Report IHMC CmapTools 2006-01 Rev 01-2008, Florida Institute for Human and Machine Cognition. Available at: http://cmap.ihmc.us /Publications/ResearchPapers/TheoryUnderlyingConceptMaps.pdf

Phillips, W.A. (1974). On the distinction between sensory storage and short-term visual memory. *Perception and Psychophysics, 16*(2), 283–290.

Phillips, W.A., and Baddeley, A.D. (1971). *Reaction time and short-term visual memory. Psychonomic Science*, 22(2), 73–74.

Paas, F., Renkl, A. and Sweller, J. (2004). Cognitive Theory: Instructional Implications of the Interaction between Information Structures and Cognitive Architecture. *Instructional Science, 32*, (1/2), 1-8.

Paas, F., Renkl, A. and Sweller, J. (2003). Cognitive Load Theory and Instructional Design: Recent Developments. *Educational Psychologist, 38*(1), 1-4.

Potter, M.C. (1993). Very short-term conceptual memory, *Memory and Cognition.21*, 156-161.

Potter, M.C. (1976). Short-term conceptual memory for pictures. *Journal of Experimental Psychology: Human Learning and Memory, 2*, 509-522.

Raney, K. (1999). Visual Literacy and the Art Curriculum. *Journal of Art and Design Education, 18* (1), 42-47.

Rieber, L. P. (1995). A historical review of visualisation in human cognition, *Educational Technology, Research and Development, 43*(1) 1042–1629.

Schnotz, W. (2002). Towards an Integrated view of learning from text and visual display, *Educational Psychology Review, 14* (1), March, 101-120.

Shepard, R. N. (1967). Recognition memory for words, sentences, and pictures. *Journal of Verbal Learning and Verbal Behavior, 6*, 156-163.

Seels, B. (1994). Visual literacy: the definition problem.In D. M. Moore and F. M. Dwyer (Eds.) *Visual literacy: A spectrum of visual learning, (*pp.97–112) Englewood Cliffs, NJ: Educational Technology Publications.

Sims, V.K. and Hegarty, M. (1997). Mental animation in the visuospatial sketchpad: evidence from dual task studies, *Memory and Cognition, 25*, 321-332.

Sless, D. (1977). Visual Thinking in Education, *A Journal of South Australian Education, 4* (2), 4-9.

Sligte, I.G., Scholte, H.S., Lamme, V.A.F. (2009). V4 Activity Predicts the Strength of Visual Short-Term Memory Representations. *Journal of Neuroscience, 29*(23), 7432–7438.

Solso, R.L. (2003). *The Psychology of Art and the Evolution of the Conscious Brain*, Massachusetts and London: MIT Press: Cambridge.

Sperling, G. (1960). The information available in brief visual presentations. *Psychological Monographs: General and Applied, 74*(11), 1-30.

Sperling, G. (1963). A model for visual memory tasks. *Human Factors*, 5, 19-31.

Sweller, J. (1988). 'Cognitive load during problem-solving: Effects on learning'. *Cognitive Science, 12* (2), 257-285.

Sweller, J. (1989). Cognitive technology: Some procedures for facilitating learning and problem-solving in mathematics and science, *Journal of Educational Psychology*, *81*(4), 457-466.

Sweller, J. (2003). Evolution of human cognitive architecture. In Ross, B. (Ed.), *The Psychology of Learning and Motivation* (pp.215-266), Academic Press: San Diego.

Tufte,E. R. (1990). *Envisioning information*, Cheshire, Connecticut: Graphics Press.

Weidenmann, B. (1989). When good pictures fail: An information-processing approach to the effect of illustrations', in Mandl, H. and Levin, J.R. (Eds.) *Knowledge Acquisition from Text and Pictures* (pp. 157-171), Amsterdam: Elsevier.

Chapter 7

GESTALT THEORIES OF VISUAL PERCEPTION AND VISUAL COMMUNICATION MATERIALS

ABSTRACT

It is well known that colour and contrast play important roles in the processing of visual information; however, Gestalt theories of perception are particularly relevant to the design of visual communications and presentations. This is because of the way in which human visual perception is underpinned by a search for visual cues within the visual field; a search that the Gestalt psychologists believed followed common patterns or 'laws'. This section describes the Gestalt 'laws' of perception and discusses how colour and contrast have the capacity to enhance or mitigate these 'laws' of perception. Colour and contrast are often integral in applied design in general, and visual communications in particular; therefore, knowledge about their role in respect to Gestalt 'laws' of perception may influence the effectiveness of the interface between visual communications design and human receptivity and response.

GESTALT THEORIES OF VISUAL PERCEPTION

Devised by the founders of Gestalt psychology: Czech psychologist Max Wertheimer (1880-1943) and German psychologists Kurt Koffka (1886-1941) and Wolfgang Kohler (1887-1967), the Gestalt 'laws' are underpinned by the notion that visual perception involves a search for visual cues and patterns. That is, when scanning an image, scene or landscape we automatically search for visual cues and patterns as a means of making sense of what we perceive; and this ongoing process is considered to be hard-wired in our visual perception system (Goldstein, 1996; Gordon, 1997; Koffka, 1935; Wertheimer, 1938). Given the way that these laws influence visual perception, they have particular relevance to visual communications design.

The Gestalt laws of perception evolved from the earlier theories of Ehrenfels, Mach, Husserl and Goethe. Referred to as the precursor of Gestalt theory, Austrian philosopher Christian von Ehrenfels (1859-1932) published *Üeber Gestaltqualitäten* (1890) and a translation of this is 'above, hyper or more than' (*Üeber*) the qualities (*qualitäten*) of the 'whole, form' (*Gestalt*). The Gestalt approach to perception came to be summarised as 'the whole is greater than the sum of the parts'. In a similar vein, Ernst Mach (1838-1916) published *The Analysis of Sensations and the Relation of the Physical to the Psychical* in which he outlined a version of phenomenalism wherein objects are logical constructions based upon sense-data – that is, perceptual phenomena and sensory stimuli (Mach, 1914). Similarly, Moravian Edmund Husserl (1859-1938), who has been referred to as the founder of phenomenology, proposed that we should put aside (in brackets, to use his term) unanswerable questions of existence and focus on a systematic analysis of experience alone. Husserl's approach became known as phenomenology and he coined the term *Lebenswelt* (lifeworld) to represent our experience of the complex, highly inter-related and ever-changing phenomena that constitutes the world in which we live (Magee, 2001).

Gestalt theories of perception focussed on how humans perceive their surroundings and what influences their perceptions, and context and the configuration of form were considered key factors (Graham, 2009; Koffka, 1935). Under Gestalt theories, visual perception involves a complex and inter-related process, wherein the perception of external stimuli occurs in tandem with cognitive processing. Both colour and contrast play key roles in terms of perception of context and configuration of form; and visual perception occurs in conjunction with a subconscious search among external visual stimuli for patterns and visual clues. Underpinned by perceptual-cognitive universals, these 'laws' of visual perception are thought to occur because "geometry is more deeply [cognitively] internalized than physics" (Shepard, 2001, p585).

Gestalt laws of perception focus on the 'whole' rather than the sum of the individual parts because we tend to search for and find meaningful 'wholes' and configurations that make perceptual sense.

For example, we tend to perceive whole words when we read rather than individual letterforms just as we tend to perceive a film as an ongoing visual and audio narrative rather than individual frames (Graham, 2009). "Shifts in spacing, timing and configuration can have profound effect on the meaning of presented information. While Gestalt visual principles are easy to grasp, they are very powerful" (Graham, 2009, p. 1). As Graham notes, ignoring Gestalt laws of perception may result in unintended outcomes thereby impacting negatively on the effectiveness of visual communication materials.

It is possible to identify Gestalt laws of perception in any given situation and they may be both consciously applied and manipulated in art, applied design and architecture to achieve specific outcomes.

In visual communication design, the four second rule is often considered paramount – that is, if an image, design or advertisement can't be read and understood in four seconds, the viewer's attention may be lost. Both colour and colour contrast in conjunction with careful application of the Gestalt laws of perception provide the means by which to ensure that the success of visual communication is not in any way hindered (Lidwell, Holden, and Butler, 2003; Samara, 2007; Smith, 2003).

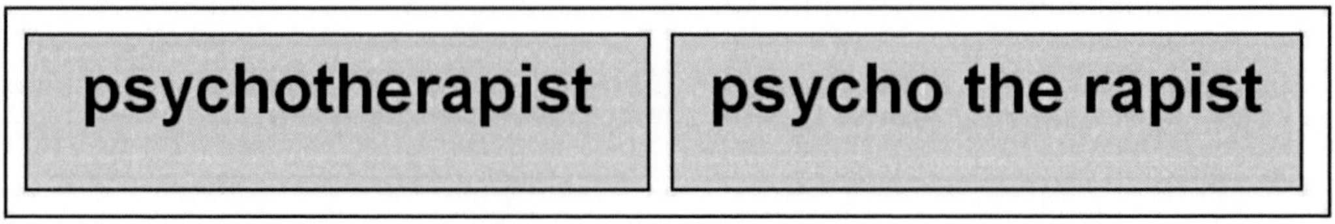

psychotherapist	psycho the rapist

Figure 7.1. Under Gestalt theory, simple changes can alter meaning (Graham, 2008).

The Gestalt Law of Pragnanz or 'Good Figure'

This law suggests that we tend to search for and perceive simple and familiar shapes when viewing an object, scene or image for the first time. Adopting Shepard's (2001) approach, the law of *Pragnanz* can be conceptualised as follows:

$$[X_{1, 2...n}] \rightarrow [X_1] \cdot [X_2] \cdot [X_n]$$

Where X_1, X_2...X_n are initially perceived as a group but after a search for patterns they become visually distinct and perceived as separate elements.

The law of Pragnanz or 'good figure' may become evident when we examine the images depicted in the following Figure. Each of these images is difficult to 'read' and we need to take time to cognitively process the various visual clues embedded within the images until we are able to make sense of the image. The first image, of a woman playing guitar, has been digitally manipulated to blur the original photograph; the second image is an untouched photograph of reeds and gumtrees reflected in a pond; and the third image features a blurred time-lapse image of cars crossing the Sydney Harbour Bridge.

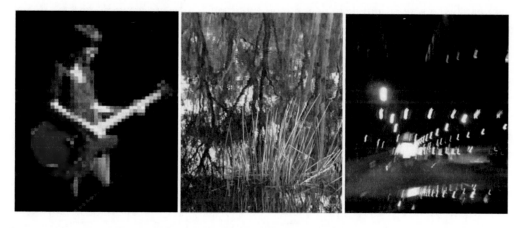

Figure 7.2. The Gestalt law of Pragnanz involves a visual search for the familiar.

Colour as well as contrast helps us visually define context and configuration of form during our perceptual search for patterns and clues. In the following Figure, random shapes begin to make more sense when colour and contrast are introduced as we visually search for and 'find' familiar shapes such as triangles and squares.

Figure 7.3. Instead of perceiving scattered shapes or lines, we tend to perceive a square.

Colour can mitigate or reinforce the Gestalt law of *Pragnanz* as per the following Figure where an odd-shaped figure begins to make sense when colour is introduced.

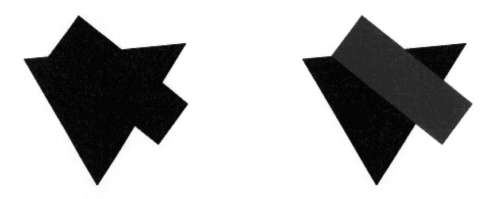

Figure 7.4. An odd-shape (left) makes more sense when colour is introduced (right).

In respect to visual communications, it is critical that images are not ambiguous unless this particular aim is intended. In an educational context it is important that images are clear and unambiguous to ensure that the communication objectives are achieved and the intended messages are successfully decoded by the intended audience.

The Gestalt Law of Proximity

This 'law' proposes that visual stimuli that are located in close proximity tend to be perceived as a group. In the following Figure, we tend to perceive three groups: the first comprised of squares, the second of rectangles and the third of squares and rectangles.

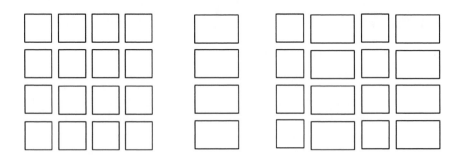

Figure 7.5. The Gestalt law of Proximity.

This law suggests that visual stimuli located in close proximity tend to be perceived as a group and Shepard (2001), who referred to this effect as "**Associativity**," provides the following conceptual model:

$$[X_1 \cdot X_2] \cdot X_3 \rightarrow X_1 \cdot [X_2 \cdot X_3]$$

where X_2 and X_3 are perceptually grouped due to proximity.

In applied design and visual communications, we tend to perceive items that are randomly located as being separate; while elements that are placed together are perceived as belonging to a group as illustrated in the following Figure.

Havana   Memphis
     London
          Chicago   Jazz
     Blues
               Nashville
     New Orleans
	Chicago Blues
	New Orleans Jazz
	Memphis
	Havana
	London
	Nashville

Figure 7.6. Items located together are perceived as a group.

The closer that visual elements are within an image or design, the more likely they will be perceived as being part of a group or pattern. This Gestalt law (along with memory and familiarity) underpins our perception that headlines belong to adjacent text; that captions belong with proximal images and clustered links that appear on a web page are related. Too much negative space between visual elements within a design serve to isolate the visual elements from one another (Graham, 2009; Lidwell et al., 2003).

In the following Figure, the main headline, secondary headline and text block of the PowerPoint slide are clearly delineated by the familiar position of these elements and their colour-coding. The law of proximity also occurs in the photographic images featured in the slide whereby the coloured panels of Ellsworth Kelly's *Color Panels for a Large Wall* are perceptually grouped together due to their consistency of size and spacing irrespective of their different colours. Similarly, the furniture placement in the Atrium of the Portrait Gallery, Washington, indicates two separate areas: the café area and the lecture area.

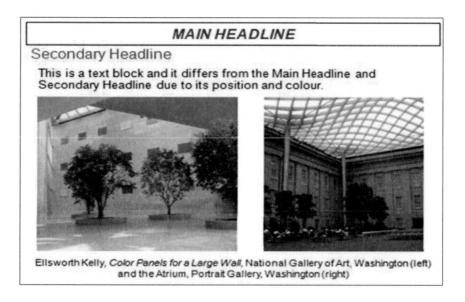

Figure 7.7. The law of proximity depicted in a PowerPoint slide.

The Gestalt Law of Similarity

This 'law' suggests that we tend to group together visual stimuli that share some level of similarity in terms of colour, tone, texture, shape, orientation or size. Under this law, elements can be depicted as follows:

$$[X_1, Y_1, Z_1] \neq [X_2, Y_2, Z_2] \neq [X_n, Y_n, Z_n]$$

where X, Y and Z are perceptually grouped because colour $(_1)$, texture $(_2)$, shape, tone, orientation, size or other $(_n)$ impose a pattern of perceived similarity.

The law of Similarity tends to over-ride the law of Proximity and, as illustrated in the following Figures, colour acts a catalyst in defining groupings among the visual stimuli.

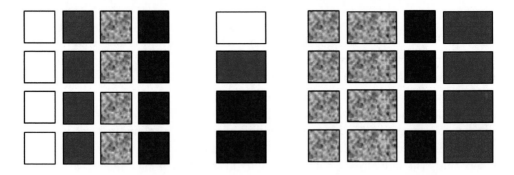

Figure 7.8. The Gestalt law of Similarity.

The law of Proximity can be used effectively in visual communications design whereby text or images that are related can be visually linked together simply by aligning them together and providing sufficient negative space around them to indicate the grouping. Colour and colour contrast can mitigate or reinforce the Gestalt law of similarity as per the following Figure where the introduction of red creates a new grouping that includes the three locations: Chicago, New York and New Orleans. In this way, the Gestalt law of Similarity has the capacity to over-ride the Gestalt law of Proximity.

Havana Memphis London Chicago Jazz Blues Nashville New Orleans	Chicago Blues New Orleans Jazz Memphis Havana London Nashville

Figure 7.9. The effect of colour on the Gestalt law of Similarity.

The Gestalt Law of Good Continuation

Under this law, visual elements that seem to be in lines (straight or curved) or appear to form familiar shapes are perceived as belonging together and can be depicted as follows:

$$[X_1 + X_2 + X_n] = [X_3]$$

where X_1, X_2...X_n are separate visual elements but are perceptually grouped to create a new visual element: X_3.

In the following Figure, two red arcs are perceptually grouped to form a circle; while three blue arcs on the right are also perceptually grouped to form a continuous line.

Figure 7.10. The Gestalt law of Good Continuation.

In visual communications design, the law of Good Continuation has been strategically used in advertising to force the viewer to re-read an ambiguous logo or image thereby prompting a possible increase in recognition. However, this effect needs to be tempered by the 'four second rule' mentioned above which suggests that if an image can't be read and understood in four seconds, the viewer's attention may be lost (Lidwell et al., 2003; Samara, 2007).

Figure 7.11. Ambiguous and unambiguous text.

The Gestalt Law of Common Fate

This law, which proposes that groups of visual stimuli that share a similar orientation or configuration tend to be perceptually grouped together, can be depicted as follows:

$$[X_1, X_2] \rightarrow [X_1] \cdot [X_2]$$

where X_1 and X_2 are perceptually separated because colour, texture, shape, tone, orientation or size impose a pattern of perceived dissimilarity.

This law proposes that groups of visual stimuli that share a similar orientation or configuration tend to be perceptually grouped together. In the following Figure, the inner circle (composed of diagonal stripes) is perceived as separate from its surroundings (also composed of diagonal stripes) because of a change in the orientation of the stripes, and colour reinforces this effect.

Figure 7.12. The Gestalt law of Common Fate – colour tends to reinforce this law.

In the following Figure, the Gestalt law of Common Fate has been used in a PowerPoint slide to differentiate different text blocks via the use of bullet points and also via the use of different colour type and italics. The same law is applied in visual communication materials via the use of frames, directional text blocks, coloured backgrounds and the like.

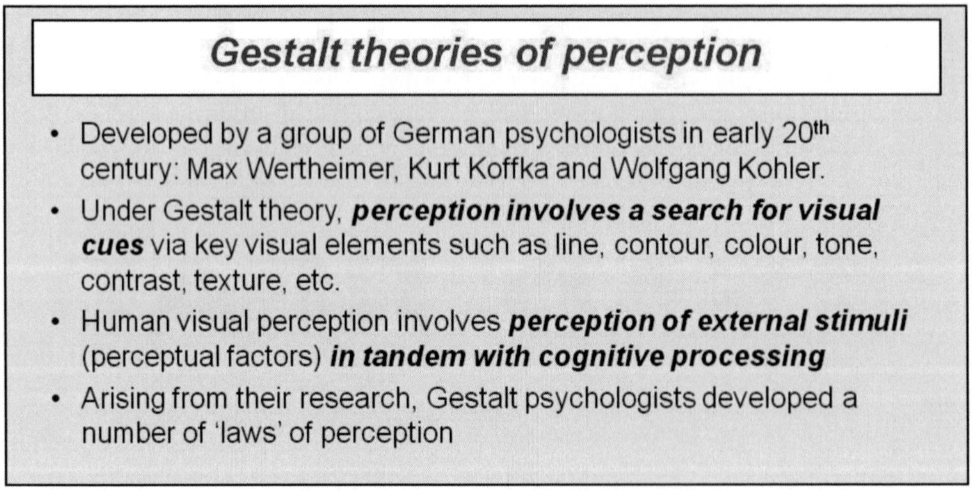

Gestalt theories of perception

- Developed by a group of German psychologists in early 20th century: Max Wertheimer, Kurt Koffka and Wolfgang Kohler.
- Under Gestalt theory, *perception involves a search for visual cues* via key visual elements such as line, contour, colour, tone, contrast, texture, etc.
- Human visual perception involves *perception of external stimuli* (perceptual factors) *in tandem with cognitive processing*
- Arising from their research, Gestalt psychologists developed a number of 'laws' of perception

Figure 7.13. The law of proximity depicted in a PowerPoint slide.

The Gestalt Law of Figure-Ground Segregation

This 'law' suggests that visual stimuli may be perceptually segregated into a figure-background separation due to the perceptual organisation of contours and outlines. Colour and colour contrast may influence which area is perceived as Figure and which as Ground: lighter, more saturated colours tend to make visual stimuli appear to advance, while darker colours make visual stimuli appear to recede to form the background. Variations of Figure-Ground are depicted in the following Figure.

Figure 7.14. Colour and contrast amplify Figure-Ground separation.

This particular 'law' can be harnessed to improve the design and effectiveness of visual communications. Specifically, when tonal contrast is stronger, the contour boundary between Figure and Ground is more easily perceived thereby creating focus.

Ambiguous Figure-Ground Images

Ambiguous figure-ground separations occur when the contours between figure and ground exist but are difficult to identify. The following Figure illustrates ambiguous figure-ground separations. On the left is the face-vase illusion devised by Danish psychologist Edgar Ruben (1886-1951) in which the outline of two faces creates the outline of a vase depending on which outline takes perceptual precedence (Rubin image cited in Hoffman, 1998, p. 92). On the right is a photograph depicting a film still featuring a guitarist from a film that was screened behind a stage on which is a drum kit and microphones. In this image, it is difficult to determine which visual elements represent the foreground and which visual elements represent the background.

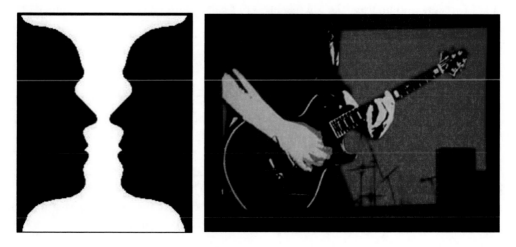

Figure 7.15. Ambiguous figure-ground images.

Figure 7.16. Ambiguous figure-ground separations.

Ambiguous figure-ground images are often used to great effect in art, film and theatre design, it is unwise to use such images in visual communications due to the negative impact they have on perception and understanding. This tends to run counter to the work of renowned designer Neville Brody, whose typeface design and graphic designs were often deliberately ambiguous: "I see my role partly as a catalyst for thought and for questioning. A lot of our work is an open-ended statement which is often not completed until the person who looks at it has reached his or her own conclusion" (Brody cited in Gibson, 2011 ¶12).

In respect to visual communication materials and PowerPoint-style presentations, immediate understanding is generally the goal and hence ambiguity is inappropriate. The following Figure features still images from films that are intriguing but difficult to decipher: *The Girl Who Played With Fire* (Alfredson, 2009) and *Zodiac* (Fincher, 2007).

Colour and contrast play important roles in visual perception and they specifically help to distinguish detail, depth, borders, and contours, plus attract focal attention and assist in visual search and detection tasks. In addition, colour and contrast also play important roles in the patterns of visual perception as per the Gestalt laws of perception.

The strategic use of colour and contrast, particularly in conjunction with the Gestalt laws of perception, are critical in visual communications design. While colour and contrast are often incorporated to support aesthetic and/or functional communication objectives, it is suggested that colour and contrast can be strategically harnessed in tandem with the Gestalt laws of perception to improve the effectiveness of visual communications design outcomes.

REFERENCES

Alfredson, D. (2009). *The Girl Who Played With Fire*. France: Zodiak Entertainment.

Fincher, D. (2007). *Zodiac*. Los Angeles: Paramount Pictures.

Gibson, B. (2011). Neville Brody: Inventing a graphic language. Retrieved 2 August 2011, from http://www.apple.com/pro/profiles/brody/

Goldstein, E. B. (1996). *Sensation and perception*. Pacific Grove, CA: Brooks/Cole.

Gordon, I. E. (1997). *Theories of visual perception*. New York: John Wiley and Sons.

Graham, L. (2009). Gestalt laws of perception: Using Gestalt theory to improve print and electronic designs. *Design Principles and Practices: An International Journal, 3*(4), 385-393.

Hoffman, D. D. (1998). *Visual intelligence: How we create what we see*. New York: WW Norton and Company.

Koffka, K. (1935). *Principles of Gestalt psychology*. London: Routledge and Kegan Paul.

Lidwell, W., Holden, K., and Butler, J. (2003). *Universal principles of design*. Beverly, MA: Rockport Publishers.

Mach, E. (1914). *Analysis of sensations and the relation of the physical to the psychical (Trans. C. M. Williams)*. Chicago: Open Court Publishing Company.

Magee, B. (2001). *The story of philosophy*. London: Dorling Kindersley.

Samara, T. (2007). *Design elements: A graphic style manual*. Beverly, MA: Rockport Publishers.

Shepard, R. N. (2001). Perceptual-cognitive universals as reflections of the world. *Behavioral and Brain Sciences, 24*, 581-601.

Smith, R. (2003). *The artist's handbook*. London: Dorling Kindersley.

Wertheimer, M. (1938). Laws of organisation in perceptual forms. In W. Ellis (Ed.), *A source book of Gestalt psychology*. London: Routledge and Kegan Paul.

Chapter 8

VISUAL PERCEPTION:
THE ROLES OF COLOUR AND CONTRAST

ABSTRACT

Human visual perception and the ways in which humans process visual stimuli are integral to effective visual communications design. This section discusses the mechanics of human visual perception as well as cognitive processing of visual information and Gestalt theories of perception given the relevance of these to the ways in which humans perceive, organize and cognitively process visual stimuli.

In addition, colour and contrast are examined in some depth as these play key roles in visual perception and hence the design of effective visual communication materials. Colour models as well as common colour-related constructs are discussed along with perceptual effects as these have relevance to visual communications design. Information is also provided about current colour theories as well as common colour combination techniques as these provide insight and guidance in visual communications design. Finally, digital technology and issues relating to digital reproduction are discussed with particular reference to visual communications design.

HUMAN VISUAL PERCEPTION

Understanding the mechanics of human visual system provides insight into the ways in which visual communication materials can be effectively designed. However, human visual perception is a complex process and remains only partially understood. Despite this, it is well known that both colour and contrast play important roles in conjunction with cognitive processing of incoming visual data; processing that occurs in a number of areas within the brain (Goldstein, 1996; Hoffman, 1998; M. Livingstone, 2002).

The visual perception process begins with the eye receiving incoming visual information in the form of light-waves. Incoming visual light-based stimuli is received by rod and cone receptors which are embedded in the human retina, the light-sensitive tissue that lines the inner surface of the eye.

The retina comprises about six million colour-sensitive cone receptors and these are found mostly in the fovea area (a cone-rich area located directly in the line of sight), as illustrated in the following Figure.

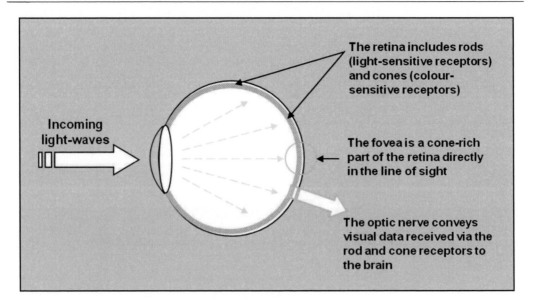

Figure 8.1. The human eye.

In addition, there are about 120 million rod receptors and these are located mostly in the peripheral area of the retina. Out-numbering cone receptors by about 20-to-1, rod receptors are light rather than colour sensitive (Goldstein, 1996; Kolb, 2003; M. S. Livingstone, 1988).

It has been suggested that our visual intelligence processes literally construct what we see and the cognitive processing functions that occur in tandem with visual perception have been referred to as "unconscious conclusions" whereby we make inferences and drew conclusions from the jumble of visual stimuli that constantly bombards our visual sense (Hermann von Helmholtz cited in Hoffman, 1998, p. 11). These unconscious inferences occur as we cognitively process incoming visual information; however, before proceeding, it is timely to discuss some factors that influence the physical process of visual perception including the impact that various types of ambient lighting have on visual perception and the effect that the natural ageing process has on visual perception.

Factors that Impact on Visual Perception

A number of external and internal factors influence both the capacity of the human eye to perceive incoming visual information and the visual quality of the information perceived, and it is important to consider these in respect to their impact on the use and effectiveness of visual teaching materials. For example, external factors such ambient lighting plus variations in natural lighting due to time of day/season impacts on visual perception, and these in turn have an impact on the visual quality of information received via the visual perception system (Cuttle, 2008; Julian, 2006; Rea, 1993).

In terms of internal factors, it is known that macular degeneration affects about 10% of people aged between 66 and 74 years, and up to 30% of people between 75 and 85 years of age. In addition, the human visual system undergoes change with advancing age and these changes are largely continuous. Specifically, there are between 1.2 and 1.5million retinal ganglion cells in the human retina and each of these receive input from about 100 rods and cones; however, retinal ganglion cells decrease in number by about 25% from age 20 to 80 years. This is compounded by a decrease of about 50% in the lateral geniculate nucleus (LGN) from age 20 to 80 years. The LGN is the area in the thalamus of the brain that receives incoming visual information from the optic nerve before relaying it on to the primary visual cortex of the brain. While it is unclear why these changes occur, it is known that visual perception of luminance contrast (light-dark contrast) and colour contrast both decline in sensitivity with age thereby reducing the visual capacity among older people. Diminished visual capacity is negatively impacted under low or poor ambient lighting conditions (Fiorentini, Porciatti, Morrone, and Burr, 1996; M. Livingstone, 2002; Newacheck, Haegerstrom-Portnoy, and Adams, 1990; Werner, Peterzell, and Scheetz, 1990).

These internal and external factors can have a huge impact on the quality of information perceived. In respect to the effectiveness of visual communication materials, while it may not be possible to halt the impact of the ageing process on human vision, it is certainly possible to address external factors (such as sources of light) to ensure that conditions for visual perception are optimum.

Sources of Light

Knowledge about the different sources and types of light and their impact within an educational context is important especially in regard to the perception of visual teaching materials. A key source of natural light is sunlight, which varies depending on time of day, the seasons and contextual setting. In the built environment, artificial light generally augments natural light, providing a more consistent level of ambient lighting. Common sources of artificial light include incandescent lights, light-emitting diodes, arc lamps and fluorescent lighting. Each of these light sources emit light at different luminous levels which in turn impact on both directed task lighting and general ambient illumination. In respect to diversity among students in terms of age range and individual visual capacity, it is important to ensure that ambient lighting is optimal within a learning environment to maximise efficiency of visual teaching materials. The following table provides a brief description of common types of artificial light sources and the applications for which they were designed.

Table 8.1. Types of artificial lighting

Combustion lighting is light produced as a result of burning fuel and includes the light emitted by candles, gas lights and fires. The level of lighting produced by combustion is considerably lower than other forms of lighting and tends to produce just as much heat as light. This type of lighting is not recommended for visual tasks as the light emitted is both inconsistent and relatively poor.	
Incandescent lighting generally consists of a glass enclosure with a filament of tungsten wire inside. When an electrical current passes through the filament and, as the filament heats up, light is emitted that approximates a continuous spectrum. A good source of light, incandescent lights include: 40–100W tungsten incandescent bulbs Glass and quartz halogens	

Table 8.1. (Continued)

Light-emitting diodes are a semiconductor and, when turned on, current flows from one side of the p-n junction (the anode) to the other side (cathode).The charge carriers (that is, the electrons and holes) release energy in the form of photons and different semiconductor materials create different coloured light from >760 wavelengths (Infrared) through the visible light spectrum up to <400 (Ultraviolet). LEDs are a good source of light.	
Arc lamps refer to a class of lamps that produce light via a voltaic arc. Two electrodes, generally made of tungsten, are separated by a gas which is ionised. A very high voltage is pulsed through the lamp to ignite the arc. Different gases are used and these include neon, argon, xenon, krypton and mercury. Arc lamps were mostly superseded by filament lamps.	
Fluorescent tube lights are gas-discharge lamps that use electricity to excite mercury vapour. The excited mercury atoms result in short-wave ultraviolet light which causes phosphor to fluoresce emitting a visible light. A good source of light, **fluorescent lights are available in a range of 'colours' including** warm-white, neutral-white, cool-white and daylight versions.	
High density discharge (HID) lamps are high pressure gas-discharge lamps such as metal halide lamps and high pressure sodium lamps. Often used in car headlamps, sports arenas, outdoor lighting and street lighting, these lamps produce high light output and, as they have a higher luminous efficiency since they produce more light than heat, they are a good source of light.	

In the following Figure, a lecture room is illustrated at two different lighting settings: full lighting (with fluorescent lights) and subdued lighting (with incandescent lights), and a noticeable difference in the perception of detail and colour in the room in obvious.

Figure 8.2. Same lecture room, different lighting levels.

Ambient Illumination Colour

Sources of light emit slightly different ambient illumination colour and this influences the perceived quality of objects, materials and settings. Different ambient colour-types are identified via the Kelvin scale and vary from 'warm' through to 'cool' as per the following Figure (Cuttle, 2008; Goldstein, 1996; Julian, 2006).

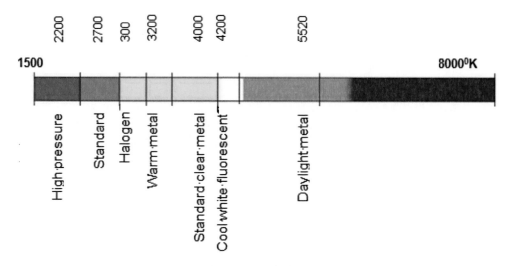

Figure 8.3. Varying ambient illumination colour as per the Kelvin scale.

On the Kelvin scale, a lower Kelvin temperature translates as a 'warmer' ambient illumination colour; while a higher Kelvin temperature translates to a 'cooler' ambient illumination colour.

Variations in ambient illumination colour produce corresponding variation in the perceived quality of objects and settings. That is, an object will appear to have a slightly 'warmer' hue under incandescent and halogen lights irrespective of its actual colour. Conversely, an object will appear to have a slightly 'cooler' hue under cool white fluorescent lights irrespective of its actual colour. It is important to take into consideration ambient illumination colour when designing visual teaching materials to ensure that variations in ambient illumination colour does not inadvertently create ambiguous illustrations, or illustrations/text that fail to convey what was intended.

Reflectance and its Impact on Ambient Lighting

The level of reflectance within the built environment in terms of surface reflectance of interior walls, ceiling, etc, influences ambient illumination and may also create varying levels of glare or gloom depending on the amount of ambient illumination. For example, a room that is painted white or a very light tone will have higher reflectance and appear brighter than if the same room was painted a darker tone.

Similarly, an interior that has good ambient illumination but is then filled with natural light at particular times of the time may become an interior with unacceptable levels of glare at certain times of the day.

To ensure that the use of visual teaching materials is optimised, it is therefore important to ensure that the learning environment has the appropriate level of illumination, plus the appropriate level of reflectance to minimise glare and gloom (Cuttle, 2008; Lam, 1992).

THE ROLE OF CONTRAST AND COLOUR CONTRAST IN VISUAL PERCEPTION

Colour and colour contrast play key roles in the visual perception process. An understanding of these roles and their importance in terms of visual perception is important irrespective of the situation or setting. However, in terms of visual teaching materials, these will be more effective if colour and colour contrast are adjusted in line with the key roles these play in human visual perception.

Visual information, which passes through to the brain from the retina via the optic nerve, continues along different pathways and through different areas of the brain. In the brain, incoming visual data as well as internal signals representing expectations, pattern recognition and so on, are processed on an ongoing basis during normal vision (Goldstein, 1996; M. S. Livingstone, 1988; Logothetis, 1999). The parvocellular pathway, which distinguishes between varying brightness levels of different hues thereby allowing for perception of shapes and borders, has a slower processing time but higher acuity or resolution. The magnocellular pathway reduces visual data to tones of black, grey and white, is sensitive to contrast (in terms of contrast between hues and luminance contrast) as well as movement, and has a faster response time but lower acuity. Some signals from both pathways are also processed in a third area, which is sensitive to colour and luminance, but not to movement, depth or shape. A coloured image on a coloured background can be easily perceived by the parvocellular system, but difficult to perceive by the magnocellular system if the colours are of equal luminance. Colour contrast between different objects allows us to identify contours, depth and shape (Ittelson, 1960; Johns and Sumner, 1948; Ratliff, 1972).

Contrast and its Role in Attracting Focal Attention

In addition, the human eye generally makes quick scanning movements on an ongoing basis when viewing a scene or performing any activity. Referred to as saccades, it is estimated that the eye makes about three scanning movements per second and these tend to occur unhindered during both focal and distributed attention (McPeek, Maljkovic, and Nakayama, 1999; O'Regan, 1992). Saccades generally involve focal attention and are facilitated by a short-term memory system; but what catches the attention of a saccade? A recent study of visual thresholds found that contrast was a key predictor variable for visual detection (Shang and Bishop, 2000). This study found that visual contrast (in terms of tonal value/luminance) was of greater influence in visual detection than size, object type and landscape type.

Contrast and its Role in Detail Detection

Contrast plays a key role in detail and depth detection. Levels of contrast between elements within a visual field help us to detect figure-ground separation, plus help us detect detail among the elements within a visual field. To illustrate the impact that contrast has in terms of legibility, the following Figure features a black text on a white background. Strong contrast allows us to easily read the text quickly and effortlessly. However, the text on the right is more difficult to read because the colours have similar tonal value and saturation level. While the hues are different, the lack of contrast hinders legibility. While this can often be an effective technique in some art or graphic design applications, diminished legibility becomes problematic for older people among whom rod receptors decrease dramatically in the seventh decade of life impairing their visual capacity (Fiorentini et al., 1996; Jackson, Owsley, and McGwin, 1999).

Figure 8.4. Visual detail is negatively impacted by weak contrast.

Fixational Reflex

The human eye has the tendency to notice and focus on objects that are bright or feature movement. Called the *fixational reflex*, it has been suggested that this occurs because the object attracting attention contrasts strongly with its surroundings and is therefore deemed significant during normal vision, indicating that cognitive processing occurs in tandem with visual perception (Boynton, 1979). In the following Figure, the images are identical except that the hue, saturation and tonal value of the lotus blossom have been digitally manipulated in the image on the left to match the contextual colours. It is obvious when we look at the image on the right that the contrasting hue and saturation of the lotus blossom relative to the surrounding colours that draws our attention.

Strong contrast attracts attention and creates focus, and this can be highly effective in visual communications design to draw attention to key areas of text and images; or to help users to navigate their way around webpages. In addition, the use of strong colour contrast can help to achieve specific outcomes in terms of signalling, attracting or diverting attention within the context of visual communications.

A recent study focussed on the use of colour in advertising indicated that higher levels of saturation and tonal value tend to influence feelings of excitement and relaxation, respectively; and this tends to result in a somewhat more favourable attitude toward the brand

(Gorn, Chattopadhyay, Yi, and Dahl, 1997). However, it is important to balance this information with the need to maintain legibility.

In the following images, the Power-point image on the left illustrates an example of less than effective visual communication. The image features lighter tones and poor contrast which, if viewed from the back of a class or large lecture room, would be difficult to read. While a bright yellow has been used to direct visual focus to the headline (*Colour Notation Systems*) and circled area (*Color Libraries*), the effectiveness of this colour is diminished because of the lack of contrast. In addition, lack of contrast between body text type colour and background colour reduces the readability; while poor quality illustration quality further detracts from the effectiveness of the Power-point image. The image at right illustrates a more effective Power-point image.

Figure 8.5. Contrasts in hue, saturation or brightness tend to attract our attention.

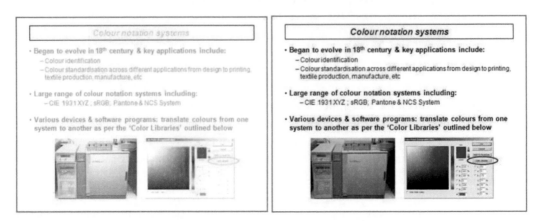

Figure 8.6. Differences in fixational reflex arising from variations in contrast.

COLOUR AND ITS ROLE IN VISUAL COMMUNICATION DESIGN

Colour plays an integral role in visual communications design; however, it is a complex phenomenon that requires extensive discussion. In an attempt to simplify colour, it has been classified into four distinct categories (conventional colour, substance colour, formula colour and spectral profile colour) and assigned three attributes: hue, saturation and tone. These provide a means of describing colour within the context of visual communication (Feisner, 2000; Gage, 1995; Green-Armytage, 2006).

Categories of Colour

Four categories of colour have been identified: conventional colour, substance colour, formula colour and spectral profile colour (Green-Armytage, 2006). Conventional colour represents those broad categories to which we assign archetypical descriptors such as *green*, *blue* or *red*. As such, these descriptors represent colours that share some similarity as per the following Figure, which features a range of *greens*.

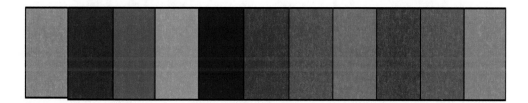

Figure 8.7. Conventional colour: Various examples of green.

Conventional colour terms are similar to the taxonomic rank of *family* wherein a colour term such as *orange* represents a family of hues that can be classified under the name *orange*. It is clear from the above Figure that the family of hues may vary considerably.

Substance colour refers to specific pigment colours and dyes that are unique and generally derived from natural sources such as *turquoise, amber, vermilion, Mummy brown* and *indigo*. Given the source diversity of substance colours, variations in colour are not uncommon. A manufacturing boom in synthetic pigments occurred shortly after the Industrial Revolution mostly as a response to issues such as cost, permanence and light-fastness of substance colours (Delamare and Guineau, 2000; Smith, 2003). Substance colours, pigments and dyes can be identified via colour notation systems.

Formula colour represents the myriad hues devised according to a specific or *ad hoc* formulas. Manufacturers of paints, printing inks and dyes such as Dulux, Berger Paints, Porter's Original Paints, plus Winsor and Newton produce and market a huge range of different colours based on in-house formulae.

These colours are often assigned a descriptive name (*Cornflower Blue, Fuchsia Pink, Canary Yellow*) which may or may not be consistent across different manufacturers. The following Figure features Epoxy Systems colours including #900 Brick Red and its RGB equivalent (Epoxy, 2011).

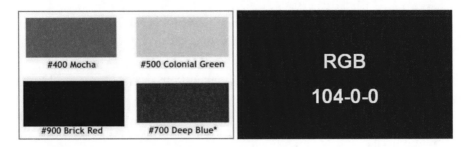

Figure 8.8. Epoxy Systems 'Brick Red' and its RGB equivalent.

CMYK colours are the basic colours used in the printing industry since the 1890s and are widely used in printing books, magazines, packaging and newspapers. Commonly referred to by their acronym, CMYK colours are Cyan (C), Magenta (M), Yellow (Y) and Black (K) as illustrated in the following Figure.

Figure 8.9. CMYK colours.

Certain formula colours can become highly recognisable over time such as the colours associated with particular brands: red coupled with white – Coca-Cola; red and yellow – McDonalds; mid-blue – Facebook; yellow – Symantec to name a few. Spectral profile colour represents colour in the form of light-waves which may be emitted by natural and artificial sources of light (Green-Armytage, 2006).

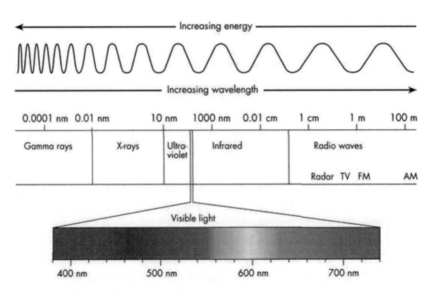

Figure 8.10. The visible spectrum segment of the electromagnetic spectrum.

The main source of natural light is sunlight, which forms the visible spectrum section of the electromagnetic spectrum. Encompassing the earth's atmosphere, this spectrum also includes Gamma rays, x-rays, radio waves and infra-red rays as illustrated in the following Figure 8.10. Spectral profile colour is the category of colour that is reproduced in most digital technology devices such as computer monitors, overhead projectors, cameras, video recorders and television monitors. There are particular issues in regard to colour reproduction within these various forms of digital technology that can impact negatively on visual communications and these issues are addressed at the end of this section. Additive colour mixing, subtractive colour mixing and optical colour mixing relate different ways in which colour can be created in terms of spectral profile colour, or substance and formula colour (Goldstein, 1996; Harkness, 2006).

Attributes of Colour

Colour is considered to have three distinct attributes and these provide useful descriptors when discussing colour and colour application. While the literature reveals different labels for these attributes, they are herein referred to as hue, saturation and tonal value as follows.

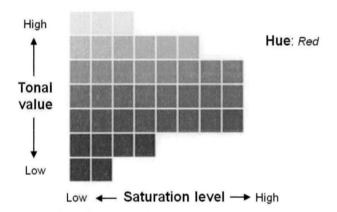

Figure 8.11. Tonal value and saturation levels of the hue: red.

By manipulating the attributes of saturation and tonal value, myriad variations of same hue can be created as per the variations of brown in the following Figure.

Figure 8.12. Brown occurs in a huge range of variations.

Hue is the attribute by which an object or substance is commonly recognised and assigned a prototypical hue-category name such as *red* or *green*. This definition of hue tends to be consistent across most colour theories (Feisner, 2000; Gage, 1995).

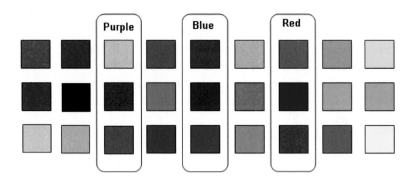

Figure 8.13. A range of Hue families.

Colour theorists over the centuries have frequently developed colour models to depict the relationship between hues as per the following Figure.

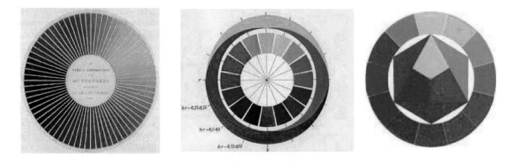

Figure 8.14. Colour wheel models of Chevreul (1855); Hering (1878) and Itten (1961).

Figure 8.15. Same image: Different levels of saturation.

Saturation is also referred to as chroma (Munsell, 1921); chromaticity (CIE, 2008); chromaticness; intensity (Albers, 1963); and the "degree of purity of a colour" (Itten, 1961, p96). A particular hue can exhibit a range of saturation levels from high saturation through to low saturation as per the Figure 8.15.

Colour saturation levels may be influenced by ambient lighting and contextual colour. That is, bright red will appear more intense if it is surrounded by green due to the influence of complementary contrast. Different saturation levels can impact on visual impressions and in the following images this apartment building at Walsh Bay, Sydney, takes on an industrial ambiance when the façade colours are de-saturated.

Figure 8.16. Same image: Different levels of saturation.

Tonal value indicates the lightness or darkness of a colour and is also referred to as tone, value and luminance (Albers, 1963; Itten, 1961; Munsell, 1921). Any hue can be depicted in a range of different tonal values as per the following tonal value chart.

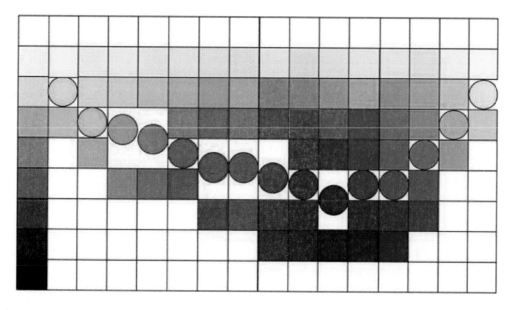

Figure 8.17. Tonal value chart.

Various software tools and devices can identify hue, tone and saturation including the Pantone and CIE systems as well as the RGB, HSL (Hue, Saturation and Luminance) and Lab colour 'dialogue' boxes found in common computer software applications.

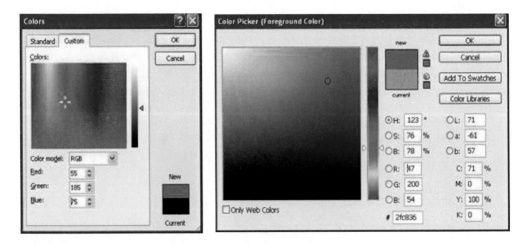

Figure 8.18. Windows and Photoshop colour 'Dialogue' boxes.

Colour Theories Relevant to Visual Communications Design

Colour has been examined and discussed since the early Greek philosophers and a plethora of colour theories exist across a range of different disciplines including psychology, physics, art and design. In general, the colour theories that emerged in the 20th century including those of Munsell, Ostwald, Kandinsky, Itten, Albers, as well as Hard and Sivik, are essentially normative theories; that is, they represent "a doctrine or ideology, a largely programmatic idea of how things ought to be done" (Moore, 1997, p. 24). As such, these theories tend to be positivist as opposed to the colour theories that emerged from the Bauhaus and Johannes Itten, which have a more post-positivist theoretical underpinning given their flexibility and focus on experimentation. It is these latter theories that are perhaps more predominant in visual communications design.

The Bauhaus, which was founded in Weimar, Germany, in 1919 by architect Walter Gropius (1883-1969), had a profound impact on architecture, design and design education during the 20th century (Bayley and Conran, 2007). In 1925 the Bauhaus moved to Dessau and Hannes Meyer (1889-1954) took over from Gropius as director in 1927. In 1932 the Bauhaus moved to Berlin with Ludwig Mies van der Rohe (1886-1969) as director from 1930 until 1933, when the school was closed by the Nazi regime.

The curriculum of the Bauhaus was underpinned by a pedagogical approach that sought to teach students design fundamentals which they could then apply to any design or architectural project and exploration and experimentation were encouraged. Colour theory and application was a key component of the Basic Course, a course that all first year students at the Bauhaus were required to complete and which was initially developed by Johannes Itten (Bayer, Gropius, and Gropius, 1975; Frampton, 1992). The Course was divided into seven main areas of study:

1. *Light-dark.* The contrast between light and dark was considered to be "the most expressive and important means of design for the artist" (Itten, 1961, p. 19). Students were encouraged to explore and apply a range of tones and to analyse paintings in terms of light-dark contrast to evaluate the effect as well as the structural role that light-dark contrast played in composition.

2. *Colour* – Colour theory and application was initially taught by Itten as well as Josef Albers and Wassily Kandinsky.

3. *Material and texture.* Students were encouraged to explore and incorporate a large range of different materials and textures.

4. *Form.* Itten asserted that the three basic forms (or shapes) are the square, the triangle and the circle. In addition, the Golden Section was studied and exercises in variation and combinations of basic forms and proportions provided students with experience in the constructive organisation of compositions.

5. *Rhythm.* Students were encouraged to use the repetition of lines, points, shapes, textures and colour to create a sense of rhythm in compositions. Deviations in direction and mass were considered to contribute to variations in rhythm.

6. *Expressive forms.* Itten considered that "if a genuine feeling is to be expressed in a line or plane, this feeling must first resound within the artist" (Itten, 1961, p. 147). Students were encouraged to experiment with line, rhythm, form and direction and analyse paintings to explore the expressive nature of form.

7. *Subjective forms.* Itten believed that each student expressed their idiosyncratic nature by using the basic elements of design differently in their compositions. The basic elements may be summarised as tone (light-dark), colour, texture, form (shape), rhythm, line, direction and mass (Bayer et al., 1975).

Johannes Itten (1888-1967), a Swiss painter and founding teacher at the Bauhaus (1919 to 1923), developed theory of colour and colour application that continues to be influential in art and design education (Gage, 1995). As a tool to explore and discuss colour, Itten developed a 12-hue colour wheel as per the following Figure.

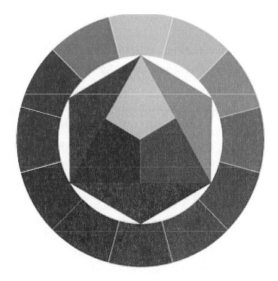

Figure 8.19. Itten colour wheel model.

Itten asserted that seven kinds of colour contrast exist and, given the role that contrast plays in visual perception and its capacity to attract or divert attention, these different types of contrast are highly relevant to the design of effective visual communications.

Contrast of Hue

Itten suggested that this type of contrast involves differences based on the attribute of hue alone. Due to its ability to attract attention, create focus and add vibrancy and diversity, hue contrast is frequently used in applied design. Strong hue contrast, which is often used in corporate logo design, improves legibility and can either divert or attract attention; it is therefore frequently used in advertisements, maps, posters and all forms of visual communications as per the following Figure.

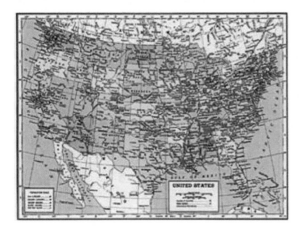 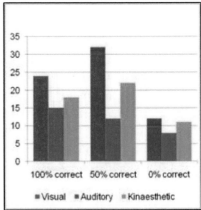

Figure 8.20. Contrast of hue.

Light-Dark Contrast

An inestimable number of variations exist between black and white and the following Figure illustrates a small sample of light-dark variations.

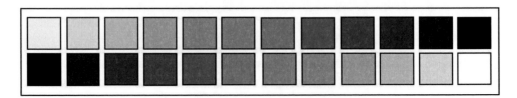

Figure 8.21. Variations of tone.

Itten suggested that light-dark contrast can be used to attract attention as well as convey ambience, depth, form and mood. Light-dark contrast can vary subtle to strong depending on variations of tonal level within a design, and tonal value can easily be manipulated to attract or divert attention as illustrated in the following Figure.

Figure 8.22. Variations in light-dark contrast and the effect on directed and focal attention.

Cold-Warm Contrast

This type of contrast occurs between colours classified as 'cool' or 'warm' (as described above). In the following Figure, 'cool' colours feature in the *Cinderella Man* poster while contrasting 'warm' colours are used to attract attention to the main figure and the film title.

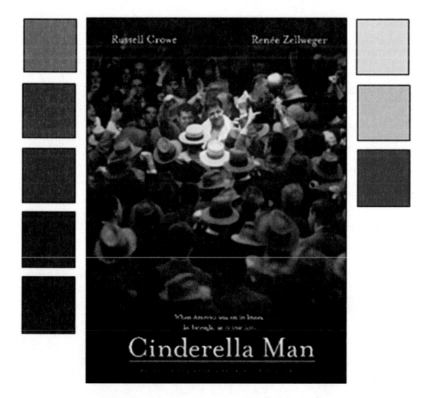

Figure 8.23. Contrast between 'cool' colours and 'warm' colours.

In the following Figure, the headline at right tends to attract more attention due to the warm-cool contrast between text colour and background colour.

Figure 8.24. Using cold-warm contrast to highlight key information.

Complementary Contrast

Itten suggested that complementary contrast occurs between **pairs of 'complementary colours' as identified by theorists such** Chevreul (1855): red-green, orange-blue and yellow-purple. Like hue contrast, complementary contrast can be manipulated to add focus and highlight key information. In the following Figure, two images include the same information; however, the key text (*Friday's lecture*) attracts more attention when the text is depicted in orange – the complementary colour to blue.

History of Rock 'N' Roll	**History of Rock 'N' Roll**
• Clarksdale & Greenville	• Clarksdale & Greenville
• Chicago & electric blues	• Chicago & electric blues
• Memphis – Friday's lecture	• Memphis - Friday's lecture
• London & the British invasion	• London & the British invasion

Figure 8.25. Using complementary contrast to highlight key information.

In the following Figure, complementary contrast between text and background has been incorporated in the image at right due to its positive impact on legibility.

Figure 8.26. Using complementary contrast to highlight key information.

Simultaneous Contrast

Simultaneous contrast is based on the perceptual effect known as simultaneous contrast whereby colour/s appear to change due to the influence of proximal colour. Simultaneous contrast may occur between complementary or contrasting colours as well as colours that exhibit differences in tonal value as per the theories of Chevreul (1855) who also championed a link between complementary colour and colour harmony.

In the following Figure, simultaneous contrast occurs between the text colour and the background colour making the text colour appear to change.

Figure 8.27. The influence of simultaneous contrast on colour appearance.

Simultaneous contrast not only makes colours appear to change in terms of hue but also in terms of tonal value, as illustrated in the following Figure.

Figure 8.28. The influence of simultaneous contrast on colour appearance.

Contrast of Saturation

Contrast of saturation relates to variations in levels of saturation among a group of colours within an image. As the eye tends to be drawn to areas that display contrast, contrast of saturation is an effective means of attracting or diverting attention and creating a focal point as illustrated in the following Figure. In this example, the image at right has been altered so that focal attention is directed to the central building which is the element in the image that contrasts from the background in terms of saturation.

Contrast of saturation can also be manipulated in text-based visual communications whereby a strong, saturated colour is used to draw attention to key information.

Figure 8.29. Contrast of saturation.

	Schedule		**Schedule**	
June:	Meeting with client	June:	Meeting with client	
July:	Finalise research brief	July:	Finalise research brief	
Aug:	Pilot study	Aug:	Pilot study	
Oct:	Main study (NSW)	Oct:	Main study (NSW)	
Nov:	Data analysis	Nov:	Data analysis	
Dec:	Report due	**Dec:**	**Report due**	

Figure 8.30. Using contrast of saturation to highlight key information.

Contrast of Extension/Proportion

This type of contrast relates to the proportional use of colour within a composition and this technique can be used to create focus and draw the eye to specific areas within an applied design context (Feisner, 2000; Kopacz, 2003; Mahnke, 1996; Shillito, 1979). In the following Figure, red is used sparingly in the *Vantage Point* poster to create a focal point.

Figure 8.31. Contrast of extension/proportion from minimal (left) to maximum (right).

Red is used strategically in the *Vanity Fair* layout to draw the eye to different sections around the page; while in the *Red* poster, red is predominant and also used strategically to link its connotative meanings to the title of the film.

COLOUR AND PERCEPTUAL EFFECTS

Colour and contrast play significant roles in a number of perceptual effects and familiarity with these effects enables the designer to either use these to achieve particular outcomes; or, avoid them if they impact negatively on the effectiveness of visual communications design. Colour has long been known to contribute to perceptual interactions when viewed in close proximity, and painters such as Leonardo Da Vinci (1452-1519) and Caravaggio (1571-1610) used this knowledge to great effect in their painting. Techniques such as *sfumato* and *chiaroscuro* involved careful use of colour and tonal contrast and enabled artists to create various visual illusions (such as depth and volume) despite access to a limited range of pigments.

Simultaneous Contrast

Simultaneous contrast occurs when the proximity of one colour tends to visually influence the perception of another colour. This perceptual effect may occur in a static situation (simultaneous contrast) or may arise when the perception of currently viewed stimuli influences or is modulated by previously viewed stimuli – referred to as successive contrast (Chevreul, 1855; Goldstein, 1996). This perceptual effect, which can occur across a range of situations and settings, is illustrated in the following Figure where two grey squares are identical but appear different due to the close proximity of a lighter grey (at left) and a darker grey (at right).

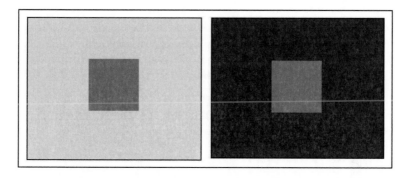

Figure 8.32. Simultaneous contrast: The inner grey squares are identical but the left appears darker than the right due to colour contrast of the proximal colour.

Lateral inhibition, which may explain why a number of perceptual effects including simultaneous contrast occur, is an effect that occurs in the retina when some receptor neurons are absorbing incoming light signals thereby inhibiting or suppressing nearby receptor neurons from transmitting signals as per the following figure (Goldstein, 1996).

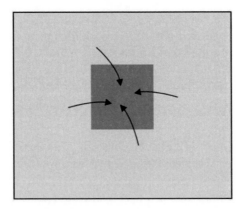

Figure 8.33. Lateral inhibition may explain why the lighter surround of the figure (left) stimulates receptor neurons causing the partial suppression of nearby receptor neurons (Goldstein, 1996).

Simultaneous contrast also occurs due to differences in hue and in the following figure, the red square at left appears marginally darker and redder than the red square at right; which appears marginally lighter and more orange due simultaneous contrast.

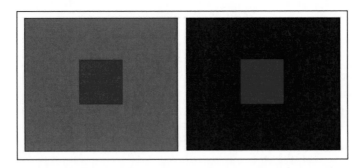

Figure 8.34. Simultaneous contrast: The inner red squares are identical but the left appears darker than the right due to colour contrast of the proximal colour.

Another example of simultaneous contrast is White's illusion illustrated in the following Figures. In this illusion, the influence and placement of proximal white and black stripes serves to either perceptually lighten or darken areas of identical grey.

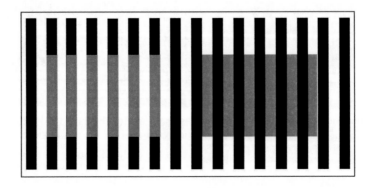

Figure 8.35. Simultaneous contrast: The inner grey areas are identical but the left appears lighter than the right due to the influence of proximal colour.

The Hermann Grid and Scintillating Grid Illusions

Some visual patterns or illusions have been linked to visual discomfort and, while the level of discomfort may vary, such illusions may induce or trigger nausea, headaches, migraine or epilepsy (Wilkins et al., 1984). To avoid visual discomfort, it is advisable to minimise the use of strong-contrast repetitive patterns in visual communications design. For example, the Hermann Grid illusion, first described by Ludimar Hermann (1838-1914) in 1870, occurs when ghost-like dark grey blobs appear at the white intersections within a pattern of repeated black squares. Similarly, the Scintillating Grid illusion, first described by Lingelbach, 1994, is another perceptual effect wherein ghost-like black dots appear in place of white dots at the intersections in the grid creating visual movement within an otherwise static illustration.

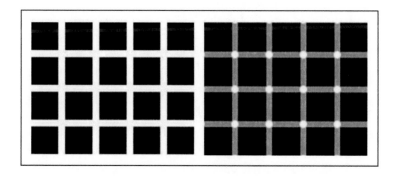

Figure 8.36. The Hermann Grid illusion (left) and Scintillating Grid illusion (right).

Colour and Equiluminance (Vibrating Colour)

Matching the tonal level (luminance) of colours within a pair or group of colours, particular if they are complementary/contrasting colours, can make them appear to visually vibrate (Holtzschue, 2006; M. Livingstone, 2002). Vibrating colours have been used to great effect by painters including Claude Monet (1840-1926), Marcel Duchamp (1887-1968) and Bridget Riley (b1931). However, it is recommended that vibrating colours are not used in visual communication design because of the negative impact they can have on the effectiveness of such communications.

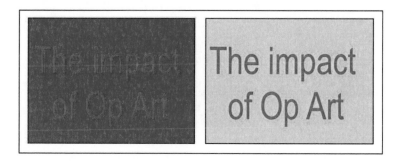

Figure 8.37. Strong vibrating colour (left) and minimised vibrating colour (right).

Form and Contour: The Effect of Colour

Hard edge contours tend to increase the level of apparent contrast between Figure and Ground (Rubin, 1921, cited in Kanizsa, 1979). The following Figure features two shapes of an identical colour; however, the square appears marginally darker in appearance than the non-linear shape due to its hard-edge contour.

Figure 8.38. Hard edge contours tend to increase the apparent level of contrast.

COLOUR COMBINATION TECHNIQUES

Colour is one of a number of design elements that can help to convey meaning in visual communications design and it can be applied in a variety of ways in visual communications. Depending on the context, colour has the capacity to convey meaning more effectively than words and the literature includes a range of colour combination techniques specifically for application in applied design as follows (Feisner, 2000; Gage, 1995; Kopacz, 2003; Mahnke, 1996; Stone, Adam, and Morioka, 2006).

Hue Similarity (Analogous Hues)

This technique suggests combining colours that share a high degree of similarity in terms of hue. While the tonal values and saturation levels of hues may vary, this technique relies on combining colours that are generally found alongside each other on colour wheel models (Hard and Sivik, 2001; Itten, 1961; Munsell, 1921). Unless tonal value and saturation are varied, there tends to be minimal contrast and hence this technique does to always contribute to effective visual communications design.

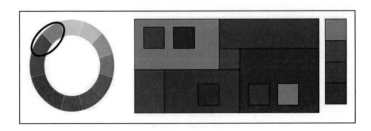

Figure 8.39. Colour combination based on hue similarity.

Combining colours based on hue similarity is also referred to as 'simple harmony' due to an assumed link between such colours and positive aesthetic response despite a relative absence of empirical evidence.

Extended Hue Similarity

This technique involves combining colours that share a high degree of similarity in terms of hue as well as additional colour/s that are marginally different in hue (Feisner, 2000; Shillito, 1979). While the tonal values and saturation levels of hues may vary, this technique combines colours that are generally found alongside each other within a larger arc area on colour wheel models and, given the likelihood of a greater range of contrasting colours, this technique tends to be more effective in visual communications.

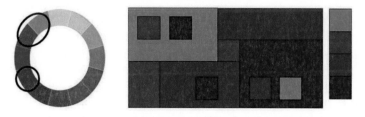

Figure 8.40. Colour combination based on extended hue similarity.

Monotone

Monotone involves using colours that share a high degree of similarity in terms of tonal value as per the following Figure (Feisner, 2000; Mahnke, 1996; Shillito, 1979). This colour combination technique provides reduced opportunities for using contrast to attract attention or improve legibility within visual communications design.

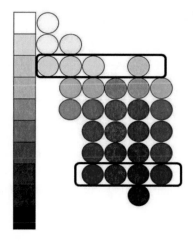

Figure 8.41. Monotone colour groups.

Monochromatic Colours

Monochromatic colour combination technique involves combining colours based on one hue with different tones and/or saturation levels (Feisner, 2000; Mahnke, 1996).

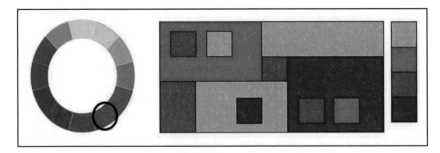

Figure 8.42. Colour combination based on monochromatic colour.

Monochromatic colour combination provides better opportunities in terms of visual communications design as it allows for a greater range of contrast to attract attention and improve legibility; however, it is a technique that needs to be applied with care to ensure that headlines and text are clearly legible.

Figure 8.43. Monochromatic colour combination in visual communications design.

Major Tonal Chords

This colour combination technique rests on combining groups of colours according to different tonal values. Major tonal chords include colours that exhibit a large range of tonal values and may be further categorised:

- High Major – mostly high or light tones with a small proportion of darker tones;
- Intermediate Major – a wide range of high, medium and low tones;

- Low Major – predominantly low tones plus a small proportion of lighter tones; (Itten, 1961; Shillito, 1979).

Most theorists consider that colour chords can help to convey an expressive quality in applied design; hence, the analogy with music. Under this technique, the tonal values of colours are usually defined as per the chart illustrated in the following Figure.

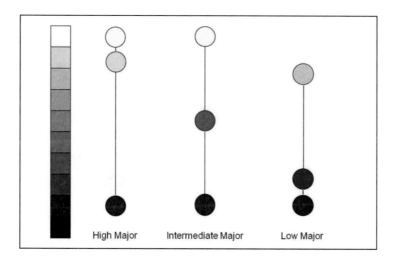

Figure 8.44. Major tonal chords.

Major colour chords provide an effective colour combination technique for visual communications design as the wide range of tones support legibility.

Figure 8.45. Examples of major tonal chords in visual communications design.

Minor Tonal Chords

Minor tonal chords represent groups of colours that exhibit a narrow range of tonal values as illustrated in the following Figure.

- High Minor: predominantly high or light tones; tends to convey a light, airy, ethereal ambience;
- Intermediate Minor: a small range of high to medium or medium to low tones;
- Low Major: predominantly low tones; tends to convey a dramatic or mysterious ambience (Itten, 1961; Shillito, 1979).

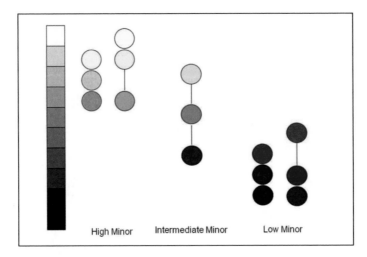

Figure 8.46. Minor tonal chords.

Minor chords of colours provide a marginally less effective colour combination technique for visual communications design because of the reduced range of tones; however, colour contrast can help to improve legibility.

Contrasting/Complementary Colour

This colour combination technique involves using groups of colours that are considered to contrasting or complementary (Feisner, 2000; Itten, 1961; Mahnke, 1996; Shillito, 1979). Different theorists have varying definitions of contrasting and complementary colour as illustrated by the colour models depicted in the following Figure.

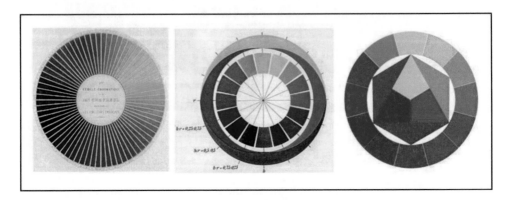

Figure 8.47. Colour models of Chevreul, Hering and Itten.

Given the way in which the human visual system works, colour contrast provides an ideal method for creating differentiation and therefore improved legibility in visual communications design. Contrasting colour combinations can involve highly saturated colours which attract attention and convey a light-hearted or youthful ambience as per the advertisements and book covers featured in the following Figure.

Figure 8.48. Colour combinations based on contrasting colour.

A range of other colour combination techniques exist and these include reduced contrasts whereby contrasting colour has been 'reduced' via the addition of a third colour. Reduced contrasts provide another way to create differentiation in visual communications design and often involve tertiary colours such as ochre, brown, slate, khaki green, etc. Tertiary colours and reduced contrasts tend to convey an 'aged' visual impression.

Of the remaining colour combination techniques in the literature (including analogous-complementary and split-complementary) double-complementary colour combinations are often used in print advertisements for high turnover consumer goods due to the attention-grabbing effect of using multiple contrasting hues. This technique involves using pairs of complementary/contrasting colours such as red-green plus blue-orange as per the following Figure (Feisner, 2000; Mahnke, 1996; Shillito, 1979).

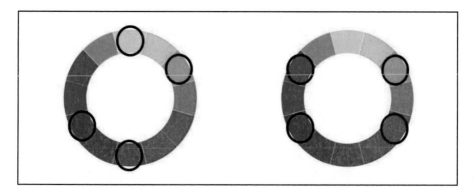

Figure 8.49. Two examples of double-complementary colour combinations.

Double-complementary colour combination was used to great effect during the 1960s and 1970s in psychedelic posters and record covers, and has influenced visual communications design since as per the following Figure.

Figure 8.50. Colour combinations based on double-complementary colours.

COLOUR AND SYMBOLIC ASSOCIATION

Colour has long been used in conjunction with symbols to create a kind of visual vocabulary or code that that can be quickly and easily conveyed and understood. Using colour in such a way can be traced back to the self-governed tribes that roamed Europe and the Picts of Northern Britain, for example, painted or tattooed their bodies using woad, a blue dyestuff derived from the plant *Isatis tinctoria* and hence came to be known as '*picti*' (Latin: painted ones) by the Romans.

Some centuries later, the Pope determined that each group that participated in the Crusades should be distinguished by different coloured symbols: England claimed the red cross on a white background; France used golden fleur-de-lys on a blue background; and Scotland claimed St Andrew's Cross (or Saltire): a white cross on an azure blue field.

Olins (1989) suggests that the coloured emblems of the Crusaders plus the tri-colour flag of the first French Republic by Napoleon Bonaparte (in 1804) and the coloured emblems of the Confederate and Republican armies of the American Civil War (1861-1865) pre-empted the widespread use of colour coupled with symbolic emblems in the commercial sector. Coloured logos are now common across public and private organisations and sporting organisations (Olins, 1989).

The speed with which many corporate logos become familiar and highly recognisable attest to the capacity of colour coupled with simple emblems to effectively convey visual information.

A number of colour theorists including Albers, Goethe and Kandinsky considered that certain colours carry specific associations which were considered to have universal applicability. For example, Albers suggested that certain colour groupings conveyed connotations such as 'Serious' or 'Melancholic' as per the following Figure.

In addition, colour associations are often culture or context-bound. Red, for example, has a range of different connotations depending on context. Firstly, red is frequently associated with revolutionary ideas, and the red star has become a global symbol associated with socialism and communism.

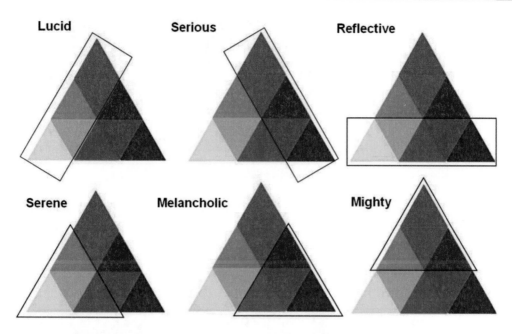

Figure 8.51. Albers' colour connotations (1963).

Such symbolic associations are evident in cover design of Che Guevara's *Motorcycle Diaries* and the print advertisement for the production of *Rock n' Roll*, Sydney Theatre Company featured in the following Figure.

Figure 8.52. Red is often associated with revolutionary ideas.

However, red is also strongly associated with romance, passion and virility in Western culture as per the illustrations in the following Figure. Plus, red is often used to symbolise danger as per Stop signs worldwide and examples of applied design such as the poster for the films *Sin City, Edge of Darkness* and *The Hurt Locker*.

Figure 8.53. Red is often associated with romance and passion.

However, red is also associated with danger and is frequently used in signage due to this particular association as per the following Figure.

Figure 8.54. Red is often associated with danger.

Similarly, gold is often used to symbolise quality, opulence and wealth in western culture, and is frequently used in advertisements to convey such connotations. However, if colour is to be used symbolically in visual communications design, it is imperative to remember that particular colour associations may not be consistent across different cultures or sub-cultures. The following Table provides some insight into the variations of colour connotation for seven colours (Aslam, 2006).

Table 8.1. Variations in colour connotation across different cultural groups

Colour	Anglo-Saxon	Germanic	Chinese	Japanese
White	Purity	-	Death Mourning	Death Mourning
Black	Mourning Fear, Expensive	Mourning Fear, Anger	Expensive Powerful	Expensive Powerful
Red	Love/Passion Fear, Anger	Fear, Anger Jealousy	Love, Luck Happiness	Love, Anger Jealousy
Blue	High quality Masculine	Warm Feminine	High quality Trustworthy	High quality Trustworthy
Yellow	Happy Jealousy	Envy Jealousy	Pure Good taste	Envy Good taste
Green	Envy, Good taste Enviro pure	-	Pure Reliable	Love Happy
Purple	Authority/Power (Church hierarchy)	-	Expensive Love	Expensive Powerful

DIGITAL COLOUR DATA AND PHOTOGRAPHIC COLOUR REPRODUCTION ISSUES

Reproduction of colour data and photographic images is often problematic and there are a number of reasons for variances that arise during reproduction of coloured data and images. Knowledge about such issues provides a starting point in mitigating them in terms of the design of visual communication materials.

Firstly, it is estimated that humans can distinguish between 2 million and 10 million different colours (Gouras, 1991; Judd and Wyszecki, 1975; Pointer and Attridge, 1998). In terms of colour data as input, Morovic and Morovic (2003) note that, given that huge range of possible (real) colours, digital sampling of such a gamut in its entirety is virtually impossible. Colour reproduction is always limited by the colour classification system used and the colour reproduction capabilities of the software and computer peripherals such as printers, projectors and the like. Hence, it is important to note that colour reproduction is always constrained by a trade-off between accuracy of reproduction and the colour systematisation method (Yendrikhovskij, 2001).

As with all digital technology data, various algorithms are used to process and reduce the file size of colour data. If colour data is considerably reduced, this reduction has a negative impact on accuracy of colour reproduction.

A second key reason for colour reproduction issues relates to the different colour systems and colour gamuts embedded within software programs (such as Microsoft, PowerPoint, etc) and digital devices such as computers, scanners, cameras, printers and projectors. A colour gamut is the colour recognition and reproduction capacity embedded within software programs and digital devices, and these are not always identical. In fact, colour gamuts are rarely the same (except in some cases where the devices are manufactured by the same company); hence, variation in colour invariably occurs when colour is transferred from one software program or device to another.

The flow of colour data from one software program or device to another is depicted in the following Figure. Colour stimuli captured via input devices such as scanners and digital cameras is converted into digital data which is then 'read' by output devices such as printers and projectors. Each device may have a different colour system and colour gamut, and therefore each step in the sequence may involve another step of colour data conversion and storage, thereby corrupting the colour data due to the number of conversions – a digital version of 'Chinese whispers' (Morovic and Morovic, 2003).

In addition, software programs such as Adobe Photoshop process colour information by converting colour information to binary form and processing the data mathematically. Photoshop generally provides the user with a selection of different modes or colour systems such RGB and CMYK as well as the Pantone system. When the user converts the colour data within an image from one mode of colour to another, the colour data is converted to Lab mode first before converting it to the specified mode. This occurs because the Lab mode provides a far greater number of colour values than other modes.

Most digital cameras, when photographing an object or environment, capture photons of light using charge couple devices (CCD). A CCD has light receiving photo-pixel elements that generate electrons in proportion to the amount of light received by each element at a rate that varies from 8 bits per pixel up to 24 bits per pixel (Miura, 2001; Vrhel, 2000).

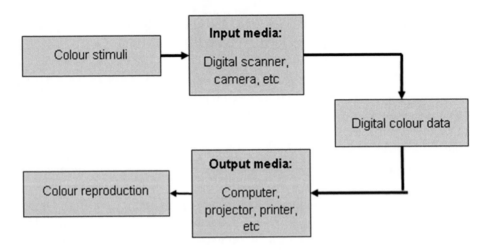

Figure 8.55. The flow of digital colour data (Morovic and Morovic, 2003).

The resulting image data is then translated into binary code and compressed for storage and subsequent processing, often as a JPEG file; a common and widely used image file format (Dipert, 1998).

JPEG file format was jointly developed by the International Telecommunications Union (ITU) and the International Organisation for Standardisation (ISO) and it evolved as an international standard for compressing image data (Skodras, Christopoulos, and Ebrahimi, 2001). The image data in a JPEG is weight-averaged using a discrete cosine transform function, usually in blocks of 8x8 photo-pixels, thereby compressing the data (Dipert, 1998; Schroeder, 1997). As some image data is lost as a result of this process, JPEGs are referred to as 'lossy' unlike an alternative method of processing image data referred to as TIFF (Tagged Image File Format). The TIFF file format that does not compress image data and is therefore known as a 'lossless' file format; however, TIFF image files require much larger storage space than JPEG files.

It is widely known that the more pixels captured per image, the greater detail and clarity per image; and the current convention therefore is to capture images at the highest possible pixel per image rate as JPEG files and ensure adequate provisions for file storage (Janesick and Putnam, 2003; Skodras et al., 2001). While images of 120 pixels per centimetre provide images of very high quality, camera manufacturers such as Pentax consider that pixel counts greater than this are beyond the detection threshold of human vision (Pentax, 2005).

Irrespective of the file format used for storage of digital colour photographic images, there will always be a discrepancy between the amount of visual data apparent in the real object or scene and the amount of visual data in the digital photograph of the object or scene. Converting and compressing digital photographic images will always result in the loss of visual colour data.

REFERENCES

Albers, J. (1963). *The interaction of color.* New Haven, NY: Yale University Press.

Aslam, M. M. (2006). Are you selling the right colour? *Journal of Marketing Communications, 12*(1), 15-30.

Bayer, H., Gropius, W., and Gropius, I. (Eds.). (1975). *Bauhaus 1919 - 1928.* London: Secker and Warburg.

Bayley, B., and Conran, T. (2007). *Design: Intelligence made visible.* London: Conran Octopus.

Boynton, R. M. (1979). *Human color vision.* New York: Holt, Reinhart and Winston.

Chevreul, M. E. (1855). *The principles of harmony and the contrast of colours: And their applications to the arts (Facsimile edition; Trans. C Martel).* Whitefish, MT: Kessinger Publishing.

CIE. (2008). CIE 1931 XYZ colour space, Commission Internationale de l'Eclairage. Retrieved 14 July 2008, from http://www.cie.co.at/

Cuttle, C. (2008). *Lighting by design (2nd ed.).* Oxford: Architectural Press.

Delamare, F., and Guineau, B. (2000).*Colour: Making and using dyes and pigments.* London: Thames and Hudson.

Dipert, B. (1998). Compression puts images on a diet. *EDN, 43*(18), 71-82.

Epoxy. (2011). Epoxy Systems - Color chart. Retrieved 2 August 2011, from http://www.epoxysystems.com/bgcolorchart.htm

Feisner, E. A. (2000). *Colour: How to use colour in art and design.* London: Laurence King.

Fiorentini, A., Porciatti, M., Morrone, M. C., and Burr, D. C. (1996). Visual ageing: Unspecific decline of the responses to luminance and colour. *Vision Research, 36*(21), 3557-3566.

Frampton, K. (1992). The Bauhaus: Evolution of an idea 1919-1932. In K. Frampton (Ed.), *Modern architecture: A critical history (3rd ed.).* New York: Thames and Hudson.

Gage, J. (1995). *Colour and culture.* London: Thames and Hudson.

Goldstein, E. B. (1996). *Sensation and perception.* Pacific Grove, CA: Brooks/Cole.

Gorn, G. J., Chattopadhyay, A., Yi, T., and Dahl, D. W. (1997). Effects of color as an executional cue in advertising: They're in the shade. *Management Science, 43*(10), 1387-1400.

Gouras, P. (1991). Cortical mechanisms of colour vision. In P. Gouras (Ed.), *Vision and visual dysfunction* (Vol. 6, pp. 179-197). London: Macmillan.

Green-Armytage, P. (2006). The value of knowledge for colour design. *Color Research and Application, 31*(4), 253-269.

Hard, A., and Sivik, L. (2001). A theory of colors in combination - A descriptive model related to the NCS color-order system. *Color Research and Application, 26*(1), 4-28.

Harkness, N. (2006). The colour wheels of art, perception, science and physiology. *Optics and Laser Technology, 38*(3), 219-229.

Hoffman, D. D. (1998). *Visual intelligence: How we create what we see.* New York: WW Norton and Company.

Holtzschue, L. (2006). *Undertsanding color.* New York: John Wiley and Sons.

Ittelson, W. H. (1960). *Visual space perception.* New York: Springer.

Itten, J. (1961). *The art of color (Revised edition, 1973).* New York: John Wiley and Sons.

Jackson, G. R., Owsley, C., and McGwin, G. (1999). Aging and dark adaptation. *Vision Research, 39*(23), 3975-3982.

Janesick, J., and Putnam, G. (2003). Developments and applications of high-performance CCD and CMOS imaging arrays. *Annual Review of Nuclear and Particle Science, 53*, 263-300.

Johns, E. H., and Sumner, F. C. (1948). Relation of the brightness differences of colors to their apparent distances. *Journal of Psychology, 26*, 25-29.

Judd, D. B., and Wyszecki, G. (1975). *Color in business, science and industry*. New York: Wiley.

Julian, W. (2006). *Lighting: Basic concepts*. Sydney: University of Sydney (Faculty of Architecture, Design and Planning).

Kanizsa, G. (1979). *Organisation in vision: Essays on Gestalt perception*. New York: Praeger.

Kolb, H. (2003). How the retina works. *American Scientist, 91*(1), 28-35.

Kopacz, J. (2003). *Color in three-dimensional design*. New York: McGraw-Hill.

Lam, W. M. C. (1992). *Perception and lighting as formgivers for architecture*. New York: Van Nostrand Reinhold.

Livingstone, M. (2002). *Vision and art: The biology of seeing*. New York: Abrams.

Livingstone, M. S. (1988). Art, illusion and the visual system. *Scientific American, 258*(3), 78-85.

Logothetis, N. K. (1999). Vision: A window on consciousness. *Scientific American* (November 1999), 45-51.

Mahnke, F. (1996). *Color, environment and human response*. New York: John Wiley and Sons.

McPeek, R. M., Maljkovic, V., and Nakayama, K. (1999). Saccades require focal attention and are facilitated by a short-term memory system. *Vision Research, 39*(8), 1555-1566.

Miura, K. (2001). Imaging and detection technologies for image analysis. *Electrophoresis, 22*, 801-813.

Moore, G. T. (1997). Towards environment-behaviour theories of the middle range. In G. T. Moore and R. W. Marans (Eds.), *Advances in environment, behaviour and design* (Vol. 4). New York: Plenum Press.

Morovic, J., and Morovic, P. (2003). Determining colour gamuts of digital cameras and scanners. *Color Research and Application, 28*(1), 59-68.

Munsell, A. H. (1921). A grammar of color. Retrieved 20 October 2003, from http:/www.gretamacbeth.com/Source/Solutions/munsell/index.asp

Newacheck, J. S., Haegerstrom-Portnoy, G., and Adams, A. J. (1990). Predicting visual acuity from detection thresholds. *Optometry and Vision Science, 67*(3), 184-191.

Olins, W. (1989). *Corporate identity: Making business strategy visible through design*. New York: Thames and Hudson.

O'Regan, J. K. (1992). Solving the 'real' mysteries of visual perception: The world as an outside memory. *Canadian Journal of Psychology, 46*(3), 461-488.

Pentax. (2005). Pentax Technical Information. Retrieved 20 October 2005, from http://www.pentax.com

Pointer, M. R., and Attridge, G. G. (1998).The number of discernable colours. *Color Research and Application, 23*, 52-54.

Ratliff, F. (1972). Contour and Contrast. *Scientific American, 226*(6), 91-101.

Rea, M. S. (Ed.). (1993). *Lighting handbook - Reference and application (8th edition)*. New York: Illuminating Engineering Society of North America (IES).

Schroeder, M. D. (1997). JPEG compression algorithm and associated data structures. <http://people.cs.und.edu/~mschroed/index.html>. Retrieved September 2003

Shang, H., and Bishop, I. D. (2000). Visual thresholds for detection, recognition and visual impact in landscape settings. *Journal of Environmental Psychology, 20*(4), 125-140.

Shillito, P. (1979). Shillito Design School syllabus: Recollections of Zena Stefanek, Shillito Design student from 1977 to 1979. Sydney: Shillito Design School.

Skodras, A., Christopoulos, C., and Ebrahimi, T. (2001). The JPEG still image compression standard. *IEEE Signal Processing Magazine, September*, 36-58.

Smith, R. (2003). *The artist's handbook*. London: Dorling Kindersley.

Stone, T. L., Adam, S., and Morioka, N. (2006). *Color design workbook*. Beverly, MA: Rockport Publishers.

Vrhel, M. J. (2000). *Color imaging: A computational model of color categorisation*. Paper presented at the 2000 International Conference on Image Processing.

Werner, J. S., Peterzell, D. H., and Scheetz, A. J. (1990). Light, vision, and Ageing. *Optometry and Vision Science, 67*(3), 214-229.

Wilkins, A., Nimmo-Smith, I., Tait, A., McManus, C., Della Sala, S., Tilley, A., et al. (1984).A neurological basis for visual discomfort. *Brain, 107*(4), 989-1017.

Yendrikhovskij, S. N. (2001). A computational model of colour categorisation. *Color Research and Application, 26*(Supplement), S235-S238.

Chapter 9

DESIGN FACTORS

ABSTRACT

Aside from the cognitive processing of information and the mechanics of human perception, there are a number of design factors that influence the effectiveness of visual communications. These include audience identification and analysis plus the clear definition of communication objectives. These serve to inform communication strategies and provide insight for the design and structure of visual communications. More specifically, design layout and various issues regarding typeface design and size also influence the efficacy of visual communications. Furthermore, the principles and elements of design and the way these are applied to visual communications can impact positively or negatively on the effectiveness of such communications.

BACK TO BASICS

Prior to discussing the elements and principles of design, there are a number of basic factors that can contribute to effectiveness of visual communications and presentations. This section discusses audience-needs maps which provide a starting point when planning visual communications. They also underpin communications objectives, which in turn provide direction for communication strategies and visual presentation structure. Visual and verbal indicators of structure are discussed as well as traditional and non-traditional delivery methods. A number of guidelines for content, layout and typeface style and size are provided along with recommendations for sound and music.

Who's the Star: Presenter, Audience or Content?

The key to successful visual communications and presentations is to keep the focus on the content and ensure that the meaning embedded within the content resonates with the audience. Duarte (2010) suggests that it is "the audience is the hero" rather than the presenter whose role is more of mentor and guide: "audience insights and resonance can only occur when a presenter takes a stance of humility" (Duarte, 2010, p. 20). By deferring to the audience, engagement is more likely: "audience insights and resonance can only occur when a presenter takes a stance of humility" (Duarte, 2010, p. 20)

Identify the Audience, the Objective and the Communication Strategy

Prior to designing visual communications, it is imperative to have some understanding of the audience, their level of knowledge and their likely attitude to the information to be presented. To achieve this, Duarte (2008) suggests taking the time to build an audience-needs map which can provide a benchmark against which the communications objectives can be assessed and tweaked. This process helps to improve levels of engagement and understanding, and therefore has a positive impact on the effectiveness of visual communications and presentations. The questions provided in the following Table provide a starting point for understanding the audience.

Table 9.1. Key questions in building an audience-needs map (Duarte, 2008)

What are they like?	Demographics and psychographics provide an indication of who the audience is and what they are like.
Why are they here?	What do they think they are going to get out of the presentation? Why are they coming to the presentation?
What keeps them up at night?	Understanding what fears the audience may have provides you with the knowledge to empathise and offer a solution.
How can you solve their problem?	What's in it for the audience? How are you going to make their lives better?
What do you want them to do?	Answer the question "so what?" from their perspective. Makes sure there's a clear 'call to action'
How might they resist?	What will keep them from adopting your message and carrying out your 'call to action'
How can you best reach them?	People vary in their preferences to receive information...Give the audience what they want and how they want it.

It is also recommended that the communication objectives are identified as these provide the starting point for devising the structure of the visual communications task. Once these have been identified, a communication strategy can be developed that suits both the audience and the objective of the task as per the following Table. Two alternative communication strategies include the State-Support-Summarise strategy and the Agenda/Roadmap strategy, as follows (Beighlie, 2005).

1. State-Support-Summarise strategy

    - Introduction: State the purpose; tell the audience what you plan to tell them;
    - Body of presentation: present key information 'chunks'; provide support and evidence for this information and indicate relevance to the audience;
    - Conclusion: Summarise the presentation; tell the audience what you told them.

2. Agenda/Roadmap strategy

- Present an agenda or roadmap for the communication task;
- State the key problem or question (in the case of presenting research findings, this may involve stating the objective of the research);
- Present and demonstrate the 'solution'; or in the case of presenting research findings, identify what was done (methods) and what was found (data);
- Summarise and discuss the conclusions; and in the case of research findings, discussion future research directions;
- Acknowledgements and references.

Table 9.2. Sample Communication strategy

Audience	Third year law students
Objective	Inform the audience of the role and responsibilities of the Chief Justice of Australia (This objective assumes a high level of knowledge about the Australian court and judicial system among the audience).
Strategy	Apply the State-Support-Summarise strategy and include specific text content supported by organisational diagrams.

Structure

Aside from communications strategies, it is important to ensure that the overall structure of visual communications and presentations is designed to attract and then maintain the audience's attention for the duration of the presentation.

Duarte (2010) suggests that visual communications and presentation fall between Reports which convey information in a topical, hierarchical, direct and precise manner; and Stories (cinematic or literature) which are more dramatic and communication occurs in an expressive or theatrical manner.

A report is considered "organise facts by topic, while a story organises scenes dramatically", and a presentation tends to be more explanatory and should alternate between facts and storytelling while communicating in a "believable, credible and engaging manner" (Duarte, 2010, p. 26). Duarte (2010) suggests incorporating the following structural elements:

a) A distinct 'beginning' to describe the topic, highlight key information, and situate the topic from a contextual perspective;
b) A 'middle' that begins with a dilemma relating to the topic or a 'call to action' that focuses on an apparent imbalance relating to the topic. This section should also provide a number of different perspectives relevant to the dilemma;
c) An 'end' that highlights the preferred solution to the dilemma and indicates the next steps post-presentation.

Visual and verbal indicators can be used to indicate structure, and the following Figure illustrates a simple method wherein visual sign-post indicators highlight the current position as well as the sequential structure of the presentation. Visual sign-posting provides an overt method of highlighting key sections within visual communications and presentations. Similarly, verbal signals also provide the audience with an understanding of structure as per the following examples (Feynman cited in Duarte, 2010, pp. 132-133).

Figure 9.1. Sign-posting the sequential structure of a presentation.

Table 9.3. Verbal indicators of structure

Introductions	New key points	Conclusions
Today's presentation is going to focus on...	The next key point to focus in is...	The key conclusions to remember are...
This presentation will highlight...	In addition, it's imperative to understand....	So, the proposal arising from today's presentation...
Today, I'll be discussing the...	The next question we'll focus on is....	But most important conclusion is...
What I'd like to do in this lecture...	Another issue that needs to be addressed is...	Finally...

Another aurally-based indictor is the practice of pausing for effect. This technique is an important means of allowing time for the audience to consider the information provided and a few seconds of silence is all that is required for an audience to stop and ponder the message. The lack of sound can also act as an aurally-based indicator to reinforce key points. In addition, humour can also be used strategically as an additional means to keep an audience engaged. Humour provides a catalyst to break tension and can also help to increase connection and engagement between presenter and audience.

Story Templates and Sparklines

Incorporating a level of drama within the context of a story template in visual communications and presentations is considered necessary by Duarte (2010) to encourage the audience to cross an imaginary threshold from passivity or relative scepticism to adopting the perspective of the presenter and accepting or embracing the knowledge delivered by the presenter.

Duarte (2010) advocates following a simple situation-complication-resolution story template to add a level of drama whereby the situation section describes 'what is'; the complication section highlights key issues that impact on 'what is'; and the resolution section describes 'what could be' and often includes 'a call to action'.

Contrast, which can transform the familiar into the stimulating, can be incorporated by juggling the tension between 'what is' and 'what could be'. Duarte (2010) provides the following descriptors to highlight contrast between 'what is' and 'what could be':

Existing point of view	:	New point of view
Past/present	:	Future
Problem	:	Solution
Need	:	Fulfilment
Information	:	Insight
Ordinary	:	Special
Question	:	Answer

In addition, Duarte (2010) suggests that other ways to incorporate drama are by shifting between the analytical and the emotional, and by swapping between traditional and non-traditional delivery methods. These shifts provide contrast which in turn creates drama.

The "sparkline" represents the form that communication may take in terms of the tensions that arise between 'what is' and 'what could be' plus the contrasts in emotion and delivery which (hopefully) highlight the key points for the audience; that is, moments when the audience achieves insight or inspiration (Duarte, 2010). The following Figure depicts techniques to vary levels of engagement beginning from an initially passive level.

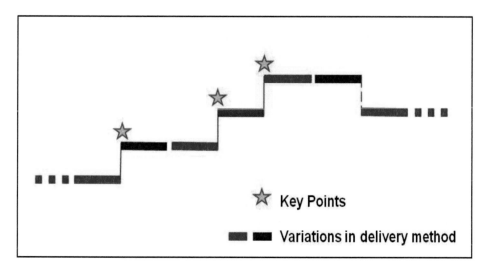

Figure 9.2. Techniques to vary levels of engagement.

Traditional vs. Non-Traditional Delivery Methods

Varying delivery methods provides a means of embedding contrast and increasing levels of engagement, and the following Table identifies different delivery methods.

Table 9.4. Traditional and non-traditional delivery methods (Duarte, 2010)

TRADITIONAL	NON-TRADITIONAL
Stage	
Be the main event	Share the main event
Hide behind the podium	Be free to roam
Use the stage as-is	Use the stage as a setting
Style	
Serious business tone	Humour and enthusiasm
Confined expressiveness	Large expressiveness
Monotone	Vocal and pace variety
Visuals	
Read slides	Minimise slides (reference only)
Static images	Moving images
Talk about the 'product'	Show the 'product'
Interaction	
Minimise disruptions	Plan disruptions
Resist feedback	Embrace real-time feedback
Request silence	Encourage exchanges
Content	
Familiarity with features	Wonderment and awe at features
Flawless knowledge	Self-deprecating humanness
Long-winded rambles	Memorable, headline-sized sound bites
Involvement	
One-way delivery	Multi-way deliver and audience involvement via asking questions, buzz groups, mini forums, etc

CONTENT AND LAYOUT

Simplicity and clarity are critical in the design of effective visual communications and it is generally recommended that the design of content and layout is limited to the essential elements only. Simplicity is recommended not just for aesthetic purposes but also to aid cognitive processing of the information provided in visual communications. However, designing effective visual communications and presentations takes time and "the amount of time required to develop a presentation is directly proportional to how high the stakes are"

(Duarte, 2008, p. 12). The following indicates the time needed for developing the average 30 to 45 minute presentation:

Research, collecting information and data	6-20 hours
Building an audience-needs map	1 hour
Generating and organising ideas	2-3 hours
Feedback and critique on ideas from colleagues	1 hour
Design/devise the structure	2 hours
Design/construct the presentation visuals	20-60 hours
Rehearse and refine presentation	3 hours (Duarte, 2008)

Simplicity and clarity can be achieved with the careful placement of elements and Duarte (2008) recommends applying the following principles to maximise effectiveness.

Table 9.5. Principles to maximise effectiveness in visual presentations (Duarte, 2008)

Contrast	Use contrast between the elements in visual communications to help the audience clearly identify the main points
Flow	Arrange elements in such as way as to ensure that the audience knows the order in which to process information
Hierarchy	Arrange elements in such a way that the audience can quickly and easily see the relationships between the elements
Unity	Establish a level of unity between elements so that the audience senses that information/elements belong together
Proximity	The audience perceives meaning from the location of elements and the relationship between groups of elements
Whitespace	**Whitespace provides visual 'breathing room'; too much visual clutter** impedes understanding

It is recommended that complex tables, graphs and illustrations are simplified to aid comprehension and avoid distraction. Putnam and Gibber suggest ungrouping elements within complicated tables, graphs and illustrations so that key information becomes the centre of attention and viewers are not bamboozled by excessive detail.

In this regard, Putnam and Gibber also recommend limiting artistic 'exuberance' and keeping visually distracting and unnecessary visual elements to a minimum (Putnam and Gibber, 2006).

Highlighting importance and meaning is critical in visual communications, and Duarte (2008) provides five key rules that help achieve clarity and effectiveness:

1. Tell the truth
2. Get to the point
3. Pick the right visual presentation tool for the job
4. **Highlight what's important**
5. Keep it simple (Duarte, 2008, p. 65)

PROGRESSIVE DISCLOSURE OF INFORMATION 'CHUNKS'

It is suggested that ideas are subdivided so that each slide represents only a few key ideas and 'progressive disclosure' is employed so that each visual or slide in a presentation sequence follows on from previous slides. Ideally, these 'chunks' should be presented in a logical sequence whereby each idea 'builds' on ideas previously presented. If visuals or slides occur in a haphazard sequence that lacks logic, the audience may become distracted and engagement levels will drop.

Seven: The 'Magic' Number?

It is recommended that slide content is limited to three to four key items or 'chunks' of information. In addition, it is ideal to limit the amount of text per slide to no more than six lines of text per slide with no more than seven words per line (Beighlie, 2005; Putnam and Gibber, 2006). To achieve this limited amount of text, Putnam and Gibber suggest condensing text and removing all but key words.

Miller's (1956) landmark paper suggested that "the span of absolute judgement and the span of immediate memory impose severe limitations on the amount of information that we are able to receive, process and remember" (Miller, 1956, p. 95). Miller asserts that the span of immediate memory for varying bits or chunks of stimulus centres around the 'magic' number seven (give or take, two) and varies depending on whether the stimulus are monosyllabic words, digits or objects. This recommendation finds support from Doidge, who suggests that the average person can remember seven unrelated items such as a sequence of words or numbers (Doidge, 2011). However, this figure is an average and, depending on preferred learning modality and other factors such as attention deficit, temporal influences, brain damage or cultural variations, this number may vary. For example, Gladwell highlighted differences in this respect between English-speakers and Chinese-speakers when memorising numbers. This difference has to do with the brevity of Chinese number words which can be spoken in less than one quarter of a second as opposed to their English equivalents which can take about one-third of a second, and this difference has an impact on the ability to memorise numbers (Dehaene cited in Gladwell, 2009).

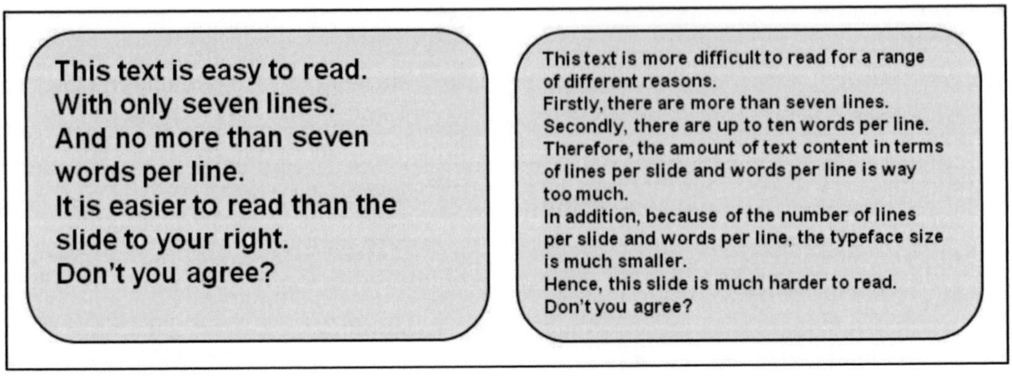

This text is easy to read. With only seven lines. And no more than seven words per line. It is easier to read than the slide to your right. Don't you agree?

This text is more difficult to read for a range of different reasons. Firstly, there are more than seven lines. Secondly, there are up to ten words per line. Therefore, the amount of text content in terms of lines per slide and words per line is way too much. In addition, because of the number of lines per slide and words per line, the typeface size is much smaller. Hence, this slide is much harder to read. Don't you agree?

Figure 9.3. Legibility is directly related to the amount of text content per slide.

It has recently been suggested that the 'magic' number of items that can be held and processed in short term memory may actually be three or four, and this number is dependent on learner-expertise plus the complexity or otherwise of the items being presented to learners (Farrington, 2011).

While the notion of cognitive load as discussed by Sweller (1988) and others is discussed in greater detail above, it is important to consider that cognitive overload can inhibit learning and reduce the amount of working memory space sufficiently enough to cause errors and reduce learning performance (Sweller, 1988).

Overall Content Timing

In terms of overall content timing, it is recommended that one slide/visual per minute is the optimum rate. However, given the technical sophistication provided by PowerPoint and Mind-mapping presentation software, the protocol of one minute per specific point and per visual/slide can become complicated when a main slide links to further slides behind the main slide which are then viewed before progressing to the next main slide. To overcome this technical issue, Radel suggests a guideline of approximately ten minutes per major concept (Radel cited in Putnam and Gibber, 2006).

Layout

It is recommended that space (or 'whitespace') is left around the perimeter of visuals and slides, and that text, images, graphs and tables are more centrally located in case the projector-screen register is not aligned. Misalignment may leave a proportion of the visual or slide projection off the screen, and information may be lost or lose legibility.

Consistency of headline, text and illustration placement as well as typeface design and size are recommended because the audience will become familiar with, and hence easily identify, such elements. In this way, consistency and familiarity contributes to greater speed and efficiency when reading overheads and PowerPoint slides, and thereby increases the effectiveness of visual communications (Beighlie, 2005).

Items Presented on the Left are Better Remembered

In relation to short-term memory, items presented on the left are better remembered and it is suggested by Della Scala et al (2010) that this indicates a statistically significant lateral bias towards the left in short-term memory rather than perception or attention in cognitively healthy adults (Della Sala, Darling, and Logie, 2010). This finding, which is the result of a large study that involved three experiments and a total of over 60,000 participants, supported the findings of earlier studies which found that healthy individuals show a preference for left space in perceptual tasks as well as mental representations of familiar material (for example, see McGeorge, Beschin, Colnaghi, Rusconi, and Della Sala, 2007).

MOVEMENT, ANIMATION, SOUND AND MUSIC

It is well known that movement attracts attention (Goldstein, 1996; Shang and Bishop, 2000). Hence, movement and animation can help to improve attention levels and increase the effectiveness of visual communications and presentations. However, it is imperative that movement and animation enhance rather than detract from communication objectives. Duarte (2008) suggests that the movement incorporated in visual communications "should seem to be familiar and should make sense" (Duarte, 2008, p. 182). To achieve this, make sure that movement is synchronised and fits with the timing and content as a lack of synchronisation can lead to distraction, confusion or cognitive dissonance. The inclusion of movement /animation can reinforce or imply particular impressions. For example Duarte (2008) refers to the way in which movement is used in film (as discussed by J. Van Sijll, *Cinematic Storytelling*) wherein fast-moving, quick cut movement can contribute to a sense of excitement and surprise; while slow-moving movement/animation may create impressions of lethargy and nostalgia. In the following Figure, the movement of two objects towards each other conveys the impression that the objects are connecting, joining or being combined; while the movement of an object from top downwards mimics the effect of gravity and conveys an impression of easy descent, and the movement of an object upwards goes against gravity and makes the ascent appear more 'difficult'.

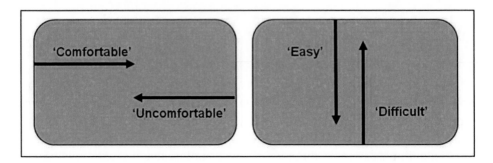

Figure 9.4. The influence of movement on impression.

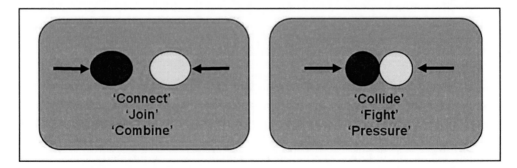

Figure 9.5. The influence of movement on impression.

Similarly, rotating objects may convey impressions of change or a shift in rank or status; while movement that suggests shrinking may imply decline or decay, and movement that implies growing may imply expansion.

In the following Figure, objects that are moving towards each other appear to be connecting or combining; while objects that move together and touch or squash each other appear to collide or be under pressure.

Movement attracts attention but can also become a distraction. Duarte (2008) suggests deleting or minimising movement or animation if it doesn't add value or serve a purpose and avoid fast-paced or too much movement as it may be confusing and distracting.

Sound and Music

Aural elements such as sound and music can add value to visual communications and presentations; however, as with movement and animation, they can also become a distraction. Key issues to consider include whether the elements contribute to the communication objectives and fit intuitively with the content as a lack of cohesion may cause discomfort or cognitive dissonance.

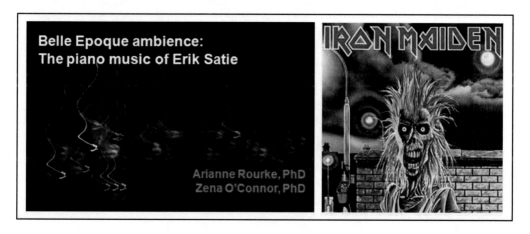

Figure 9.6. Avoid cognitive dissonance between content and sound/music.

TYPEFACE DESIGN

In general, serif fonts, italics, underlined words, capitalised words, low contrast text and thin lines contribute to poor legibility. Design features that contribute to better legibility include sanserif fonts, the use of colour and bold for emphasis, a mixture of lower-case and upper-case fonts, high contrast colours and thick lines (Putnam and Gibber, 2006).

Aside from the serif versus sans serif debate, certain aspects of typeface design are considered to support legibility while others have a negative impact on legibility. For example, typefaces that feature thin strokes or thin structural elements (vertical, horizontal or diagonal) tend to reduce legibility especially if type size is small and this can become problematic for people with reduced visual capacity. The specific typeface qualities that support legibility include consistent stroke widths, open counterforms (not condensed), wider horizontal proportions, distinct forms and extended horizontal strokes (Nini, 2006). In the following Figure, the thin strokes that feature in Bodoni tend to fade or disappear for those with reduced visual capacity leaving text difficult to read. Typefaces such as Arial Black that feature strong strokes (vertical, horizontal and diagonal) improve readability.

Figure 9.7. Typeface structure and legibility: Bodoni v. Arial Black.

Evidence-based research as well as subjective preference indicates that certain typefaces are deemed more readable than others. Specifically, the typefaces Arial, Helvetica, Verdana and Adsans are considered more readable than Times New Roman. In addition, the font created by the American Printing House for the Blind (APH) recommends the use of APHont typeface which was developed specifically for people with low vision (Russell-Minda et al., 2007). In terms of compatibility across different computer software platforms (Microsoft Word, PowerPoint, Apple, etc), Beighlie recommends Arial, Courier, Courier New, Helvetica, Monaco, MS San Serif, MS Serif, Palatino, Times, Times New Roman and Verdana (Beighlie, 2005).

Figure 9.8. Recommended typefaces.

Typeface Legibility: Serif V. Sans Serif

Serifs are the structural details on the ends of the strokes that make up the individual letters or symbols as illustrated in the following Figure.

Figure 9.9. Structural serif details (circled).

Typefaces are generally categorised into those with serifs and those without (sans serif), and it has long been held that the presence or absence of serifs impacts on readability. Specifically, sans serif typefaces are considered to be less legible than serif typefaces because they are thought to impact negatively on decipherment while the presence of serifs are considered to enhance decipherment and hence readability (McLean, 1980; Rubinstein, 1988). The following Figure features common serif and san serif typefaces.

Recent research has indicated that the presence or absence of serifs has minimal impact on reading speed and readability; however, when text is small or distant, serifs were found to contribute to a marginally improved level of legibility (Arditi and Cho, 2005). Similarly, a systematic review of research evidence on the impact of typefaces on the legibility of text found research evidence does not support strong conclusions about the legibility of serif or sans serif fonts; however, "there appears to be a subjective preference among readers with low vision for sans serif fonts" (Russell-Minda et al., 2007, p. 411).

Figure 9.10. Serif and sans serif typefaces.

Typeface Size

Visual ability tends to be highly variable and ideal reading thresholds are individualised and dependent on the font style. However, for people with normal vision, at a reading distance of 40 centimetres (16 inches), type sizes ranging from 9 to 14 points are considered optimal while readers with decreased visual capacity require at least 16 to 18 point type (Legge, Rubin, Pelli, and Schleske, 1985; Russell-Minda et al., 2007). In regards to overhead projections and PowerPoint slides, legibility is dependent on room size and viewing distance and Beighlie recommends the following:

>200 seats   Headlines: 42-48 point and Main Text: 36 point
<200 seats   Headlines: 36 point and Main Text: 28 point
<50 seats   Headlines: 32 point and Main Text: 24 point (Beighlie, 2005)

Putnam and Gibber provide some quick tests to ensure that slides are legible at point of delivery, as follows (Putnam and Gibber, 2006):

- The 'Floor test' – viewing an A4 slide printout from 2m distance
- The 'Back of the room' test – viewing an A4 printout from the back of the room.

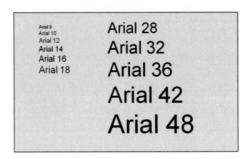

Figure 9.11. Optimal type sizes: Printed text (left) and PowerPoint (right).

Text-Background Colour

Strong contrast has a positive impact on readability particularly for readers with poor or low vision (Russell-Minda et al., 2007). Human vision declines with age and, aside from conditions such as macular degeneration, the pupil shrinks with age and less light enters the eye affecting particularly in low light environments. In addition, the lens of the eye starts to lose elasticity between the ages of 40 and 50 resulting in a decreased ability to focus and a loss of acuity (Nini, 2006). Therefore, strong contrast and strong colour contrast is recommended for text-background colour combinations. Recent research indicates that particular web-based text-background colour combinations have a stronger impact on readability and retention with higher levels of contrast generally leading to higher readability ratings and marginally higher retention scores (Hall and Hanna, 2004). This study also found that, while different colour combinations did not significantly affect retention rates, preferred colours (such as blues and chromatic colours) led to higher ratings of aesthetic quality and these higher rating were significantly related to purchase intention. In terms of specific colour combinations, the conventional combination of black on white was found to score highly in terms of readability and retention; as opposed to white on black, which rated lower on readability. Readability was generally aligned with 'professional' in an educational or commercial context; and strong contrast chromatic colour combinations (especially combinations featuring blue) were found to rate highly on readability as well as aesthetics and purchase intentions in commercial web-based contexts.

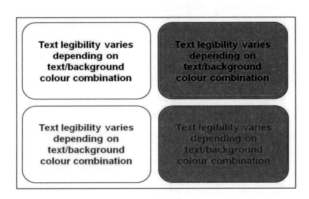

Figure 9.12. Text/background colours influence legibility.

ELEMENTS AND PRINCIPLES OF DESIGN

Design can be defined in two ways: Firstly, design refers to the process that utilises and applies the elements and principles of design in tandem with specific theoretical paradigms related to the design process such as 'truth-to-materials', 'form-follows-function', planned obsolescence or environmentally-sustainable design. Of perhaps more relevance to the design of visual communications, design can be considered to be visual elements embedded within a design composition (such as a graphic design, advertisement, website, etc) and an awareness of the order and arrangement of those elements (Raizman, 2003). In relation to the design of visual communications design, design can also be extended to include the ways in which the elements of design encode the visually-based communication objectives. Ascertaining the effectiveness of visual communications design depends on how successfully visually-based communications are decoded by the intended target audience.

'Good' Design: An Effective Interface between Design and Human Experience

It has been suggested that "vision is construction" and, in respect to the design of visual communications, the elements and principles of design play a key role in terms of how we perceive, decode and construct visual communications (Hoffman, 1998, p. 8). However, defining the elements and principles of design is challenging as the literature provides a range of different definitions some of which are broad and general; while others are more specific and practical. From a broad perspective, British design guru Terence Conran (b.1931) decreed that "good design...is intelligence made visible"; however, the notion of 'good design' is also problematic (Bayley and Conran, 2007, p. 10). However, Samara (2007) suggests that proclamations of 'good' or 'bad' in respect to design have to do with overall quality rather than subjective assertions that have to do with preference or personal taste for aesthetics, functionality or honesty in design (Samara, 2007). Hence, aligning quality and 'good design' can be both contextually and temporally relative.

Within the context of this discussion, 'good design' is considered to represent an effective interface between visual communications design and human experience, wherein the encoding and decoding processes function successfully, and the communications objectives embedded within visual communications design are achieved. This level of success depends on an understanding of human experience within the context of this interface – as the founder of Apple Computers, Steve Jobs (1955-2011): "The broader one's understanding of the human experience, the better designs we will have" (Jobs cited in Conran, 1996, p. 231).

From a different perspective, Samara (2007) considers that a number of rules exist that underpin 'good design'; rules that relate to aesthetics and/or functionality and which may be applied or broken depending on context. These rules begin with the design concept and include the following:

1. Communication: "Communicate – don't decorate" and ensure that a design communicates a message or idea to its intended audience or market and not just the designer (Samara, 2007, p. 11);

2. Cohesion: "Speak with one visual voice" and ensure that elements within a design relate to each other in some way;
3. Strategic use of focus: Use the elements of design to create a simple hierarchy of focus without creating a visually confusing design;
4. Strategic use of colour: Use colour to direct attention to key design elements and support both aesthetic and functional objectives;
5. Strategic use of contrast: Again to draw attention to specific elements and to support aesthetic and functional objectives;
6. Strategic use of negative space: provides visual 'breathing space' and the less-cluttered result supports aesthetic and functional objectives;
7. Strategic use of type: Use two and a maximum of three typefaces within any one piece of graphic visual design; treat type another kind of image; and use reader-friendly type;
8. Strategic use of balance, contrast and rhythm: Repetition and symmetry of design elements can lead to designs that are boring and not memorable.

However, the interface between design and human experience is complex and open to the influence of a number of factors such as perceptual and environmental context; temporal factors including changing trends; as well as individual and cultural differences. In view of this it is unlikely that there will be one and only one solution to any design problem and the design process therefore has to do with finding multiple alternative solutions within a given context rather than simply identifying the most aesthetically-pleasing, functional or cost-effective design solution.

Aesthetics vs. Functional Design: Mutually Exclusive?

Any discussion about the principles and elements of design invariably involves a discussion about aesthetics and functionality, and this discussion often puts aesthetics and functionality at opposite ends of a continuum as though these two aspects are diametrically opposed or either mutually exclusive.

Aesthetics play a critical role in applied design. Stebbing (2005) considers that humans possess a basic and common 'aesthetic sense' that identifies and appreciates patterns of similarity and diversity in organic forms (Stebbing, 2005, p. 16). Occurring in tandem with evolution and linked to recognition, Stebbing further argues that this aesthetic sense centres on 'perceptual primitives' represented by the basic principles evident in both design and organic form. Aesthetics cannot be downplayed in relation to the interface between visual communications design and human experience, and its importance is reflected in the notion that design is "98% common sense and 2% aesthetics" (Bayley and Conran, 2007, p. 10). To a certain extent, this is possibly why many designers abide by the dictum, 'God is in the details'[1] Evidence supporting the importance of aesthetics is found in the 'aesthetic-usability effect', a phenomenon whereby people tend to have a preference for more aesthetically-

---

[1]This dictum was attributed to a key figure of Modern design and architecture Mies van der Rohe as per Rohe's obituary in the New York Times, 19 August 1969 (Whitman, 1969). However, it has also been attributed to Gustav Flaubert (Titelman, 1996).

pleasing designs and tend to perceive aesthetically-pleasing designs as easier to use (Lidwell, Holden, and Butler, 2003). Similarly, Conran considers it the designer's responsibility to improve the quality of life through the design of products that are functional, affordable and aesthetically-pleasing: "Design is art that works" (Bayley and Conran, 2007, p. 13). Raymond Loewy (1893-1986), renowned 20th century industrial designer, summed up the importance of aesthetics from a commercial perspective: "Ugliness does not sell" (Loewy cited in Conran, 1996, p. 162).

Tufte (2005) argues that functionality in visual communications is critical and his discussion of analytical design within the context of visual communications includes a focus on completely different principles; principles that relate to content and how content is functionally presented such as the presentation of comparisons, contrasts and differences between data or content; the ways in which causality, mechanism, explanation or systematic structure are presented; the ways in which relationships are presented; and the ways in which text, numbers, images and diagrams are integrated as a whole. In addition, Tufte (2005) suggests that documentation and evidence are integral elements within visual communication materials and should not be overlooked or ignored. For Tufte, the focus is not about 'truth-to-materials', 'truth-to-process' or truth-to-form' but 'truth-to-content'.

From a broader perspective, the first designer to be honoured with a one-man show during his lifetime at the New York Museum of Modern Art, Charles Eames (1907-1978), suggested that design is "a plan for arranging elements in such a way as to best accomplish a particular purpose" (Faimon and Weigand, 2004, p. 13). This definition is echoed by Raizman (2003), who suggested that design represents the order and arrangement of the elements of an object, product or example of visual communication (Raizman, 2003). However, these comments beg the question: What are the elements and principles of design? To begin an exploration of the elements and principles of design, a key starting point is the curriculum of the Bauhaus, a highly influential 20th century design school (Bayley and Conran, 2007; De Noblet, 1993; Hauffe, 1998).

Bauhaus Design

A guiding principle embedded in the curriculum of the Bauhaus[2] was Walter Gropius' (1883-1969) belief in a unified approach to art, design and architecture whereby a student who learned the elements and principles of design could apply these to whatever task they chose in design, art or architecture (Bayer, Gropius, and Gropius, 1975).

Gropius embraced creative expression and technology, and saw these as being able to co-exist in tandem whereby "the interwoven strands of the practical and formal" aspects of design occurred within a context where creativity and industry work hand-in-hand (Bayer et al., 1975, p. 29). To this end, standardisation was seen as the means by which art, design, architecture, manufacturing and construction could be realised, and standardisation was

---

[2] The Staatliches Bauhaus, which was founded in Weimar, Germany, in 1919 by Gropius, was an amalgamation of the Weimar Academy of Art and the Weimar School of Applied Arts whose director was Henry van der Velde. In 1925 the Bauhaus moved to Dessau and Hannes Meyer took over as director in 1927; in 1932 the Bauhaus moved a third time to Berlin and Ludwig Mies van der Rohe was director from 1930 until 1933 when the school was closed by the Nazi regime.

embedded within the design process along with "Simplicity in multiplicity" (Bayer et al., 1975, p. 28).

All students at the Bauhaus were required to complete the Basic Course, initially devised by Johannes Itten: "I took personal charge of this preparatory course in the autumn of 1919. Generously, Walter Gropius left me a completely free hand in its arrangement and content" (Itten, 1963, p. 7). A number of others including Wassily Kandinsky and Josef Albers contributed to the Basic Course after Itten's involvement (BDF, 2010; Frampton, 1992). In line with the philosophy of the Bauhaus, a key aim of the Basic Course was "to acquaint [students] with the basic principles which underlie all creative activity in the visual arts", after which students were considered sufficiently informed to continue their studies in a range of areas including architecture, metalwork and graphic design (Bayer et al., 1975, p. 34).

The Bauhaus Basic Course had three main aims: Firstly, to encourage students to realise their creativity; secondly, to provide students with a range of experiences and career-related skills; and finally to convey fundamental ideas about the principles and elements of design for subsequent application in a broad range of architecture and design-related contexts (Itten, 1963). The Basic Course was divided into seven main areas of study:

1. *Light-dark*. Light-dark contrast was considered to be "the most expressive and important means of design for the artist" (Itten, 1961, p19). Students were encouraged to experiment with a range of tones and analyse paintings in terms of this contrast;

2. *Colour*. The primary colours were considered to be: red, yellow and blue; and secondary colours: orange, green and purple. In addition, "seven distinct contrast effects in the world of colour" were included in the Basic course (Itten, 1961, p42);

3. *Material and texture*. Students were encouraged to explore a large range of different materials and textures and incorporate them as key elements in compositions;

4. *Form*. The key basic forms were considered to be the square, the triangle and the circle. In addition, exercises in variations and combinations of basic forms within the context of the Golden Mean proportion provided students with experience in construction and organisation of compositions based on the notion of standardisation;

5. *Rhythm*. Students were encouraged to use the repetition of lines, points, shapes, textures and colour to create a sense of rhythm in their work. Deviations in direction and alignment created variations in rhythm and led to "simplicity in multiplicity";

6. *Expressive form*. Students were encouraged to experiment with line, rhythm, form and direction as well as analyse paintings to explore the expressive nature of different compositions. Itten considered that "if a genuine feeling is to be expressed in a line or plane, this feeling must first resound within the artist" (Itten, 1961, p147);

7. *Subjective form*. Itten believed that each student expressed their idiosyncratic nature by using the basic elements of design differently in their compositions.

The curriculum of the Bauhaus provided an educational programme that "made a major contribution to the formation of the modern industrial designer" (De Noblet, 1993, p. 24). As a result, the seven areas of study listed above came to feature in the curriculum of many subsequent design schools such as the Shillito Design School, and remain integral to the design of visual communication to this day (Shillito, 1979).

Design According to Itten: Balancing Contrasts

Itten, who was influenced by the ancient Greek philosophers and Eastern philosophy (Zoroastrianism in particular), championed the notion of balance in both design and life (Itten, 1963). For Itten, balance and contrast between opposites represented compositional logic that underpinned design: "The basis of my theory of composition was the general theory of contrast. The *chiaroscuro* (light-dark) contrast, the material and textures studies, the theory of forms and colours, the rhythm and the expressive forms were discussed and demonstrated in terms of their contrast effect (Itten, 1963, p. 12). Itten described contrast in respect to a set of possibilities of contrast: "The students had to approach the contrasts from three directions: they had to experience them with their senses, objective them intellectually, and realise them synthetically" (Itten, 1963, p. 12). These possibilities of contrast involved various constituents of design such as:

Point	Light-Dark
Line	Large-Small
Direction	High-Low
Volume	Motion-Rest
Thick-Thin	Much-Little
Broad-Narrow	Soft-Hard
Transparent-Opaque	Light-Heavy
Rough-Smooth	Hot-Cold (Itten, 1963)

These possibilities of contrast can occur in a range of different manifestations and can be modified or used strategically to direct visual attention in visual communications design.

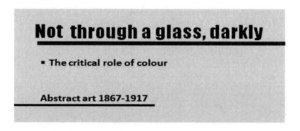

Figure 9.13. Using Line, Point, High-Low and Large-Small to direct visual attention.

Itten considered Light-Dark contrast to be particularly effective given the way in which this contrast can be modified to direct visual attention in applied design.

Figure 9.14. Using Light-Dark contrast and colour to direct visual attention.

Light-Dark contrast can also be varied to convey different 'moods' and impressions, as per the techniques of *chiaroscuro* and *sfumato* which were used to great effect by painters such as Caravaggio and Leonardo Da Vinci. In addition, Direction can be used to create emphasis and reinforce particular elements of communication as per the following Figure.

Figure 9.15. Using Direction and Light-Dark contrast to direct visual attention.

Elements of Design

Principles and elements of design have varying definitions and functions. However, the elements of design are herein considered to be specific, discrete visual constituents that can be manipulated by the designer within a framework underpinned by the principles of design. The elements of design are therefore defined as those championed by Phyllis Shillito, founder of the Shillito Design School, whose curriculum was undoubtedly by the Bauhaus (Shillito, 1979)

Table 9.6. Key elements of design

Line	Line may vary from thick to thin, coloured to achromatic
Direction	Direction may vary from left to right, diagonal and organic
Proportion/size	Variations in proportion/size of form/shape, line, etc
Texture	Texture may vary from smooth-rough and familiar-unfamiliar
Form/shape	Variations in form/shape from organic to abstract, geometric
Tone	Variations in tone from light through to dark
Colour	Colour may vary in terms of hue, saturation as well as tone

The elements of design represent key visual constituents that can be modified and varied within the context of broader design principles.

Principles of Design: Underlying Syntax of Visual Grammar

It has been suggested that humans may be hard-wired to recognise "deep fundamental principles of analytical design" that contribute to the effectiveness or otherwise of design and that these principles "are not tied to any particular language, culture, style, gender or technology of information display" (Tufte, 2006, p. 10). As such, these principles of design, are a type of "visual grammar" (Stebbing, 2005, p. 20). It has also been suggested that "concepts of opposition and balance...and the golden mean" are aspects of design that "may be part of the fundamental structure of our brain programs" wherein visual characteristics such as contrast, rhythm, balance and proportion represent a biological, evolutionary foundation (Stebbing, 2003, p. 3). From an analysis of fifty key texts from the literature on design, art and architecture, Stebbing identified a number of basic principles considered to be fundamental to both organic form and the creation of visual composition within the context of design, art and architecture: *Contrast, Rhythm (or pattern), Balance (and symmetry) and Proportion* along with *Unity/Harmony, Movement and Expression* (Stebbing, 2004).

Furthermore, Stebbing suggests that the first four principles (*Contrast, Rhythm, Balance and Proportion*) are evident in organic form as well as visual design compositions; with the latter three principles relating to perceptual effects that may arise from organic form or visual creations. Stebbing acknowledges that these principles are Western-centric and makes reference to Cho (2001) who suggests that the "grand principles of design" include *Harmony, Unity, Balance, Emphasis, Rhythm, Proportion, Contrast* and *Symmetry* (Cho, 2001, p. 63).

Similarly, Shillito suggested that the elements of design can be applied within the framework of particular design principles and these were identified as *Rhythm, Unity-Variety, Balance* and *Abstract-Realism* (from full realism to modified/shattered realism to pure abstraction) (Shillito, 1979). Shillito often referred to patterns of similarity in terms of form/shape, line, direction, tone, colour, etc, as 'harmony'; a term used interchangeably with *Unity* to represent visual cohesiveness.

Table 9.7. Key principles of design

Rhythm	The presence or absence of repetition in terms of line, form/shape, direction, etc
Unity/Variety	The presence or absence of visual cohesiveness in terms of similarity or variety of form/shape, line, colour, tone, etc
Balance	The presence or absence of symmetry/asymmetry arising from the overall arrangement of form/shape, line, etc
Abstract/Realism	From unadulterated realism to modified/shattered realism through to the absence of realism (pure abstraction).

Key principles of design can be used to vary or modify the way in which images, illustrations of text blocks can be placed within visual communications. Experimentation with the principles of design may improve or detract from the effectiveness of visual communications and presentations.

The placement of objects and text within the visual frame can be varied to suggest symmetrical balance (along with its associations of static 'reliability') or modified to suggest asymmetrical balance, a more dynamic form of balance. Similarly, illustrations to support visual communication objectives may require an abstract or semi-abstract treatment. In the following Figure 9.17., an image that depicts a realistic representation has been varied to depict a modified, abstracted version of the same image. In this way, the design has been varied to support the visual communication objectives relevant to the task.

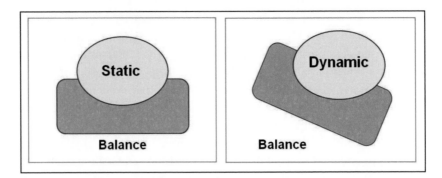

Figure 9.16. Symmetrical and asymmetrical balance.

Figure 9.17. Realism and modified realism (Poster design: Ron Baumannwww.ronbauman.com).

The objectives of visual communications and presentations can vary across a range of purposes and different audiences. The elements of design detailed above provide the means by which the visual constituents can be varied during the design process to suit the communication objectives. Similarly, the principles of design provide a framework within which the elements of design can be modified and arranged to appeal to audience needs as well as address communication objectives in visual communication materials.

REFERENCES

Arditi, A., and Cho, J. (2005). Serifs and font legibility. *Vision Research, 45*(23), 2926-2933.

Bayer, H., Gropius, W., and Gropius, I. (Eds.). (1975). *Bauhaus 1919 - 1928*. London: Secker and Warburg.

Bayley, S., and Conran, T. (2007).*Design: Intelligence made visible*. London: Conran Octopus.

BDF. (2010). Bauhaus History. Retrieved 4 May 2010, from http://www.bauhaus-dessau.de/index.php?history

Beighlie, B. (2005). Research imaging solutions (Information Technology Department, Harvard Medical School). Retrieved 5 September 2011, from http://hms.harvard.edu/ec_res/nt/E297EE41-7913-4FF4-B9D9-C7BC9D4844E4/YourPoint.pdf

Cho, D. (2001). Four stages of design revolution: Expansion of the design domain and the development of grand principles of design. *Exploring emerging design paradigms: Proceedings of the ICSID 2001* 84-152.

Conran, T. (1996). *Terence Conran on design*. London: Conran Octopus.

De Noblet, J. (Ed.). (1993). *Industrial design: Reflections of a century*. Paris: Flammarion.

Della Sala, S., Darling, S., and Logie, R. H. (2010). Items on the left are better remembered. *The Quarterly Journal of Experimental Psychology, 63*(5), 848-855.

Doidge, N. (2011). *The brain that changes itself*. Melbourne, VIC: Scribe Publications.

Duarte, N. (2008). *Slide:ology: The art and science of creating great presentations*. Sebastopol, CA: O'Reilly Media.

Duarte, N. (2010). *Resonate: Present visual stories that transform audiences*. New Jersey: John Wiley and Sons.

Faimon, P., and Weigand, J. (2004). *The nature of design*. Cincinatti, OH: HOW Design Books.

Farrington, J. (2011). From the research: Myths worth dispelling. *Performance Improvement Quarterly, 23*(4), 113-116.

Frampton, K. (1992). The Bauhaus: Evolution of an idea 1919-1932. In K. Frampton (Ed.), *Modern architecture: A critical history (3rd ed.)*. New York: Thames and Hudson.

Gladwell, M. (2009). *Outliers: The story of success*. Sydney: Penguin Books.

Goldstein, E. B. (1996). *Sensation and perception*. Pacific Grove, CA: Brooks/Cole.

Hall, R. H., and Hanna, P. (2004). The impact of web page text-background colour combinations on readability, retention, aesthetics and behavioural intention. *Behaviour and Information Technology, 23*(3), 183-195.

Hauffe, T. (1998). *Design: A concise history*. London: Laurence King.

Hoffman, D. D. (1998). *Visual intelligence: How we create what we see*. New York: WW Norton and Company.

Itten, J. (1961). *The art of color (Revised edition, 1973)*. New York: John Wiley and Sons.

Itten, J. (1963). *Design and form: The basic course at the Bauhaus and later (Revised edition, 1975)*. New York: John Wiley and Sons.

Legge, G. E., Rubin, G. S., Pelli, D. G., and Schleske, M. M. (1985). Psychophysics of reading I: Normal vision. *Vision Research, 25*(2), 239-252.

Lidwell, W., Holden, K., and Butler, J. (2003). *Universal principles of design*. Beverly, MA: Rockport Publishers.

McGeorge, P., Beschin, N., Colnaghi, A., Rusconi, M. L., and Della Sala, S. (2007). A lateralized bias in mental imagery: evidence for representational pseudoneglect. *Neuroscience Letters, 421*(3), 259-263.

McLean, R. (1980). *The Thames and Hudson manual of typography (Vol. 1)*. London: Thames and Hudson.

Miller, G. A. (1956). The magical number seven, plus or minus two: Some limits on our capacity for processing information. *The Psychological Review, 63*(2), 81-97.

Nini, P. (2006). Typography and the aging eye: Typeface legibility for older viewers with vision problems. Retrieved 30 August 2011, from http://www.aiga.org

Putnam, L., and Gibber, J. (2006). PowerPoint Design and Delivery. Retrieved 20 August 2012, from http://www.columbia.edu/cu/psychology/courses/6200/extras/PPT_Design_ Delivery_students.pdf

Raizman, D. (2003). *History of modern design*. London: Laurence King.

Rubinstein, R. (1988). *Digital typography: An introduction to type and composition for computer system design*. Boston, MA: Addision Wesley.

Russell-Minda, E., Jutai, J. W., Strong, G., Campbell, K. A., Gold, D., Pretty, L., et al. (2007). The legibility of typefaces for readers with low vision: A research review. *Journal of Visual Impairment and Blindness, 101*(7), 402-415.

Samara, T. (2007).*Design elements: A graphic style manual*. Beverly, MA: Rockport Publishers.

Shang, H., and Bishop, I. D. (2000). Visual thresholds for detection, recognition and visual impact in landscape settings.*Journal of Environmental Psychology, 20*(4), 125-140.

Shillito, P. (1979). Shillito Design School syllabus: Recollections of Zena Stefanek, Shillito Design School student from 1977 to 1979. Sydney: Shillito Design School.

Stebbing, P. D. (2003). A grammar of visual composition and its biological origin. *Communication and Cognition, 36*(3/4), 353-390.

Stebbing, P. D. (2004). A universal grammar for visual composition?*Leonardo, 37*(1), 63-70.

Stebbing, P. D. (2005). Creating a real meeting of cultures and media in the art and design curriculum through the identification of universals of aesthetic behaviour. In E. Salmi and J. Lannato (Eds.), *Graphic design: Cumulus Working Paper* (pp. 16-20).

Sweller, J. (1988). Cognitive load during problem solving: Effects on learning. *Cognitive Science, 12*(2), 257-285.

Titelman, G. (1996). *Dictionary of popular proverbs and sayings*. New York: Random House.

Tufte, E. (2006). *Beautiful Evidence*. Cheshire, CT: Graphics Press.

Whitman, A. (1969). Obituary: Mies van der Rohe. *New York Times, 19 August, 1969.*

Chapter 10

CONCLUSION

There has been much emphasis in the literature on the importance of developing visual literacy skills, there has however been less concern about how developing these skills can assist students to better understand visual material utilised in teaching. There are few comprehensive resources that assist educators to know why and how to go about using visual material in instruction to promote the fundamental educational goal of purposeful learning. This book has aimed at addressing this shortfall by providing an extensive review of the literature concerning this premise and also by providing educators with some practical advice on how to effectively use visuals in their teaching.

Back in 1999 Rakes argued that, "with the availability of graphic images through multimedia computer-based resources the impact of visuals on the learning process is rapidly becoming more profound" (p.14). More than a decade on with the wide adoption and integration of online learning and teaching in university courses it has become even more prevalent that educators include teaching visual literacy skills to their 21st century student cohort.

These visual skills it has been argued do not just happen, many students do not come to university with the ability to interpret and communicate their knowledge and understanding of the visual imagery used in teaching. For as Schnotz (2002) proposed, "it is not enough that learners possess the cognitive schemata of everyday knowledge required for understanding pictorial illustrations" (p.116), they need also to have acquired domain specific prior knowledge and the skills to apply it.

These skills need to be taught by educators who themselves are aware of the best material and methods to adopt to promote visual literacy skills and to facilitate effective purposeful learning. Sinatra (1986) suggested, visual literacy is the "active reconstruction of past visual experience with incoming visual messages to obtain meaning" (Sinatra, 1986, p5). The onus is placed on the learner to create visual recognition, however there are many methods that educators can adopt to assist with the goal of obtaining 'meaning'. For as Ausburn and Ausburn (1978) acknowledged decades before, the "superficiality of pupils' comprehension of much of what they view, suggests that higher order visual literacy skills do not develop unless they are identified and taught" (Ausburn and Ausburn, 1978, p. 288). With the avalanche of visual imagery in the multimedia bombarding our world, it is even more evident that students need to develop the ability to recognise visual subtleties; to read and understand the visual messages used to communicate disciplinary knowledge and understanding and to transfer these skills to other situations outside of the classroom.

In addition, there are many factors that impact on the effectiveness of visual learning materials in higher education and this book has explored some of these factors. "Vision is construction" and, in respect to the design of visual communication materials, colour, contrast and the elements and principles of design play key roles in terms of how we perceive, decode and construct visual communications (Hoffman, 1998, p. 8).

An understanding of these key roles enables the designer of visual materials to improve the effectiveness of such materials and ensure that communication objectives are met. In addition, the cognitive processing functions that occur in tandem with visual perception often involve "unconscious conclusions" whereby we make inferences and draw conclusions from visual stimuli (Hermann von Helmholtz cited in Hoffman, 1998, p. 11). A thorough and practical understanding of the roles of colour, contrast and the elements and principles of design also enables the designer of visual communication materials to avoid inappropriate or erroneous "unconscious conclusions" and ensures that visual communications messages are encoded and decoded effectively.

This book has also discussed many ways in which visuals can be used to promoting 'active' not 'passive' learning were students become more engaged in the learning process and hence more enthusiastic and more motivated to learn. As Bligh (2000) suggested it "has long been known that active methods of learning are more effective than passive ones" (p.254).

Teaching is all about communication, it is important therefore that educators use the most efficient and effective methods to relay their disciplinary knowledge and understanding to students. It has been suggested that using visuals in teaching is one reliable method for succinctly communicating this knowledge and understanding to students especially if effectively utilised to reinforce and add meaning to lectures and classroom activities. To do this well educators need to also develop their visual literacy skills, so that they can read the messages that images portray to promote quality learning.

As Stokes has suggested, if "visual literacy is regarded as a language, then there is a need to know how to communicate using this language, which includes being alert to messages and critically reading or viewing images as the language of the message" (Stokes, 2002, p. 12 p12). It is envisaged that this book will provide useful information to assist educators in higher education towards achieving the goal of effectively utilising visuals in teaching to promote worthwhile meaningful learning in higher education.

REFERENCES

Ausburn, L., and Ausburn, F. (1978). Visual literacy: Background, theory and practice. *PLET, 15*(40), 291-297.

Bligh, D. A. (2000).*What's the use of lectures?* San Francisco: Jossey-Bass.

Hoffman, D. D. (1998). *Visual intelligence: How we create what we see.* New York: WW Norton and Company.

Rakes, G. C. (1999, Sept). Teaching visual literacy in a multimedia age, *TechTrends*, 43(4), 14-18.

Schnotz, W. (2002). Towards an integrated view of learning from text and visual display.*Educational Psychology Review* 14(1), 101-120.

Sinatra, R. (1986). *Visual literacy connections to thinking, reading and writing.* Springfield, IL: Charles C. Thomas.

Stokes, S. (2002). Visual literacy in teaching and learning: A literature perspective. *Electronic Journal for the Integration of Technology in Education, 1*(1), 10-19.

AUTHORS' BIOGRAPHIES

Dr Arianne Jennifer Rourke - is a senior lecturer in the School of Art History and Art Education at the College of Fine Arts, UNSW. She Co-ordinates the Design History Theory and Aesthetics core courses in the Bachelor of Design and Co-ordinates the Internship and Research paper courses in the Master of Art Administration. Her research is in Cognitive load theory, visual literacy, learning style modalities, expert/novice differences and online teaching and learning examining ways of improving instructional design towards the long-term retention of learning. Dr Rourke has published widely her experimental research into teaching and learning in higher education and has recently co-edited a book with Kathryn Coleman titled: 'Pedagogy Leads Technology, Online Learning and Teaching in Higher Education: New Pedagogies, New Technologies' with Common grounds publishing. She holds the following degrees: BA (Vis. Arts), *AMCAE*; BEd (Art), *SCAE*; MA(History), *UNSW*; MA (Hons) *Macq*; MHEd, *UNSW*; EdD, *UNSW* and is currently a candidate completing a MPhil (HE) at UNSW.

Dr Zena O'Connor- After her initial training in design at the Shillito Design School (a landmark Bauhaus-style design school in Sydney), Zena's career path has since straddled the commercial and academic sectors. Zena's early experience as a designer included textile and visual communications design with occasional forays into product and furniture design, and she has worked for SBS Television, the Powerhouse Museum and National Textiles. Research has always been integral to Zena's design activities and in 2006 she established a research consultancy: Design Research Associates. Zena's main research interests include colour theory and application, visual literacy and learning modalities, design history, and environmental design. In addition, Zena teaches colour theory and application as well as visual communications design at the University of Sydney and the College of Fine Art (University of New South Wales). Zena holds a Bachelor of Business degree (UTS); Master of Design (UTS) and a Ph.D. (Sydney).

INDEX

D

N

O

P

U

T